I0795916

IMAGES
of America

CHIPPEWA FALLS
MAIN STREET

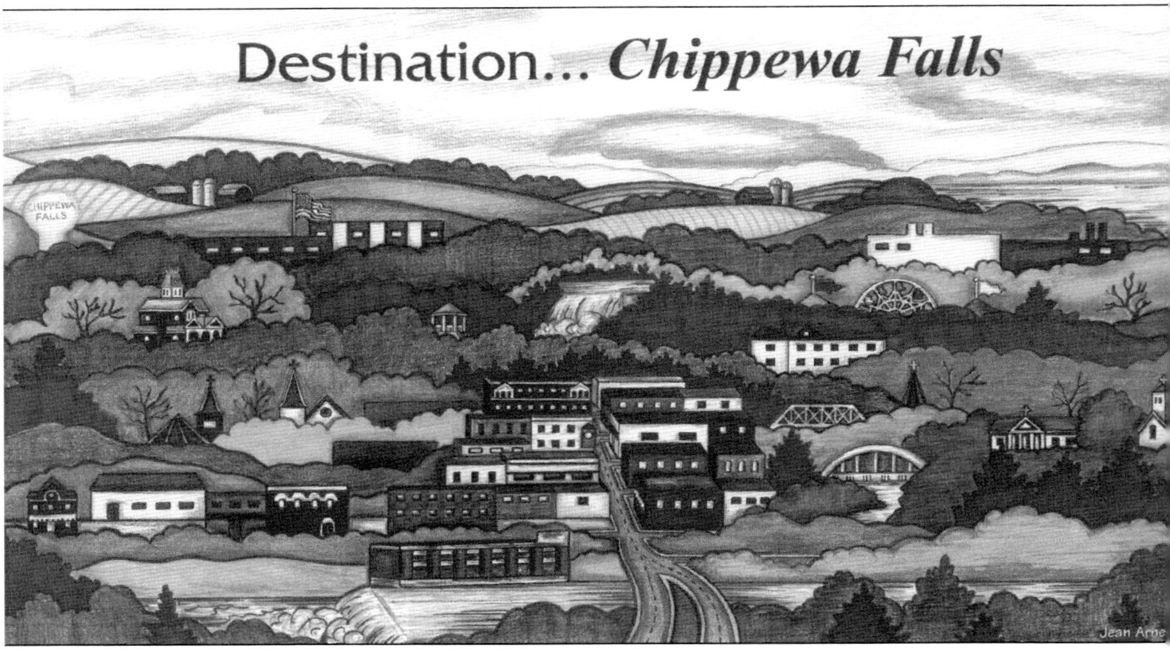

"Destination" as defined in *Roget's International Thesaurus* can be an address, an end, a goal, or an objective. Chippewa Falls, Wisconsin, is all of these. In 2000, in recognition of its historic preservation accomplishments, the National Trust for Historic Preservation designated Chippewa Falls as one of a Dozen Distinctive Destinations in the United States. Chippewa Falls Main Street, Inc., commissioned local artist Jean Arneson to create a panoramic view of Chippewa Falls, a city in a valley with historic architecture, surrounded by rolling hills and farmland and bounded by the scenic Chippewa River waterfront. This friendly, unique, and picturesque community invites you to make Chippewa Falls your destination.

IMAGES
of America

CHIPPEWA FALLS
MAIN STREET

Chippewa Falls Main Street, Inc.

Evalyn Wiley Frasch, Lead Author
Lucyann LeCleir
Jim Schuh
Nancy Schuh

ARCADIA
PUBLISHING

ISBN 978-0-7385-3354-4

Published by Arcadia Publishing
Charleston, South Carolina

Printed in the United States of America

Library of Congress Catalog Card Number: 2005920902

For all general information contact Arcadia Publishing at:
Telephone 843-853-2070
Fax 843-853-0044
E-mail sales@arcadiapublishing.com
For customer service and orders:
Toll-Free 1-888-313-2665

Visit us on the Internet at www.arcadiapublishing.com

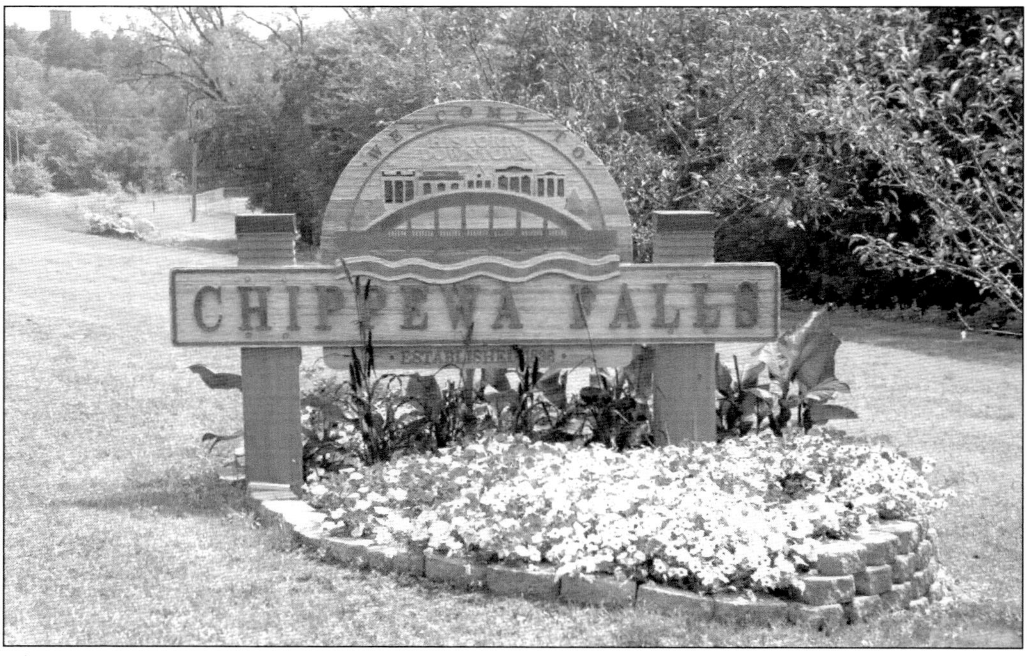

Chippewa Falls Main Street designed and installed two welcome signs in downtown Chippewa Falls. The logo on the sign incorporated the image of the Marsh Rainbow Arch Bridge, historic buildings, and the important words "Welcome to Historic Downtown Chippewa Falls, established in 1869." (Courtesy of Dave Gordon.)

Contents

Acknowledgments

One of the objectives of the Main Street program is to increase the appreciation of our irreplaceable historic architecture and of our unique local history. We hope this book will help to accomplish this goal.

We are grateful to the following businesses and organizations that assisted with their time, guidance, knowledge, resources, and photographs.

Chippewa County Genealogical Society
Chippewa County Historical Society (CCHS)
Chippewa County Sheriff's Department (CCSD)
Chippewa Falls Area Chamber of Commerce (CFACC)
Chippewa Falls Main Street, Inc. (CFMS)
Chippewa Falls Museum of Industry & Technology (CFMIT)
Chippewa Valley Museum (CVM)
Chippewa Valley Newspapers' *Chippewa Herald*
City of Chippewa Falls Fire Department (CFFD)
City of Chippewa Falls Public Library
Jacob Leinenkugel Brewing Company (JLBC)

We want to thank everyone who submitted photographs for consideration. Photo credits are noted with each picture. For the purpose of brevity we may have used the above abbreviations.

Chippewa Falls Main Street thanks the dedicated team who created this publication, our second pictorial history.

Lead Author: Evalyn Wiley Frasch
Other team members who assisted her with writing, collecting photographs, interviewing, researching, editing, and layout are:
Dave Gordon, computer wizard extraordinaire
Lucyann LeCleir
Arley Engel
Nancy Schuh
Mary Kay Brown (Main Street Administrative Assistant)
Jim Schuh, Executive Director

We also thank the spouses for their patience and understanding.

The Main Street Board of Directors, staff and volunteers hope that you enjoy our second pictorial history as much as we enjoyed collaborating on it. The local profits from this book help to fund Main Street projects.

INTRODUCTION

By the late 1860s, after the Civil War, settlers pushed westward to new lands, adventure, and the lure of wealth. The world was more accessible with the completion of both the Suez Canal and the transcontinental railroad in the United States.

In 1869, the city of Chippewa Falls, the chief sawmill town on the Chippewa River, was incorporated. Although the city did not see its first railroad line until 1875, it was a bustling lumber community with hotels, boarding houses, saloons, various mercantile establishments, public schools, churches, banks, and a fledgling brewery.

Frenchtown, on the southern shores of the Chippewa River, was home to our first European settlers—brave, peaceful, and industrious French Canadians. This first settlement became the area's hub for stage lines, steamboats, and the ferry that ran to Duncan Creek and the new developments across the river attracting land speculates and modest homesteaders. Many would stop for refreshments at the Rousseau House, a tavern named for its popular owner Charles Rousseau, before and after their trips. Pictured, looking north from Frenchtown, is an early bridge that crossed over the falls of the Chippewa River. (Courtesy of CCHS.)

In the decades that followed, Chippewa Falls continued to grow in popularity, population, and influence. At one point it was the fastest-growing city in Wisconsin. Despite hardships, natural and manmade, the city persevered through the fickle ebb and flow of progress like the mighty river it is named after. One hundred and thirty-five years later, it remains a progressive community that values its history, its uniqueness, and the pioneering spirit that drives its citizens to this day.

These historical photographs are a conduit for our citizens and guests to see our glorious past. The authors of this pictorial history hope that the light of the past and the stories of our ancestors will inspire new thoughts, aspirations, and a passion for our history and our future.

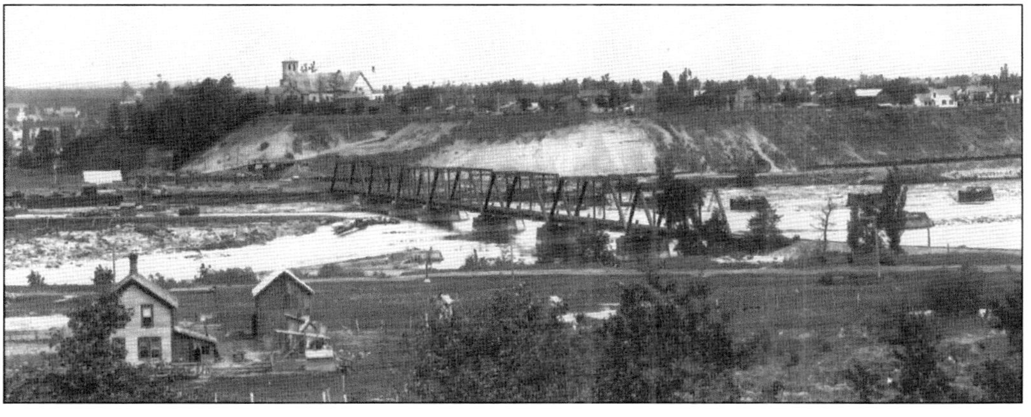

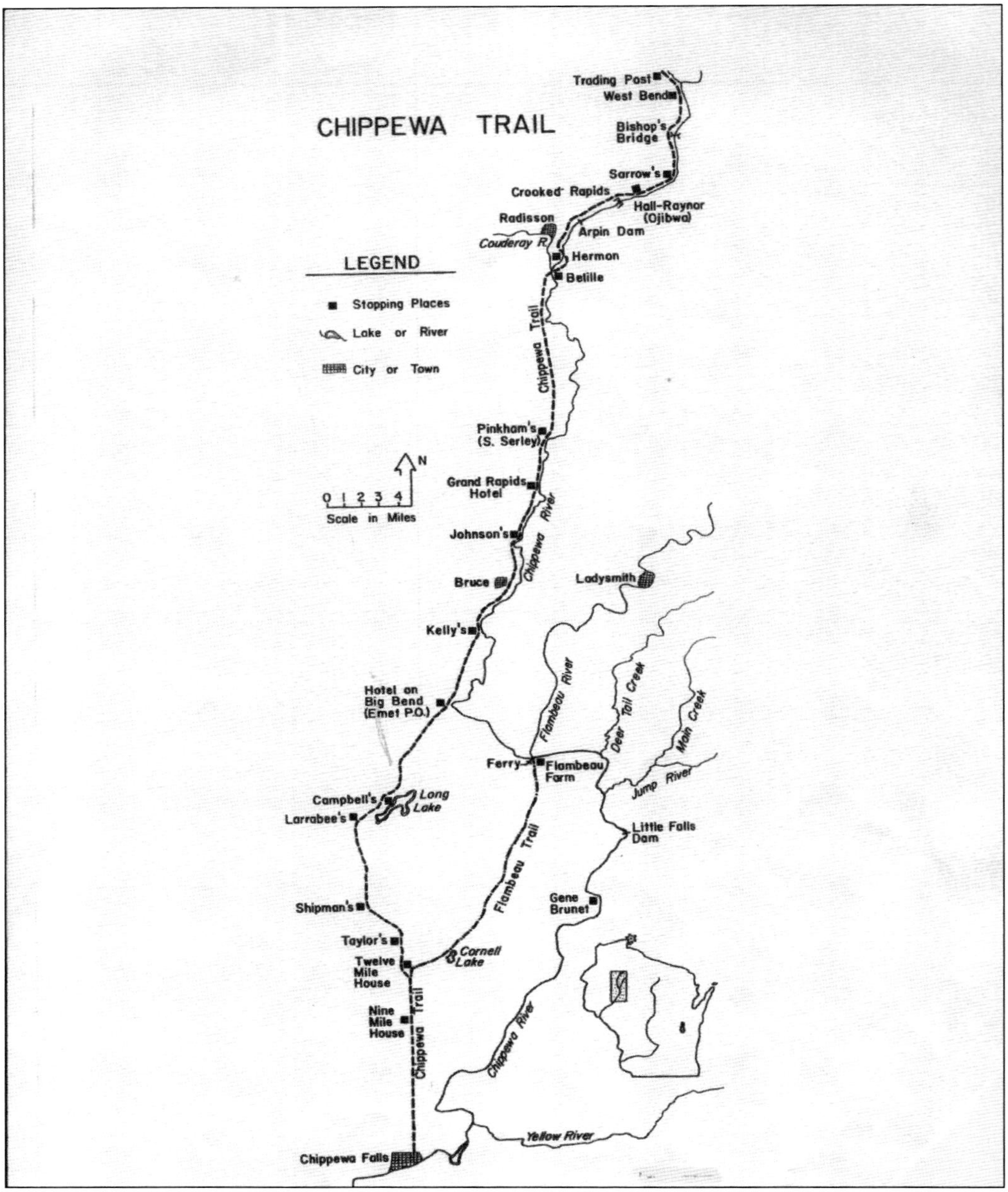

Every morning in the fall and early winter, 40 to 50 tote teams loaded with supplies purchased from merchants in the city left Chippewa Falls, bound for lumber camps, some of them hundreds of miles above Chippewa Falls. (Courtesy of Arley Engel.)

One

Turn of the Century

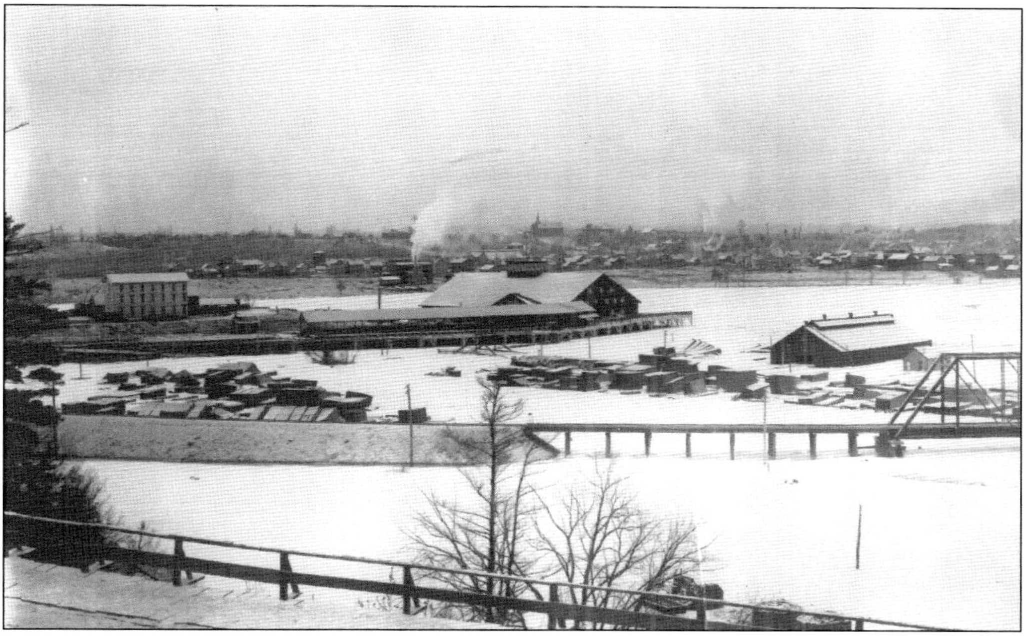

In 1836, Jean Brunet built the first sawmill on the Chippewa River for Hercules Dousman of Prairie du Chien, in essence, fixing the location of what would become the city of Chippewa Falls. From 1836 until 1911, sawmills on that site converted the strong, light, seemingly endless supply of pine into commercial lumber. During its continuous history of lumbering, the sawmill was flooded, burned, and rebuilt, while its many owners struggled to carry on the business on which the growing city depended. Hiram Allen and Frederick Weyerhaeuser were the most committed. In 1886, after the mill burned, Weyerhaeuser rebuilt the three-story structure into the largest sawmill under one roof in the world. After many decades, the pine resources of the Chippewa River basin were exhausted and the mill closed in 1911. Frederick Weyerhaeuser moved to Tacoma, Washington, where he had incorporated the Weyerhaeuser Company in 1900. Some people followed the lumber industry west, while many more remained in the Chippewa Falls area to pursue new business interests and to carve out farms on the cutover lands. (Courtesy of Arley Engel.)

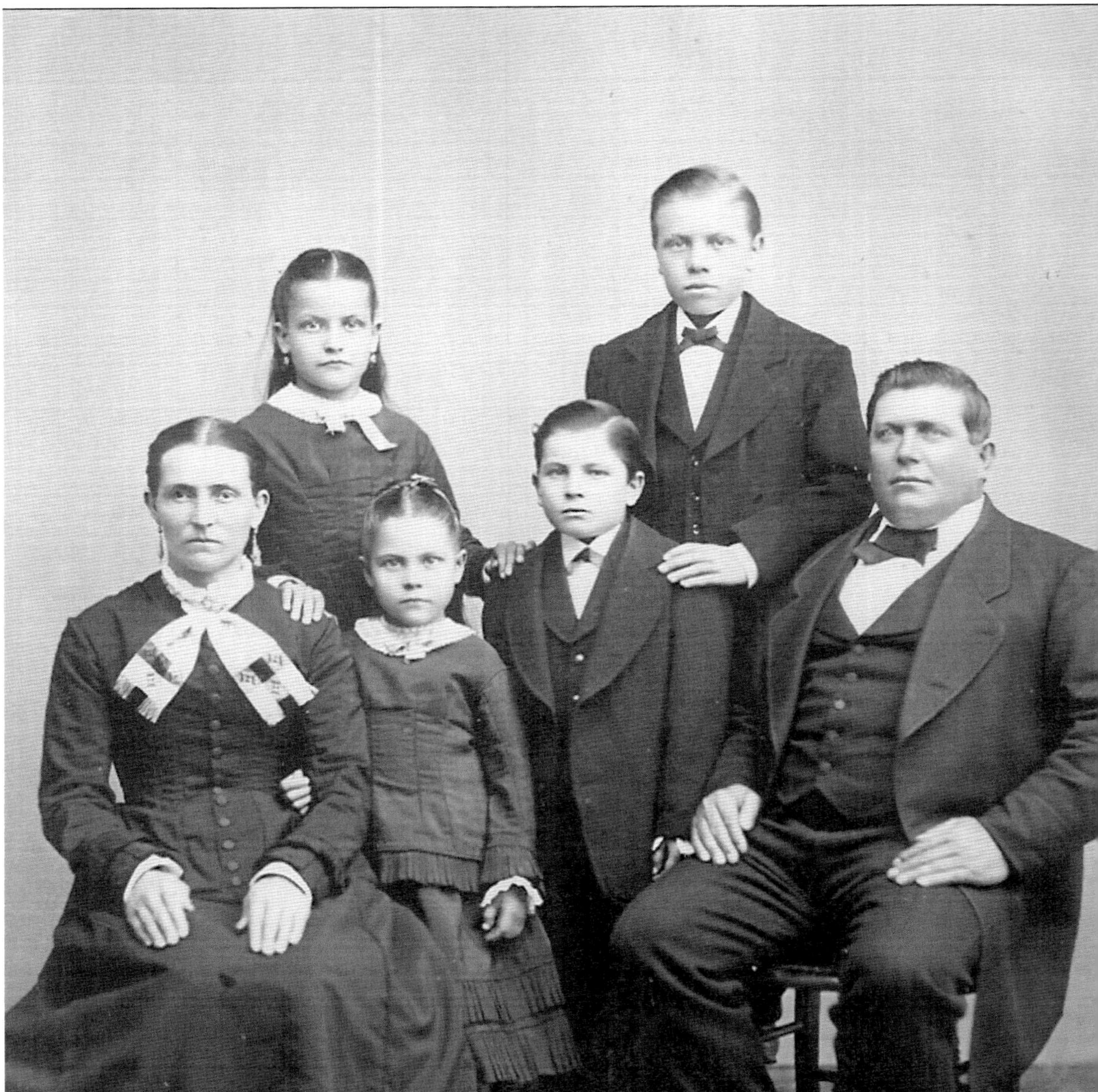

In 1867, Jacob Leinenkugel, having learned the brewery business from his father and wishing to establish his own brewery, moved to Chippewa Falls with his wife, Josephine, and son, Matt. He purchased property along Duncan Creek from Hiram Allen, and built a home for his family. The entire family endeavored to build up the brewery. The boys worked with their father in the brewery, while the girls helped cook meals for the brewery workers; however, after completing eighth grade, Rose and Susan began to work full-time in the brewery. Pictured (from left to right) are Josephine, Rose, Susan, William, Matt, and Jacob Leinenkugel. (Courtesy of JLBC.)

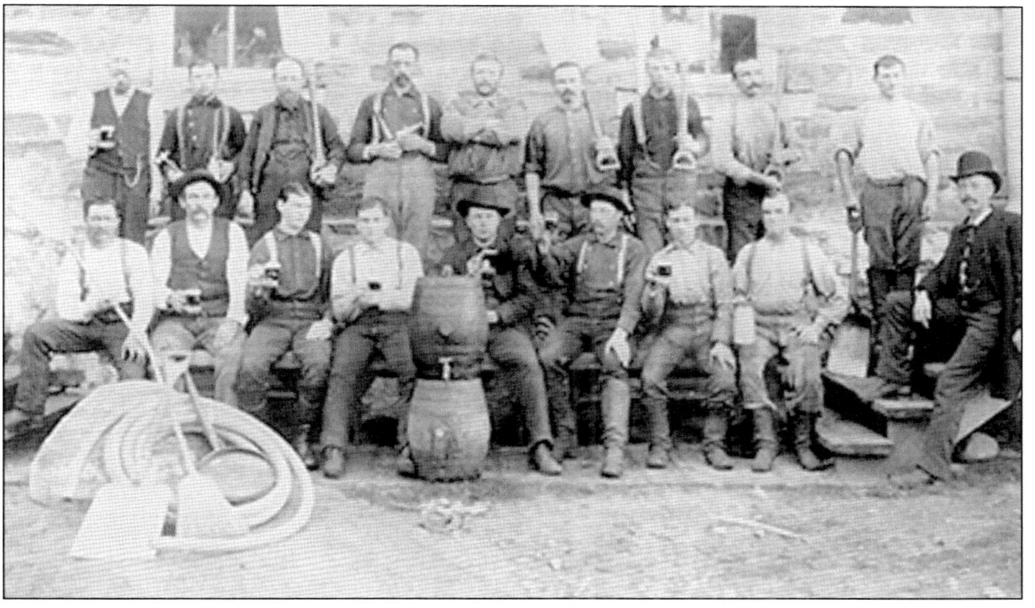

During the early years of the Spring Brewery, Jacob Leinenkugel brewed the beer and John Miller delivered the barrels to customers on their small cart pulled by a horse named Kate. As Chippewa Falls grew, so did Leinenkugel's Brewery. Dormitories were built on the brewery property to accommodate the male workers, many of whom lived apart from their families. Pictured is Matt Leinenkugel, in the center behind the barrels, with brewery workers enjoying their Bock beer. (Courtesy of JLBC.)

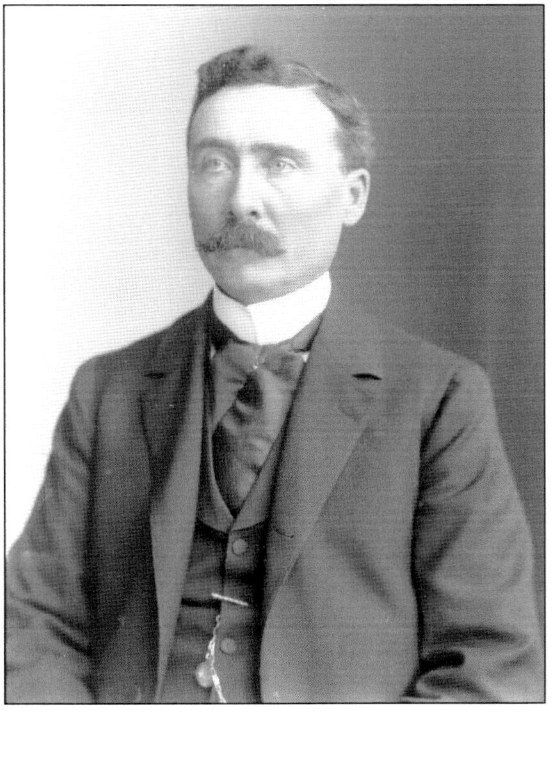

Born in Fox Lake, Wisconsin, in 1857, John Anderson graduated from the University of Wisconsin in 1879 and served as principal of Mauston High School before coming to Chippewa Falls in 1881 to practice law. He was a mayor, a city attorney, and for eight years a county judge. Judge Anderson was perhaps best known as the biographer of Father Charles Francis Xavier Goldsmith. (Courtesy of Dolores Beaudette.)

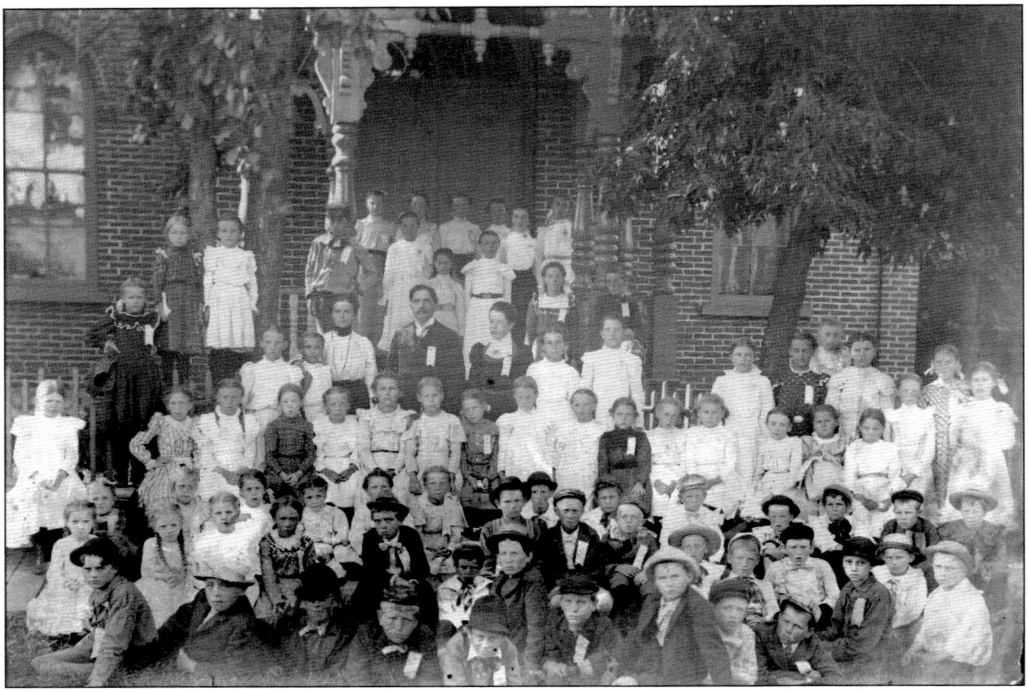

Organized in 1873, with its first small frame church on Jefferson Avenue, the Lutheran congregation decided to build a more centrally located church in 1884. They chose a lot on East Columbia Street and erected a brick building, completing a chapel on the south side of the church in 1912. Reverend A.P. Lea taught church school during the summer months. Also known as the Norwegian Lutheran Church, it then became the Scandinavian Lutheran Church. In the 1930s it was renamed Central Lutheran Church, a name that reflects its historic location and purpose. The picture below shows the church as it appeared from the 1940s through the 1970s. (Courtesy of (top) Central Lutheran Church and (bottom) CCHS.)

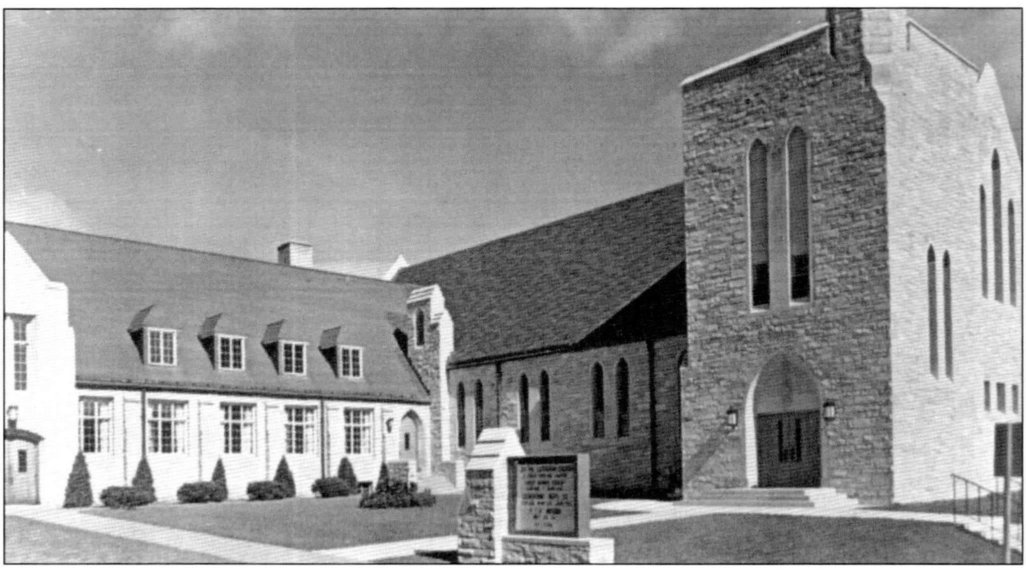

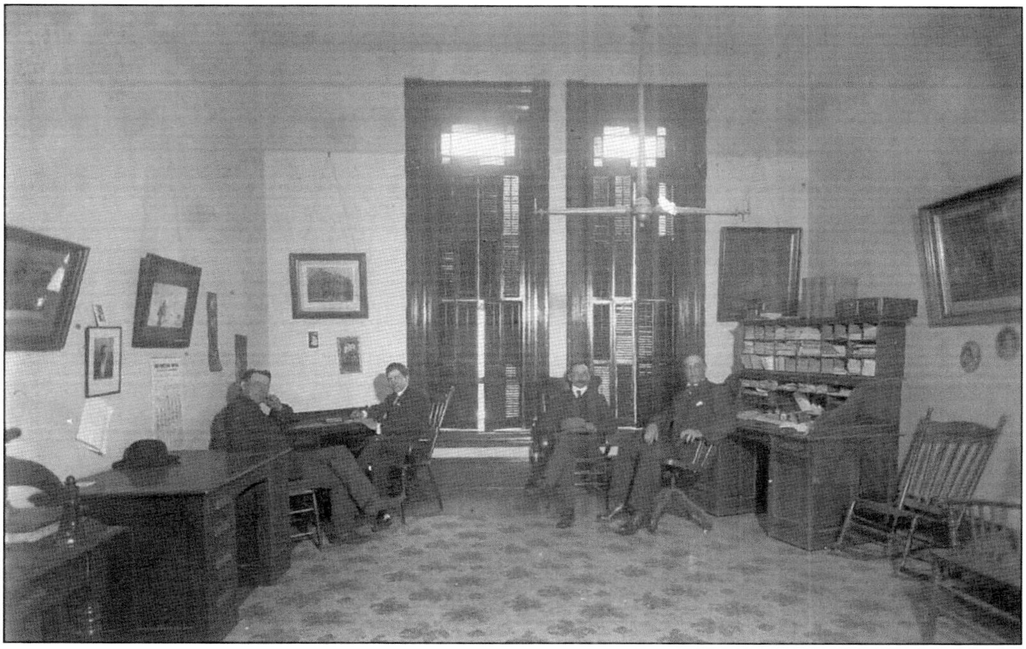

Recognizing the needs of young men for intellectual, social, physical, and spiritual guidance, especially during the tumultuous lumbering era, concerned individuals petitioned the Wisconsin State YMCA for permission to establish a YMCA in Chippewa Falls. After it was chartered in 1883, members began meeting on the second floor of 119 North Bridge Street. Pictured in 1904, these members gathered in one of the seven rooms set aside for YMCA activities, including a library with daily, weekly, and monthly papers, magazines, and books, one of which may have been *The Adventures of Huckleberry Finn* by Mark Twain, published in 1884. Below is the present-day YMCA located on Jefferson Avenue, which continues the tradition of providing social and physical activities for Chippewa Valley residents. (Courtesy of CCHS and Dave Gordon.)

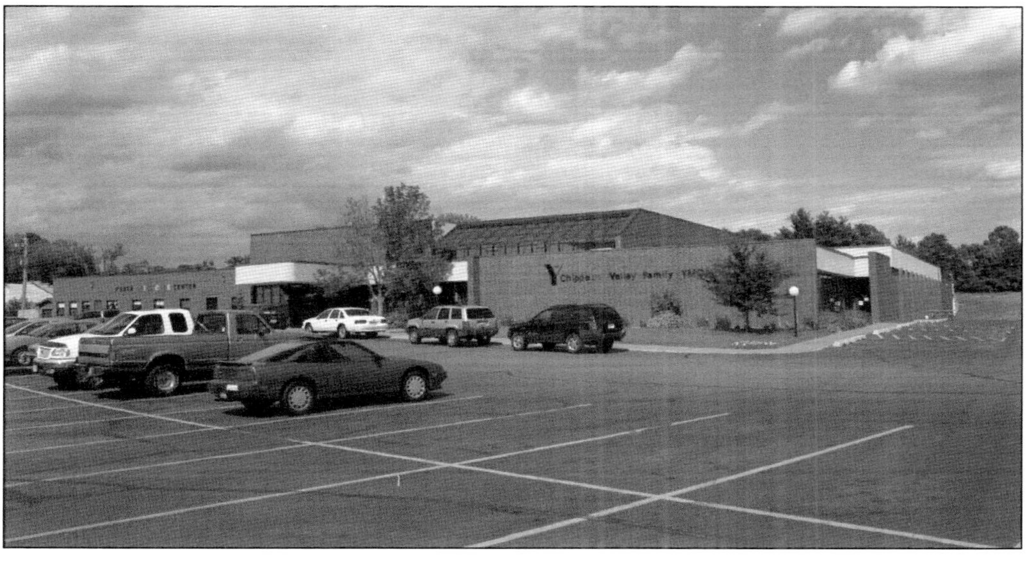

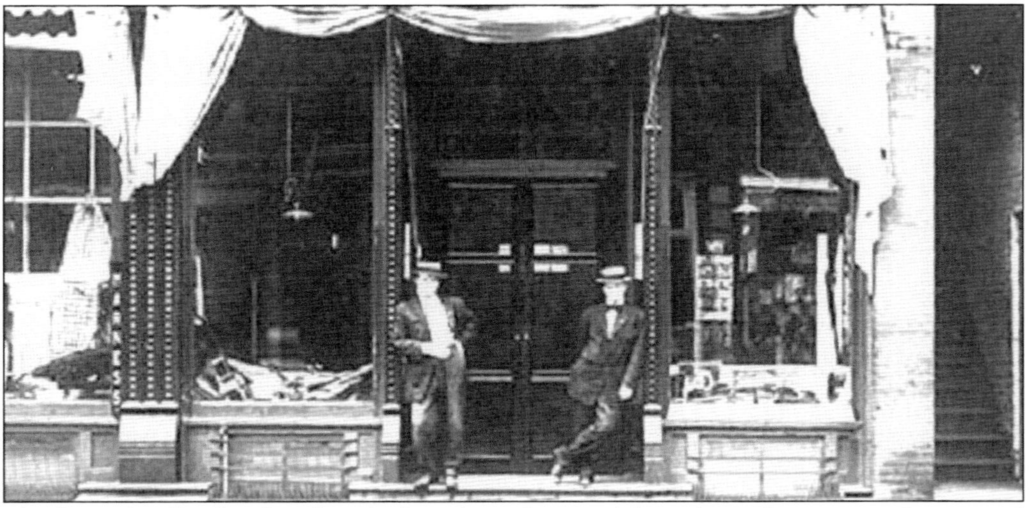

The fame of Helland violins dates back to the early part of the eighteenth century and originated in Telemarken, Norway. Knute and Gunnar Helland, great-grandsons of founder Joseph Helland, immigrated to the United States and settled in Chippewa Falls in 1909. Knute and Gunnar Helland are pictured *c.* 1918 outside the Helland Brothers Music Store, where they crafted violins made from maple and spruce for musicians throughout the country. (Courtesy of CCHS.)

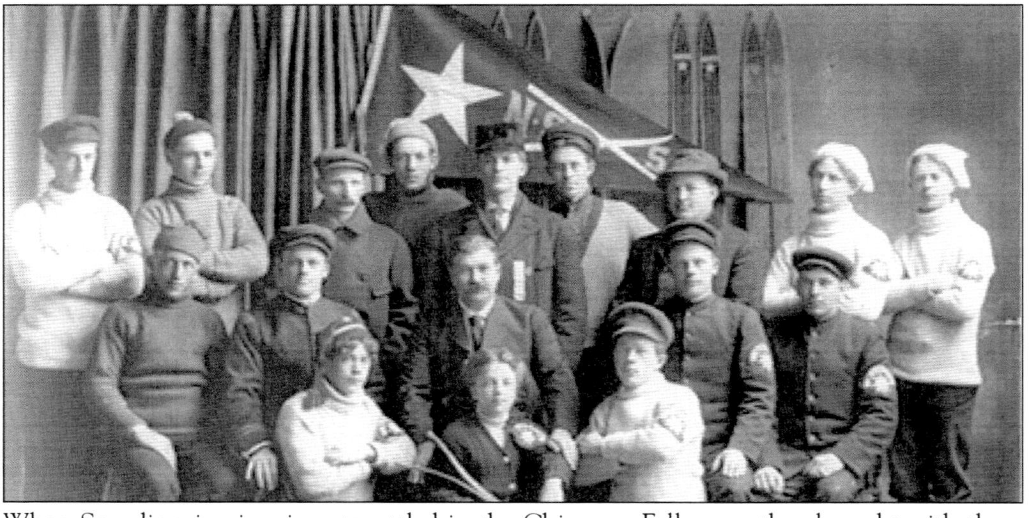

When Scandinavian immigrants settled in the Chippewa Falls area, they brought with them the traditions of their homelands, including the sport of ski jumping. In 1909, Oscar Gunderson broke the world record with a jump of 138 feet. The ski club was so prominent in making the sport popular in America that it hosted the Annual Ski Tournament in 1912, which attracted 70 entries from all over the country. Members of the North Star Ski Club pictured in this *c.* 1915 image are: (standing, left to right) Lars Haugen, Guy DeLong, Halvor Sampson, Albert Sands, Archie Putnam, Sever Remol, Rudy Emerson, Elstrom, and Anders Haugen; (seated, second row, from left to right) Anton Bergerson, Knute Helland, Julius Hovland, Gunnar Helland, and Oscar Gunderson; (front row, from left to right) Einar Lund, Ether Bergeson, and Harold Lund. (Courtesy of CCHS.)

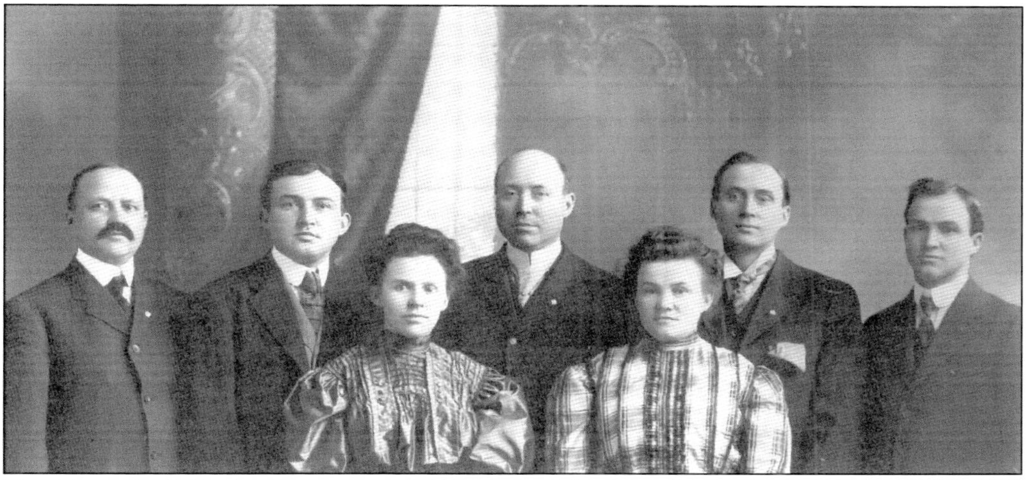

The Chippewa Falls Art Company took this picture of the Joas family in 1912. Pictured from left are Leonard, George, Lucy, Frank, Anna, Joseph, and Christopher Joas. By 1946, the Joas Insurance and Real Estate Agency, located at 107 W. Spring Street in a building constructed and used by L.C. Stanley, was a thriving and respected business in Chippewa Falls. (Courtesy of Joe Joas.)

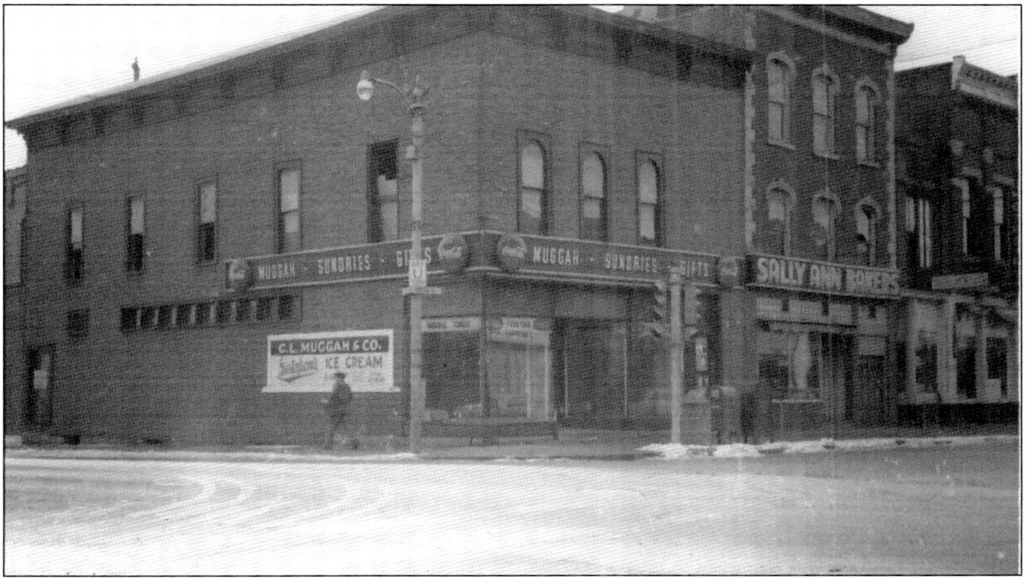

On the busy corner of Bridge and Spring Streets, Muggah Drug was established in 1908 by C.L. Muggah and became home of the famous Rexall lines of drugs and drug novelties. The popular drugstore won the confidence of the public "strictly on the merits of the goods." C.L. Muggah served as vice president of the Chippewa Falls Commercial Association. (Courtesy of CCHS.)

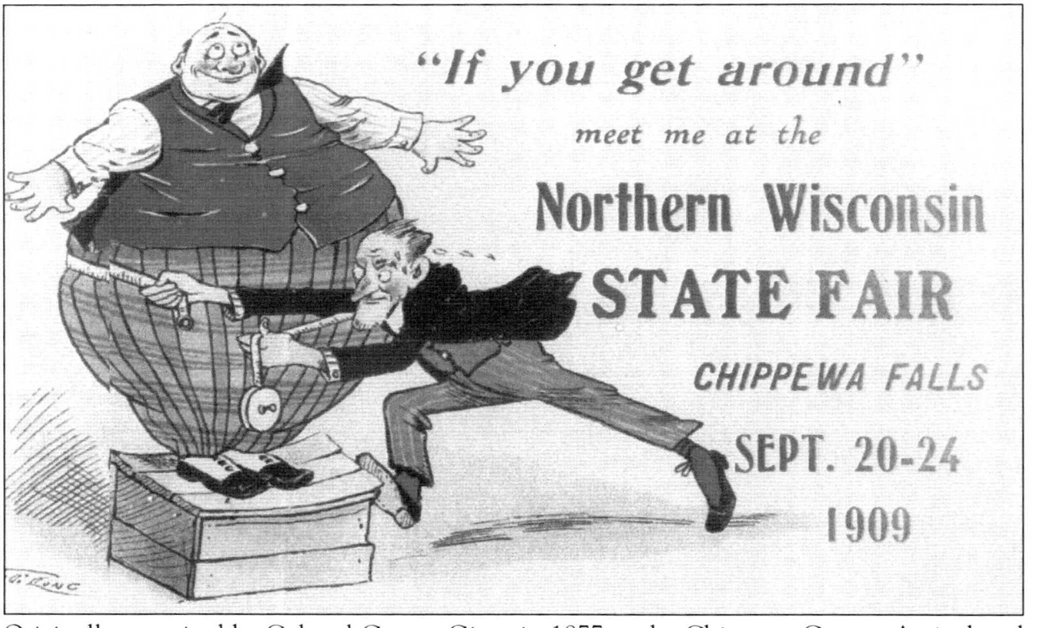

Originally organized by Colonel George Ginty in 1877 as the Chippewa County Agricultural Society, the Northern Wisconsin State Fair's purpose was to showcase the abundant agricultural products of the area. Fruits, vegetables, as well as horses, cattle, pigs, and sheep were exhibited, while harness races entertained the crowds. The theme "Meet Me at the Northern Wisconsin State Fair" appeared each year on creatively-produced posters. (Courtesy of CCHS.)

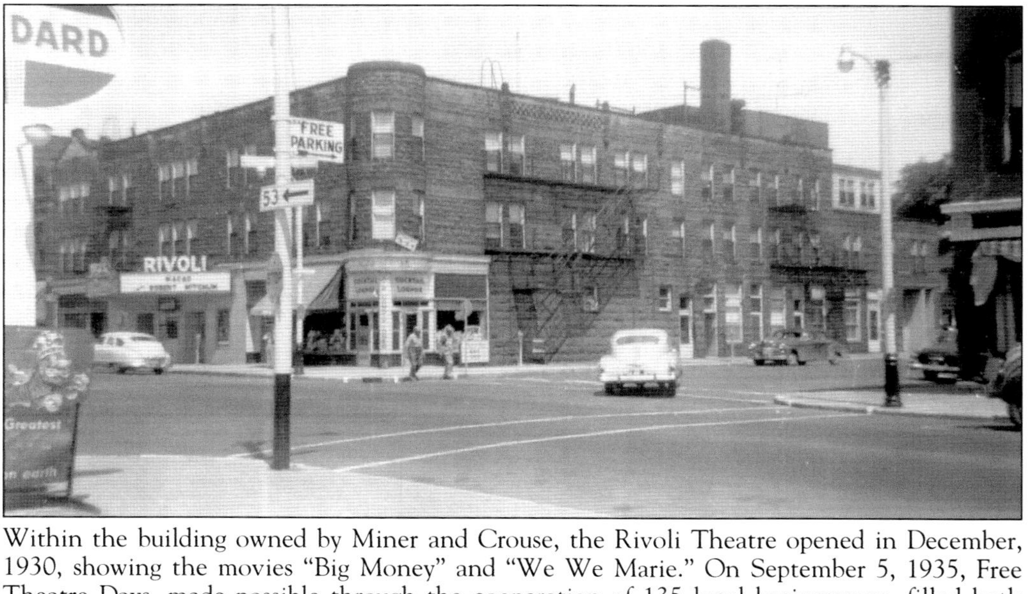

Within the building owned by Miner and Crouse, the Rivoli Theatre opened in December, 1930, showing the movies "Big Money" and "We We Marie." On September 5, 1935, Free Theatre Days, made possible through the cooperation of 135 local businessmen, filled both the Rivoli and Loop Theatres to capacity. In 1939, the Chamber of Commerce sponsored free movies for rural school children whose schools were closed that day to enable them to attend. (Courtesy of Dave and Kris Martineau.)

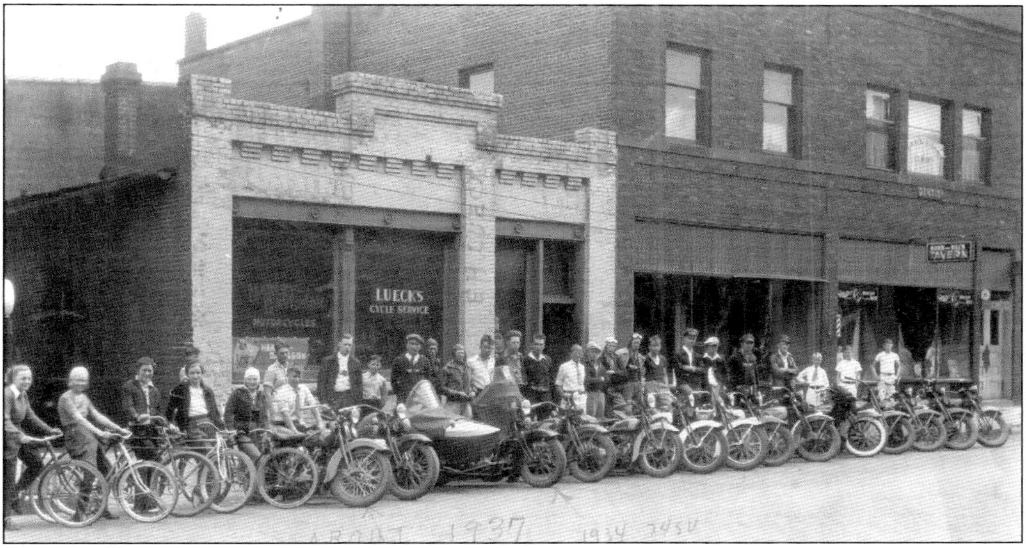

The Harley-Davidson Motor Company, organized in 1908 by William Harley and Arthur Davidson in Milwaukee, had an outlet for their fledgling motorcycles in Chippewa Falls. Walter and Ehrich Lueck opened a sporting goods store on Bay Street in 1912 and sold boats, motors, bicycles, and Harley-Davidson motorcycles. In this *c.* 1937 picture, proud owners display their Schwinn bicycles and Harley-Davidson motorcycles outside Lueck's at 7 E. Spring Street. (Courtesy of the Carl Lueck Family.)

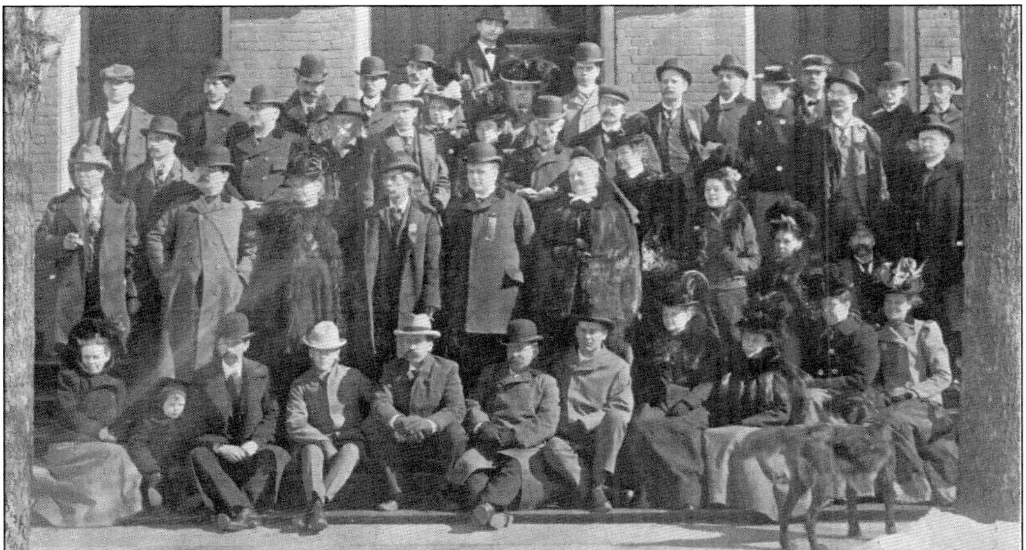

One of the oldest organizations of its kind, the Wisconsin Press Association met often in Chippewa Falls. Established as a social organization, rather than a business organization, members gathered for a week each year for a banquet and ball. The Northern Wisconsin Press Association held its meeting in Chippewa Falls in 1900, perhaps with editors present from the *Blair Press*, *Sparta Herald*, *Melrose Chronicle*, *Greenwood Gleaner*, the *Chippewa Times*, and the *Chippewa Herald*. (Courtesy of CCHS.)

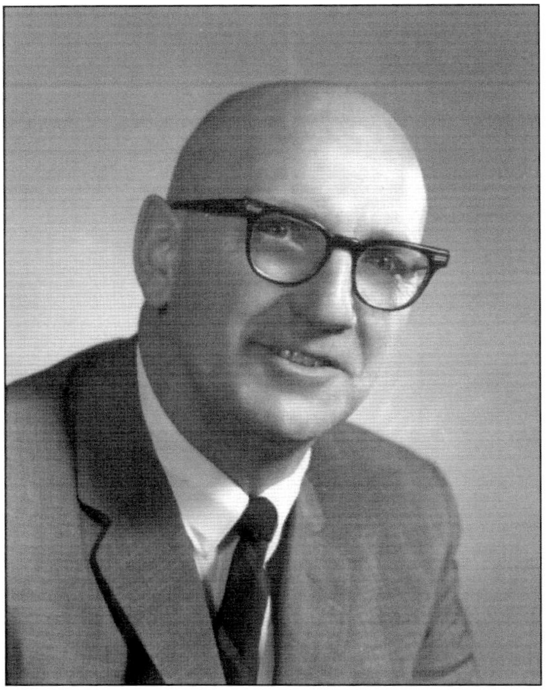

In 1946, Holly Meier began his career at the *Chippewa Herald Telegram* at the sports desk, and then moved on to the city courthouse beat, before becoming editor in the 1950s. His "Off the Beat" column highlighted his honest but folksy writing style which made life come alive on paper, according to his publisher, John Lavine. When Holly Meier died in 1985, the *Chippewa Herald* staff acknowledged that "a part of this newspaper's soul" went with him. (Courtesy of the *Chippewa Herald*.)

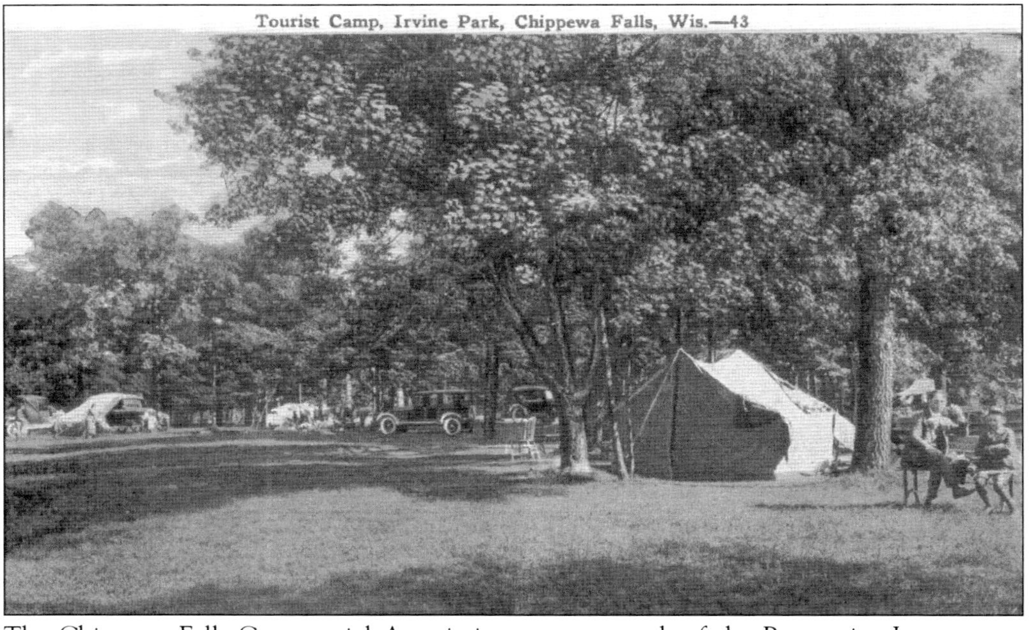

The Chippewa Falls Commercial Association, an outgrowth of the Progressive League, was responsible for the many improvements to the tourist campground at Irvine Park. In the 1930s the association made possible the up-to-date kitchens equipped with gas ranges, free gas for cooking, and shower baths, all of which were designed to make the tourist campsite a favorite stopping place for transcontinental visitors on the Yellowstone Trail, as well as summer visitors to Upper Wisconsin. (Courtesy of Gail Shipman.)

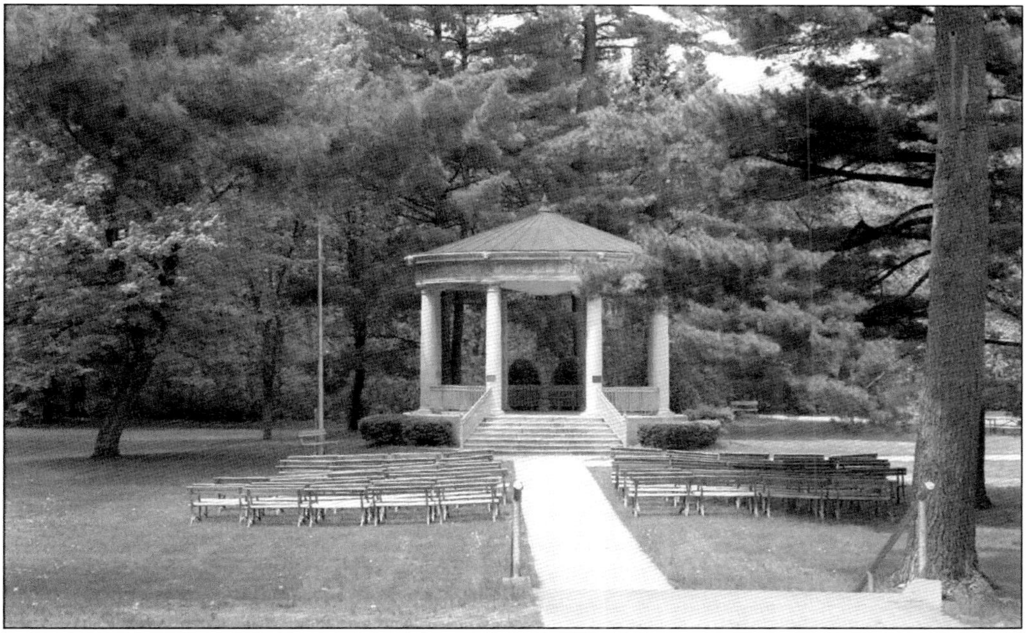

Dedicated in May, 1924, "To Our Soldiers and Sailors," the $10,000 band stand was constructed of Bedford stone and given to the city by William Irvine, who had managed the Chippewa Lumber and Boom Company for Frederick Weyerhaeuser. The dedication ceremony, attended by 15,000 people, included an acceptance speech by Mayor Eugene O'Neil who declared, "Generations yet to come will remember and bless the giver and his gift of inestimable worth." (Courtesy of Dave Gordon.)

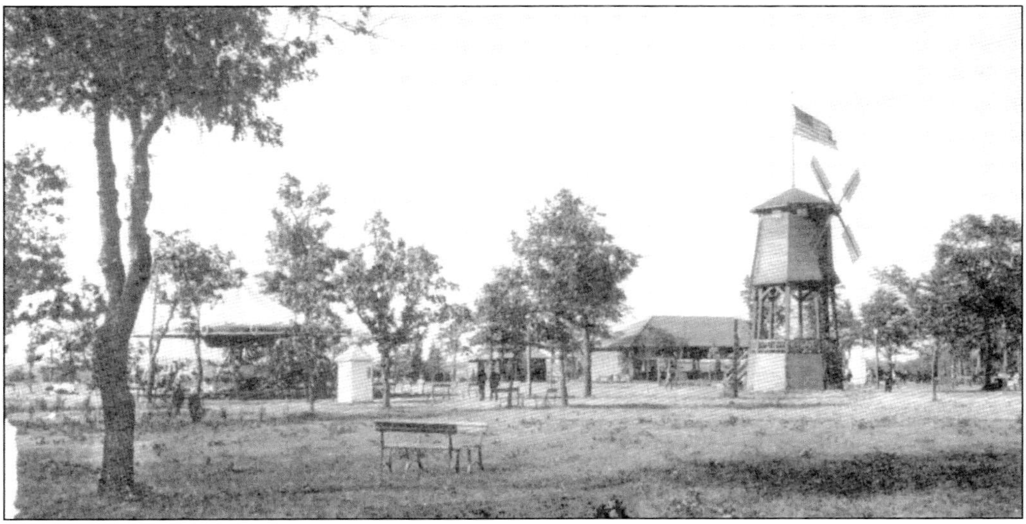

The first dam creating the 80-acre Lake Hallie was built in 1843 as a reservoir for the Blue Mills sawmill. In about 1910, when the mill closed, the Chippewa Valley Electric Railway developed Electric Park as an excursion destination for picnickers and fishermen. Electric Park, with a shelter ringed with lights, a bathing beach, dance hall, movie tower in a windmill, and boat rides, sparked recreational use of the lake. (Courtesy of CVM.)

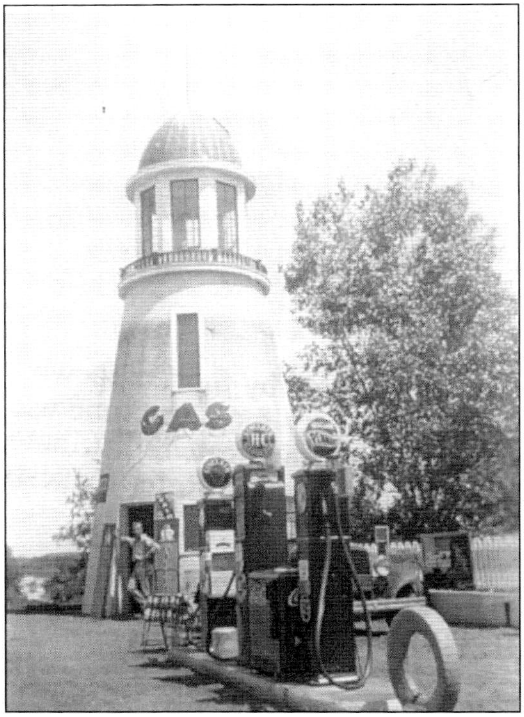

On Highway 29, the Lighthouse Gas Station advertised "Good Service—Drive In, Drive Out Satisfied." After its life as a gas station, and with the construction of Highway 29 necessitating the removal of the gas pumps, Norman Valley converted the lighthouse into a root beer stand. In 1967, Al Przybylski, owner of O'Neil Creek Campground in the town of Eagle Point, purchased and carefully relocated the 15-ton structure to the campground for use as a refreshment stand. (Courtesy of CCHS.)

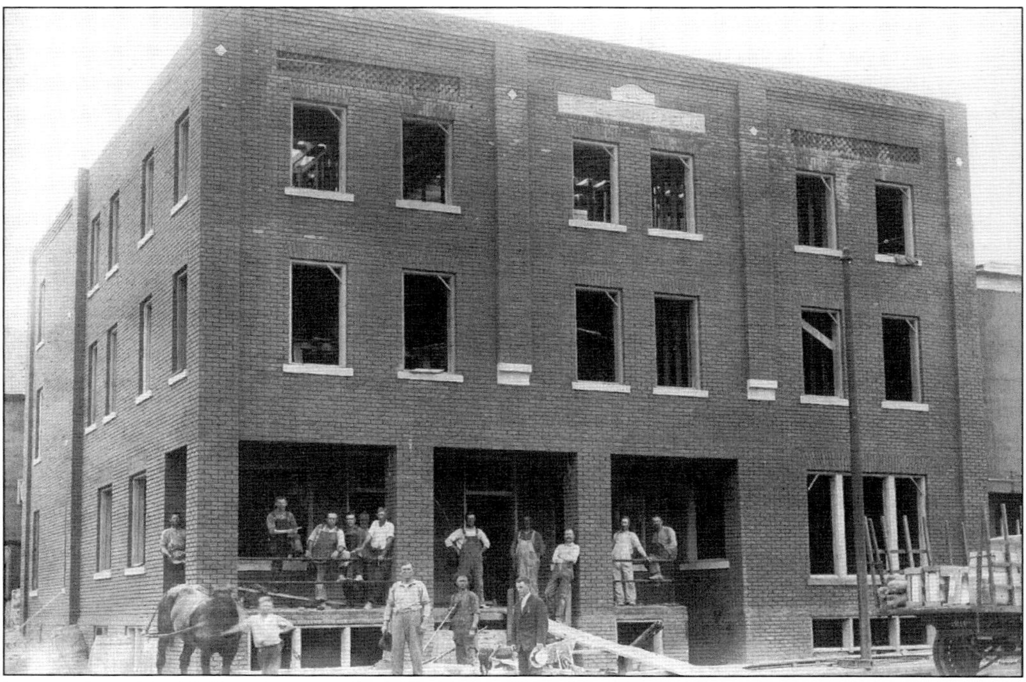

Located at 16–18 Bay Street, the Chippewa Hotel was constructed in 1915 and, upon its completion, it advertised hot and cold water and telephones in all rooms. Rates ranged from $2.25 to $2.50, while rooms with baths were available for $3.00 a night. (Courtesy of CCHS.)

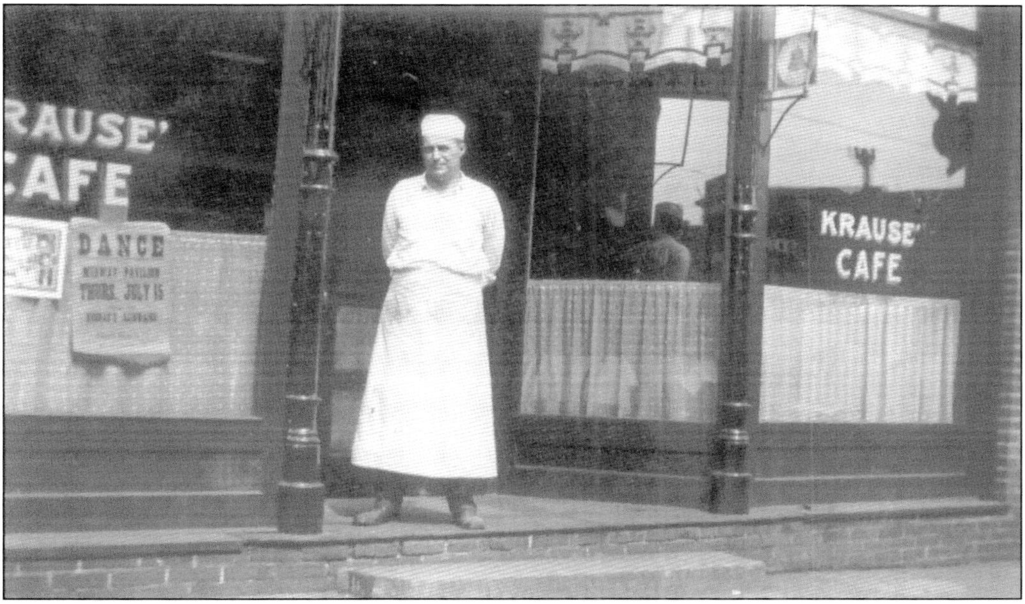

In 1920, Alvin Krause became the chef at the Hotel Northern. Four years later, he opened his first restaurant on the 300 block of Bridge Street, opposite Hotel Northern. Standing in the doorway of his first café in 1925, Al Krause advertised "Good Eats at Moderate Prices with Real Hospitality." Throughout his career, Al Krause enjoyed the reputation of operating a good restaurant with good food. (Courtesy of Audrey Krause Mattison.)

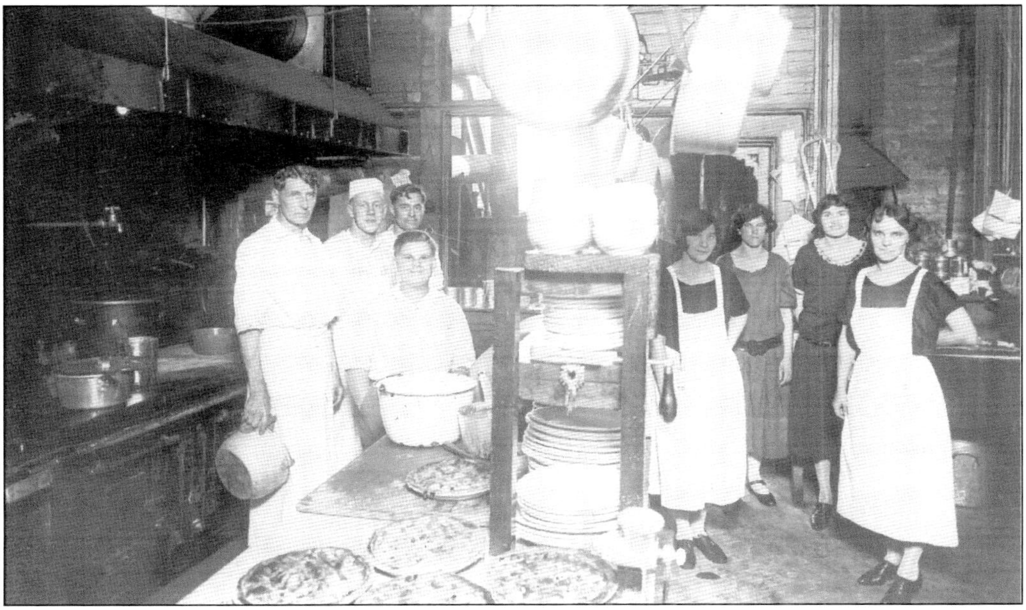

From this photograph taken on July 10, 1925, it is clear that the kitchen of Krause's Café was the focal point of the restaurant. Out of the kitchen came good food such as fried spring chicken with mashed potatoes and buttered new wax beans and, for dessert, fudge square á la mode. (Courtesy of Audrey Krause Mattison.)

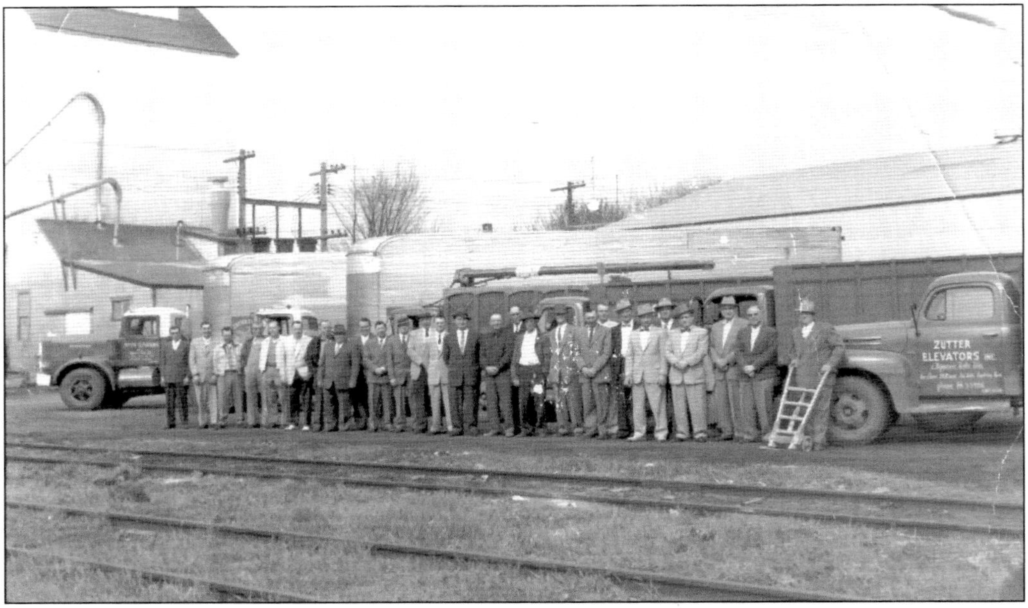

Since 1933, Zutter Elevators have served both rural and city people. It was the farm headquarters for the famous Chip-a-way Feeds and Seeds. With elevators in Chippewa Falls, Eagleton, Jim Falls, and Elk Mound, the company also sold lawn products, paint, fertilizer, binder twine, fruit, and poultry equipment. The main office and store in Chippewa Falls were located at 11 E. Spring Street while the Zutter Elevator was on the East Hill, where these employees have gathered. (Courtesy of Don and Mona Zutter.)

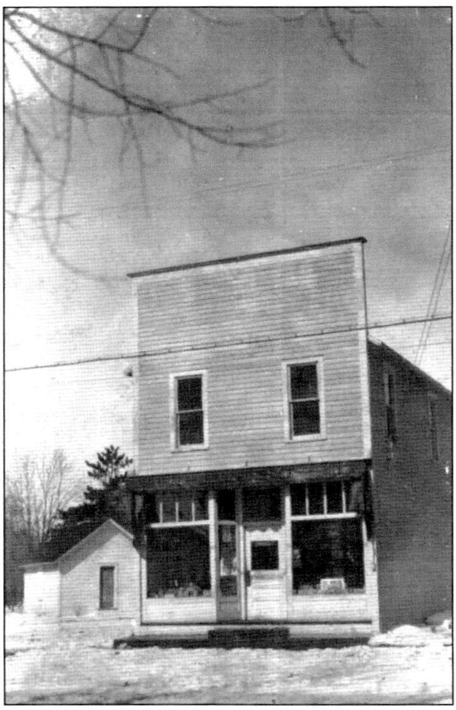

In 1874 in Chippewa Falls, there were three grocery stores, three meat markets, three bakeries, and two "fruit and confectionary" stores, all located downtown. By the turn of the century, neighborhood stores proliferated. Redard Brothers Store, pictured c. 1920, was located at 704–706 E. Grand Avenue. Presently, this historic building houses Bresina's Old Home Restaurant. (Courtesy of David R. Redard.)

Clint and Wirt Redard stand before well-stocked shelves from which customers could choose coffee, sugar, spices, canned goods, and preserved and dried fruits, c. 1919. Many generations of children have delighted in the extensive "penny candy" selection found in the long glass showcases. (Courtesy of David R. Redard.)

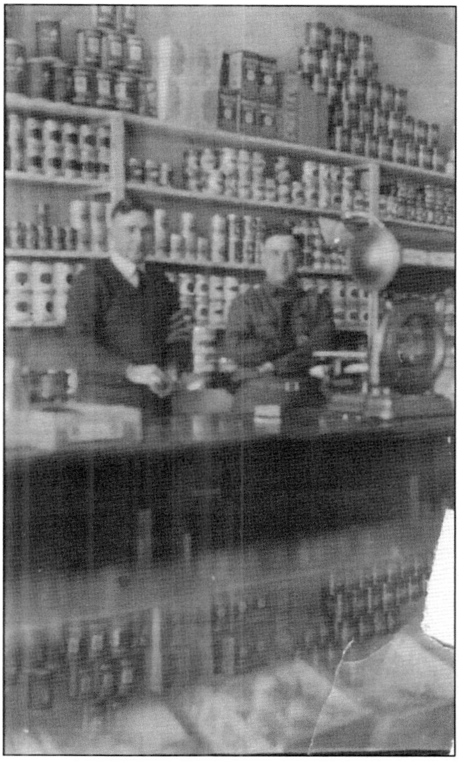

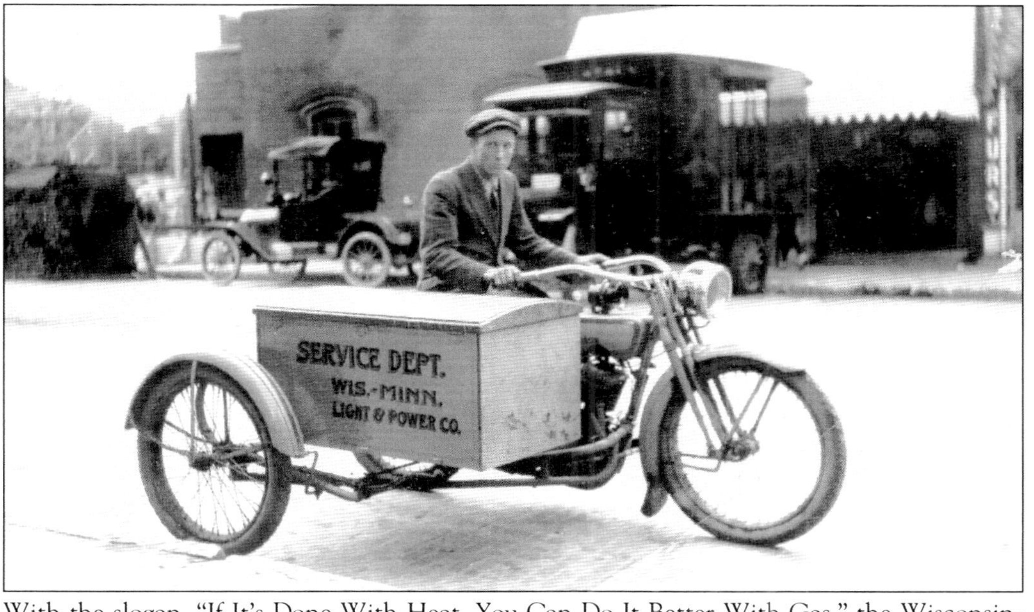

With the slogan, "If It's Done With Heat, You Can Do It Better With Gas," the Wisconsin-Minnesota Light and Power Company offered gas and electric appliances to the community. The modified Harley-Davidson motorcycle advertised the availability of its service department on wheels. (Courtesy of the Carl Lueck Family.)

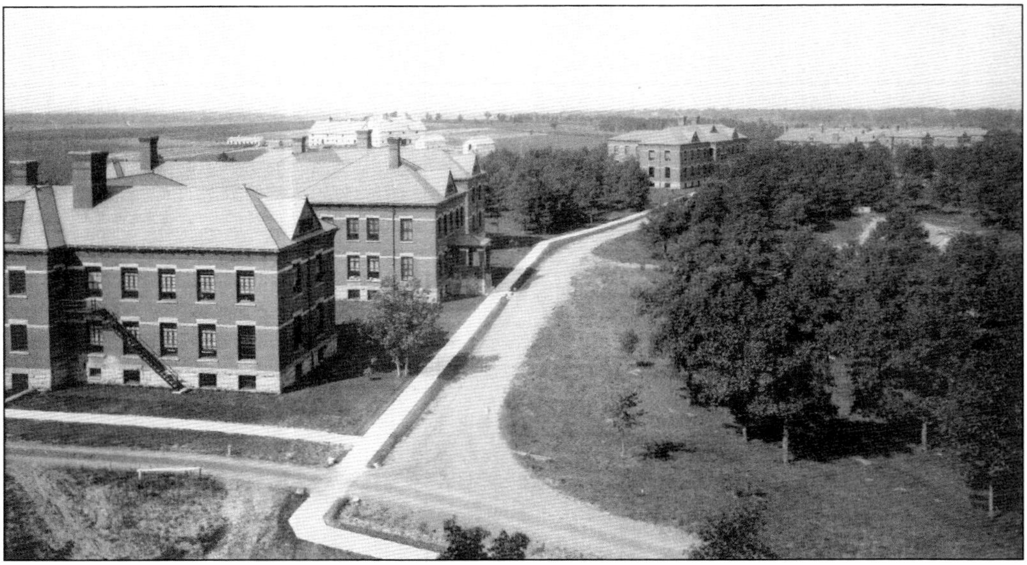

In 1897, the conditions which called for admission into the Wisconsin Home for the Feeble Minded were "the mentally afflicted child who absorbs the attention of the mother to the detriment of other children" and the widowed father unable to take care of his children financially. Each child received such care and treatment as their condition required and such education as they were capable of receiving. (Courtesy of C.J. Bejin.)

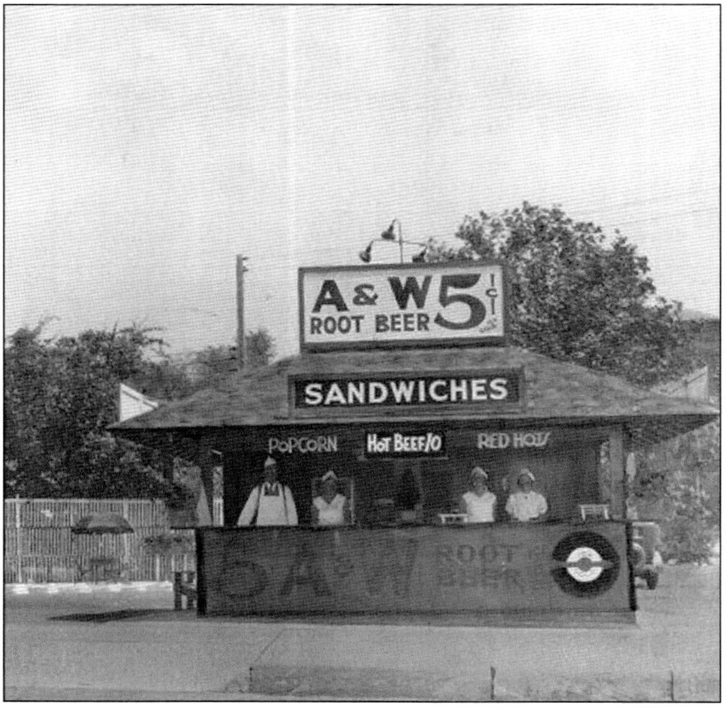

The first A&W Root Beer franchise in Chippewa Falls began in the 1930s, under the ownership of William and Selma Rudy. Pictured at its first location on the corner of River and Bridge Streets, frosty mugs of root beer were poured by Norman and Edna Kaste, who purchased the business in 1934. The building was moved to 904 Bridge Street in the early 1950s. (Courtesy of Marlys Ostby.)

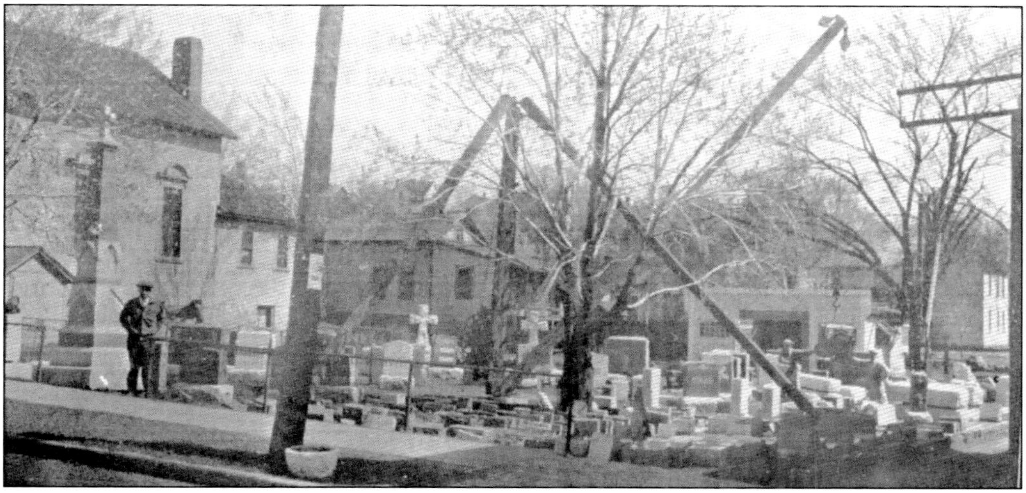

Emil Johnson founded Johnson Monument Company in 1921, when he took over the stock and business of the Henry L. Brooks Granite Company, a marble and granite manufacturing business begun in 1882. Johnson Monument is pictured at its 10 W. Columbia Street location. The company took pride in the quality of its craftsmanship, many examples of which could be found in cemeteries throughout northwestern and central Wisconsin. (Courtesy of CCHS.)

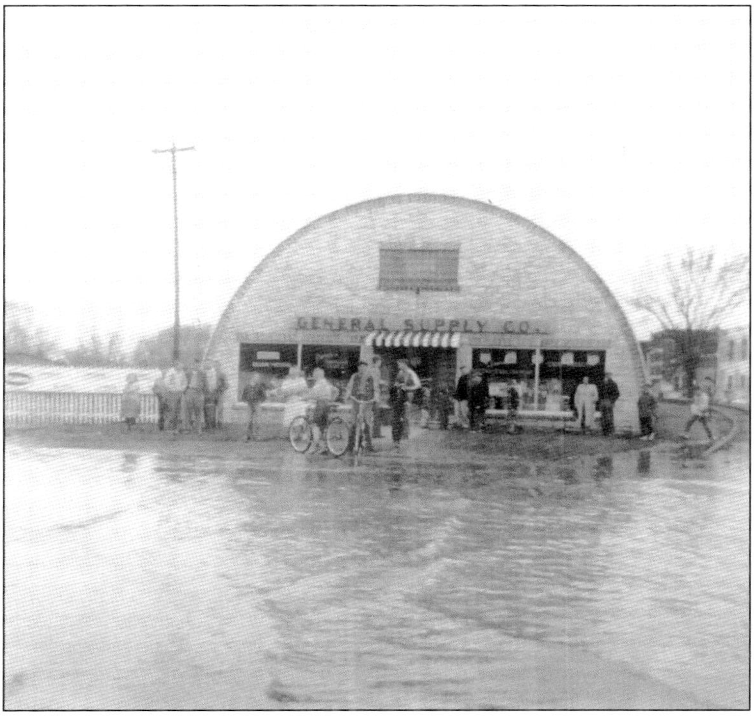

Frank Mrozinski established General Supply Company at 10 South Bridge Street in 1946, to provide a complete stock of building materials from floor coverings to plumbing and electrical supplies to chrome and stainless steel moldings and Glidden paint. When the business closed in 1978, Louis Paul Hebert purchased the building and moved it to new a location on County Highway S, north of Chippewa Falls. (Courtesy of Cuddy Grace Mrozinski.)

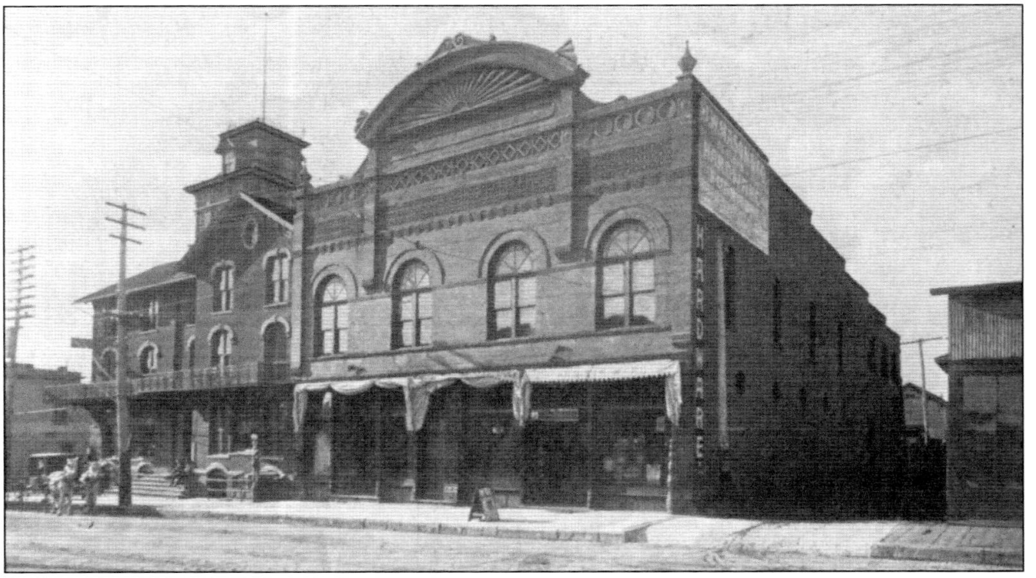

In 1903, the Mason Block was a prominent landmark in Chippewa Falls. Hardware, stoves, ranges, paints, glass, glassware, art, and furniture were all available at the A.C. Mason & Company mercantile. "If It Comes from Mason's, It's Good" was the slogan under which the business operated. The head of the enterprise, A.C. Mason, supported the progressive efforts of the Chippewa Falls business community. To the left of A.C. Mason & Company is the Hotel Stanley. (Courtesy of CCHS.)

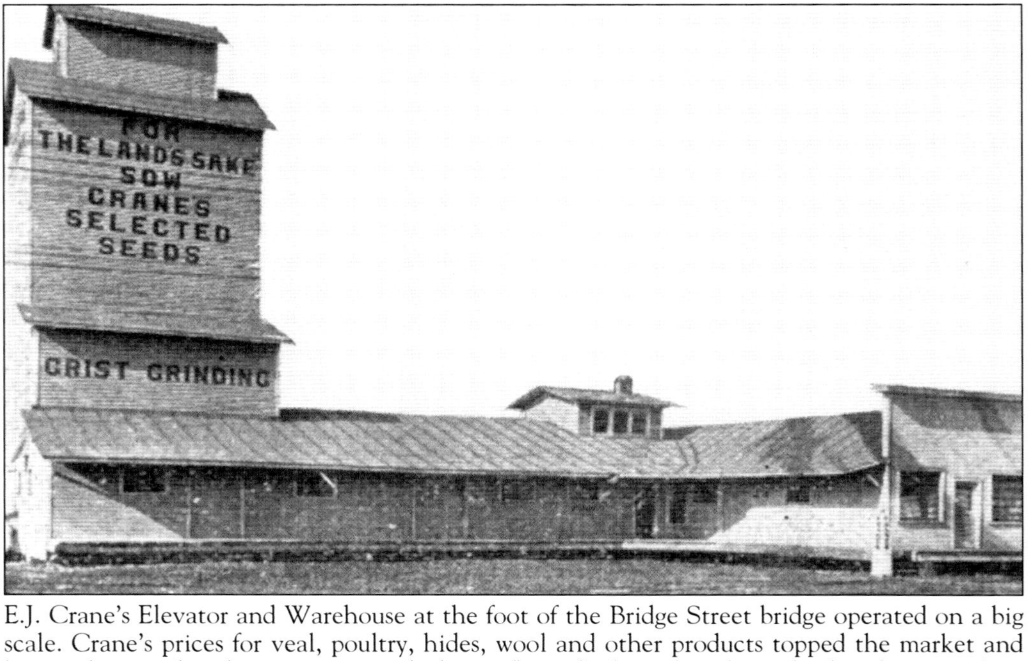

E.J. Crane's Elevator and Warehouse at the foot of the Bridge Street bridge operated on a big scale. Crane's prices for veal, poultry, hides, wool and other products topped the market and he set the merchandising pace as a dealer in flour, feed, seeds, salt, and other farm supplies. (Courtesy of CCHS.)

Two

The Three Rs

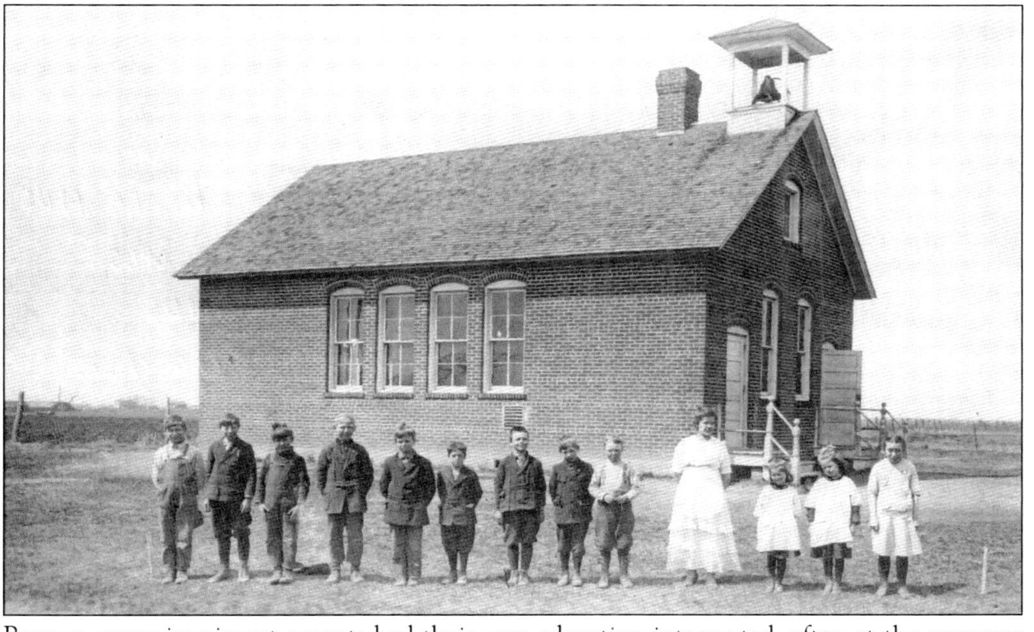

Because many immigrant parents had their own education interrupted, often at the grammar school level, they felt strongly that their children should have the advantages of higher education. In 1858, the first school superintendent was hired who, in turn, hired the first teacher. The first district schoolhouse was built on the corner of Bay Street and Grand Avenue in 1858 for students within the village of Chippewa Falls. The Catholic church created its own school in 1881. The rural districts grew rapidly as farms were established on the cutover lands. In 1924, in Chippewa County, there were 122 one-room rural schools. The daily tasks of rural school teachers showed a sense of dedication and commitment. The Rasmus School, pictured in 1916, was attended by (left to right) Herman Rasmus, Leo Collette, Willi Winter, Eddie Winter, Ingolf Rasmus, Charles Towle, Prim Collette, Norman Smith, Henry Downs, teacher Elizabeth Rasmus, Margaret Rasmus, Maryann Rasmus, and Frieda Schroeder. (Courtesy of John and Steve Rasmus.)

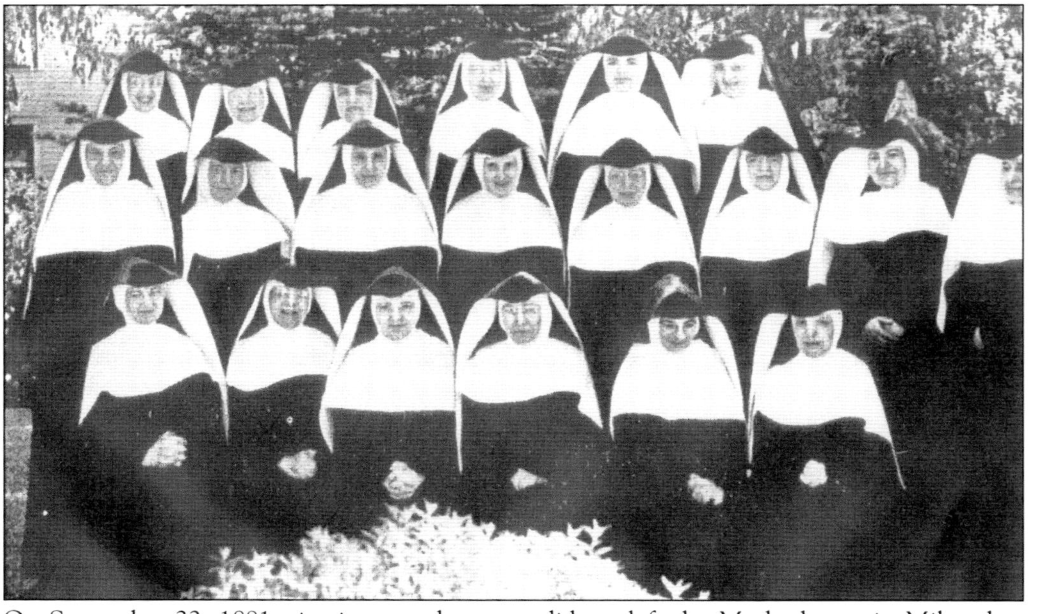

On September 22, 1881, six sisters and two candidates left the Motherhouse in Milwaukee on the Wisconsin Central Railroad for Chippewa Falls where they were to begin instructing children of the Catholic faith. The Teaching Sisters opened their school on September 27, 1881, with 500 students in attendance, a large number of whom were of French descent. Pictured are the 1954–1955 Sisters of Notre Dame who taught in the parochial high school and grade schools. (Courtesy of CCHS.)

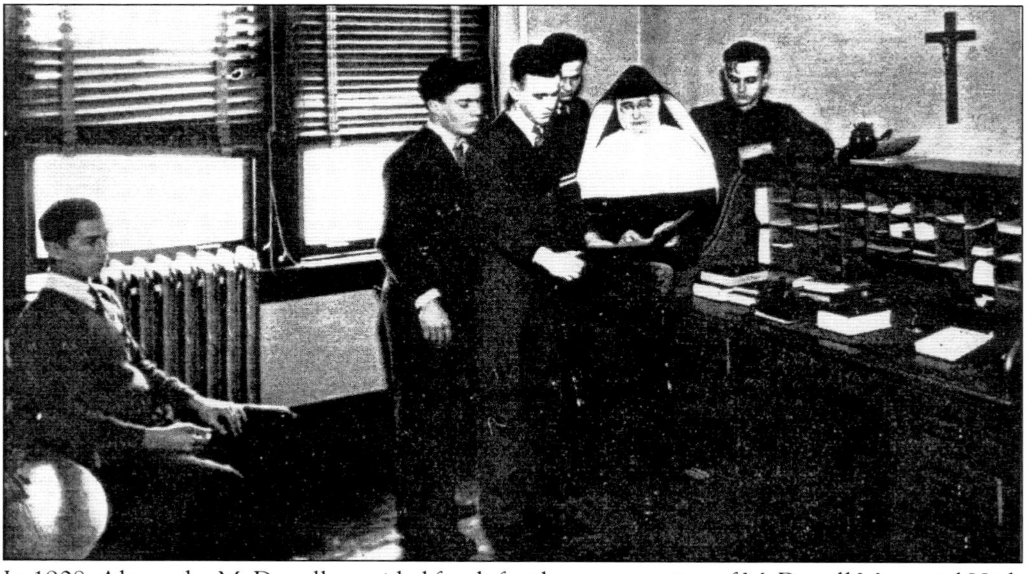

In 1908, Alexander McDonell provided funds for the construction of McDonell Memorial High School. The principal in 1936, Sister Mary Filiona is pictured in her office, being interviewed by seniors (left to right) Raymond Schmidmayr, Lawrence Carrell, Victor Mason, Eugene Picotte, and Euclid Therou. (Courtesy of CCHS.)

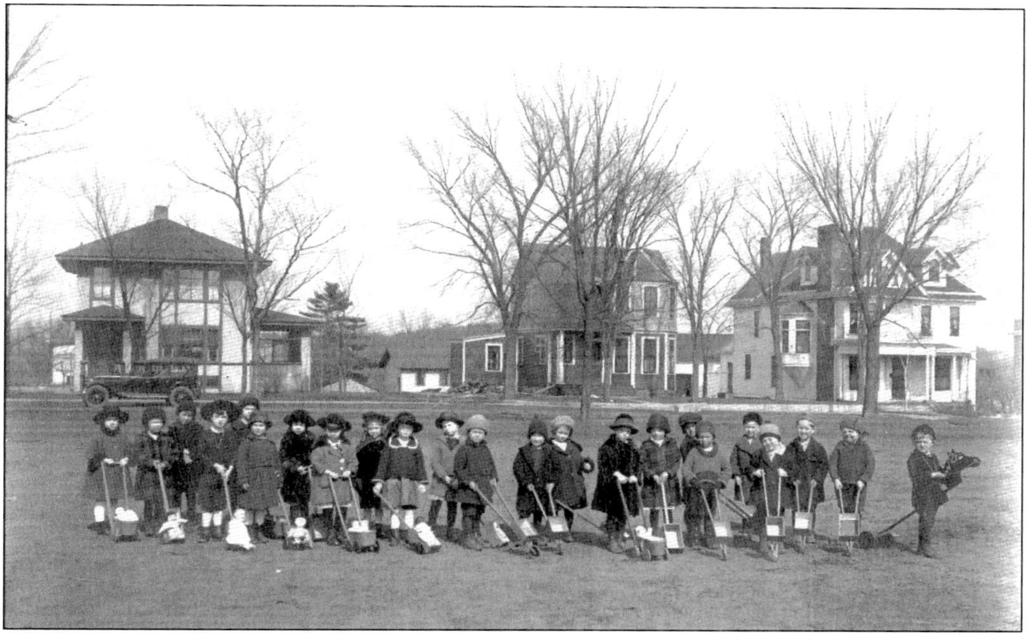

From 1870 through 1889, school attendance had more than doubled. When Chestnut School was built in 1882, the First Ward School, the Second Ward School, and the Columbia Street School were already addressing the educational needs of a rapidly growing community. The South Side Schools maintained a separate school system until 1887 when it was incorporated into the city system. With the houses on Park Place behind them, Chestnut School students line up with their doll carriages and wheelbarrows on the school grounds. (Courtesy of Kris and Dave Martineau.)

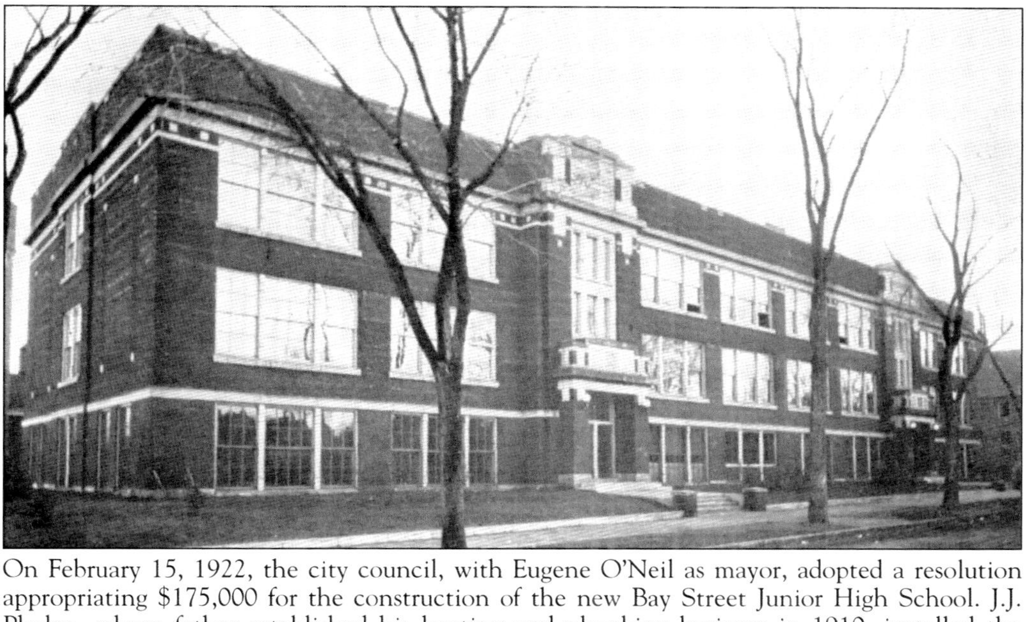

On February 15, 1922, the city council, with Eugene O'Neil as mayor, adopted a resolution appropriating $175,000 for the construction of the new Bay Street Junior High School. J.J. Phalen, whose father established his heating and plumbing business in 1910, installed the heating and ventilation system in the new school. (Courtesy of CFMIT.)

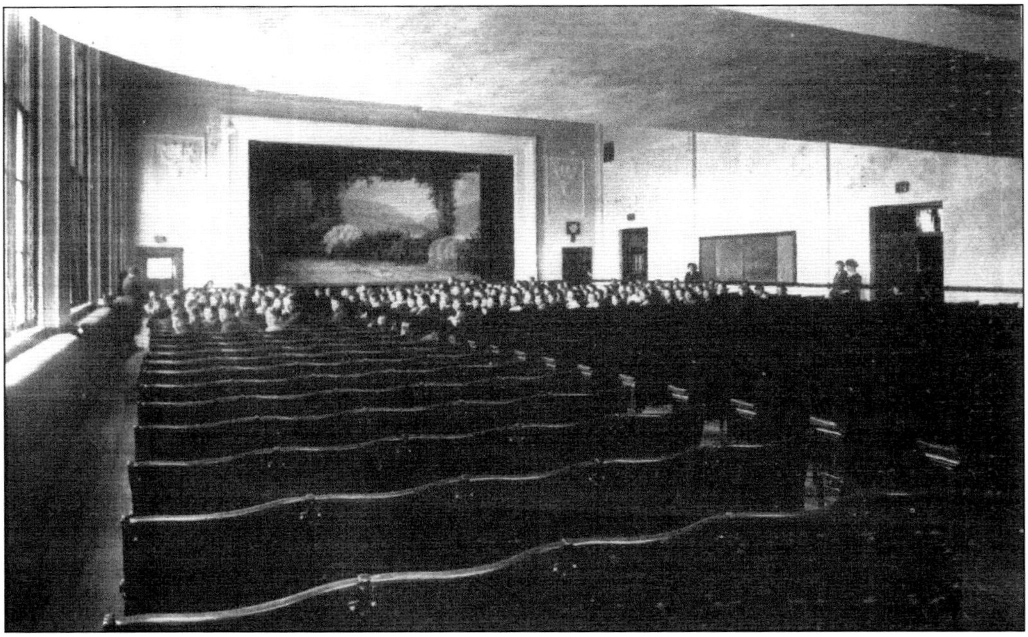

On June 2, 1944, the Junior High Auditorium was site of the Senior High School graduation exercises. Verene Voll gave the salutatory address "Youth Has Power," while Lester Kurth, the valedictorian, gave the address "My Sons Too?" At McDonell High School's graduation, Judge Rinehard and Father William Daniels spoke to the senior class. (Courtesy of CCHS.)

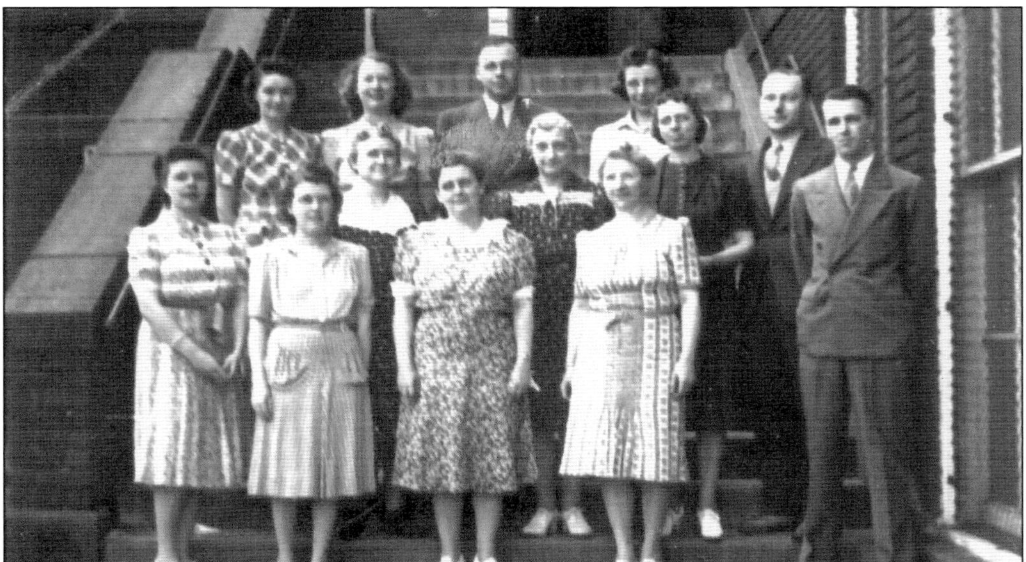

Pictured above are the faculty of the Junior High School in the mid-1930s. They are, from left: (first row) Miss Packard, Miss Viola Petrie, Miss Mary Davis, Miss Gertrude Haven, and Ward Bakken; (second row) Mrs. Esther Fehr, Miss Mary Notham, Miss Rose Durch, and Harold Zorn; (third row) Miss Francis Larson, Miss Kuyper, Mr. Adams, and Miss Genevieve Johnson. (Courtesy of Bernard Willi.)

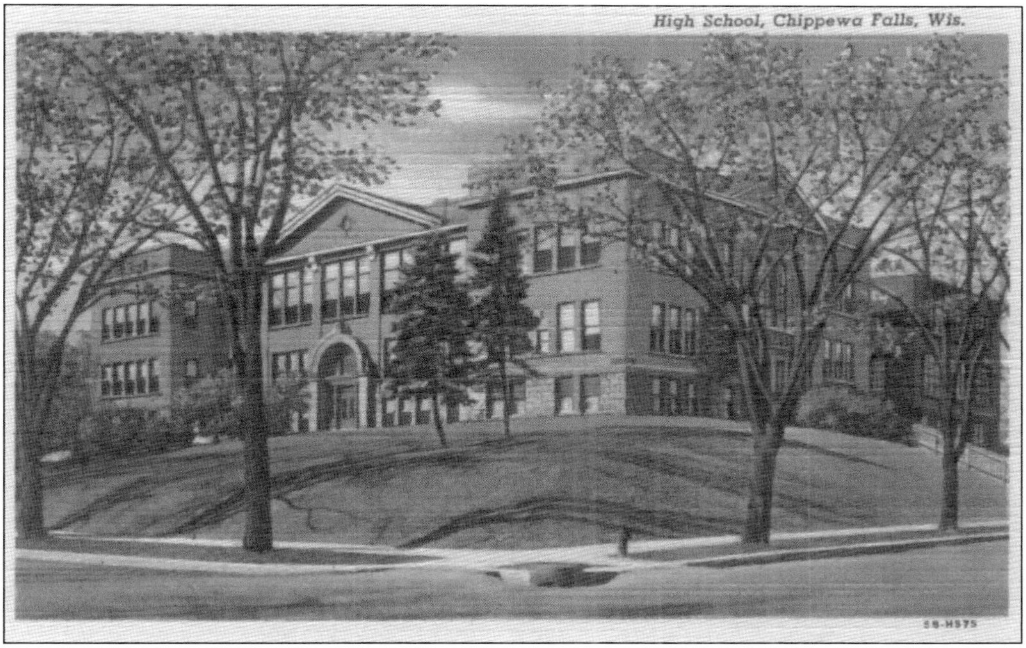

In 1906, the new Chippewa Falls Senior High School was built on the northwest corner of Bridge and Cedar Streets on the site of George Winans' 1873 home. In 1938, an addition was made at the back of the school to house the vocational school. When a new high school was built on Terrill Street in 1958, the old high school was demolished, but the vocational wing continued to serve the school district for many years. (Courtesy of Gail Shipman.)

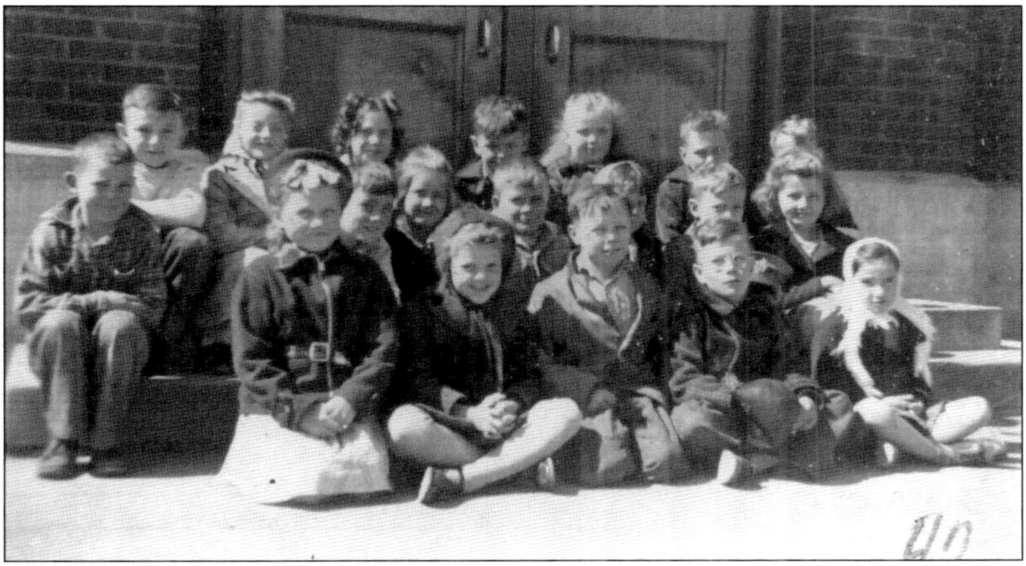

Huddled on the front steps of First Ward School in 1942, students in the second grade class gathered to have their class picture taken. Those who were identified are (back row, from left) Roger Meier, Delores Crystal, Lucille Norman, unknown, Marlene Mells, Bill Smith, and Richard Christenson. (Courtesy of Arley Engel.)

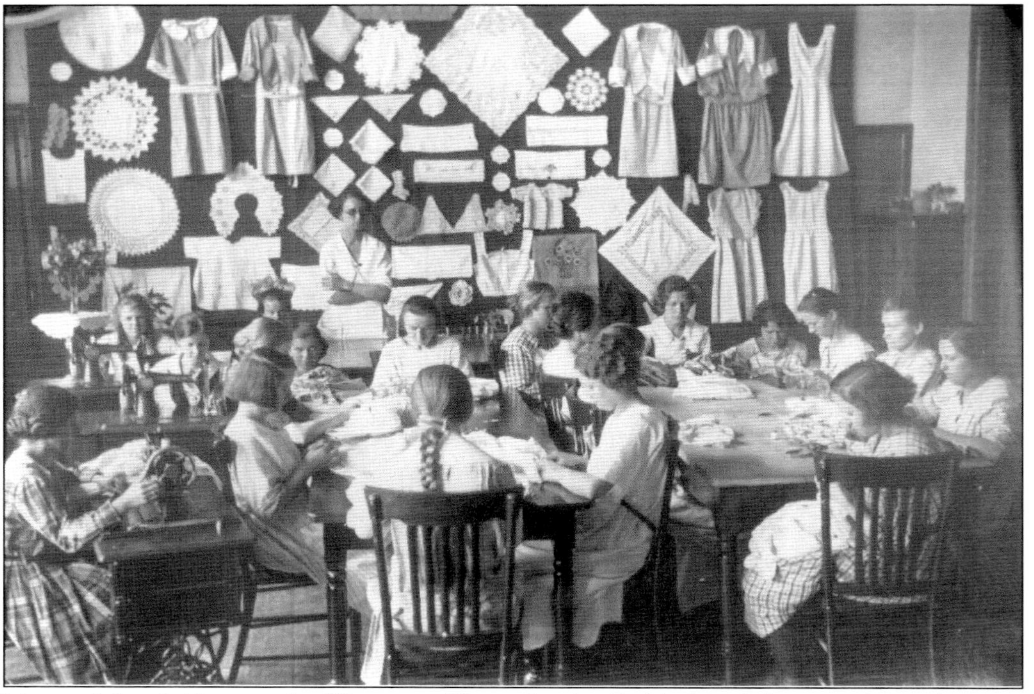

Many of the children in the Wisconsin Home for the Feeble Minded received an education in the industrial arts, furnishing supplies for the institution. While boys learned caning and basketry, girls were trained to do fine needlework. Pictured on the wall are samples of the needlework produced by the girls for use at the home. (Courtesy of CCHS)

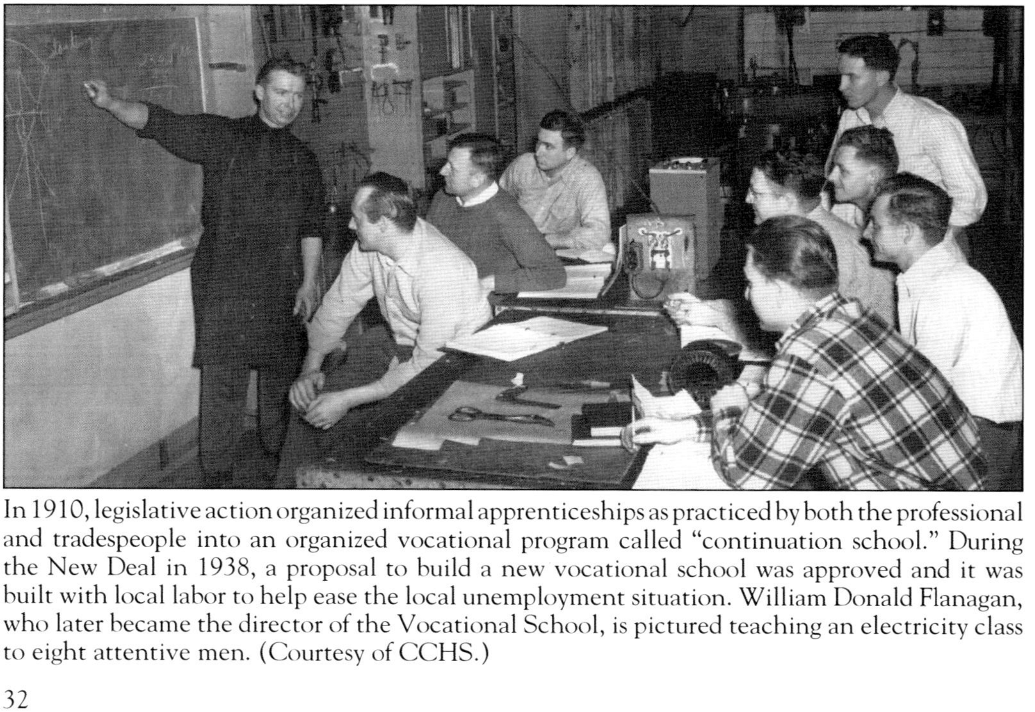

In 1910, legislative action organized informal apprenticeships as practiced by both the professional and tradespeople into an organized vocational program called "continuation school." During the New Deal in 1938, a proposal to build a new vocational school was approved and it was built with local labor to help ease the local unemployment situation. William Donald Flanagan, who later became the director of the Vocational School, is pictured teaching an electricity class to eight attentive men. (Courtesy of CCHS.)

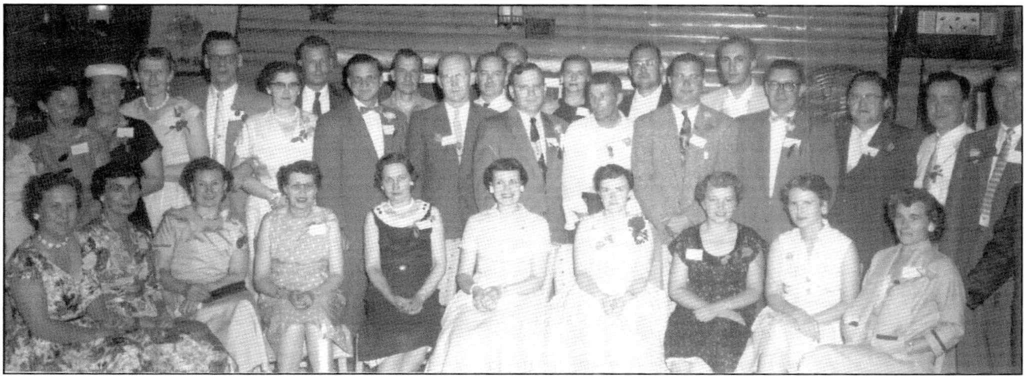

Members of the class of 1936 are pictured at their 20-year reunion, from left: (front row) Winifred Wells Domer, Crescence Loiselle Meyers, Pearl Zutter Larson, Bernadine Rheingans Furrer, Margaret Procknow Dunne, Lou Lange Anderson, Priscilla Lemay Durch, Myrtle Polzin Sparkes, Laura Kappus Flesch, and Florence Priest LeDuc; (middle row) Clarice Willenbockel, Katheryn Kassabaum Smola, Nihla Ness Brahm, Isabelle Rohrssen Mahlstadt, Nihla Meslow, LaVerne Mueller, Norman Sandvick, Henry Zeck, Gene Soden, Hugh McCausland, Robert (Bartz) Tepp, Ted Spitzenberger, Art Moline, Glen Nelson, and Rolland Johnson; (back row) Arlan Ripplinger, Earl White, Carl Krejci, Lorry O'Connell, Robert Nicolls, Jean Lohrie Lyons, Wilfred Klatt, and Gilbert Roycraft. (Courtesy of Jim and Nancy Schuh.)

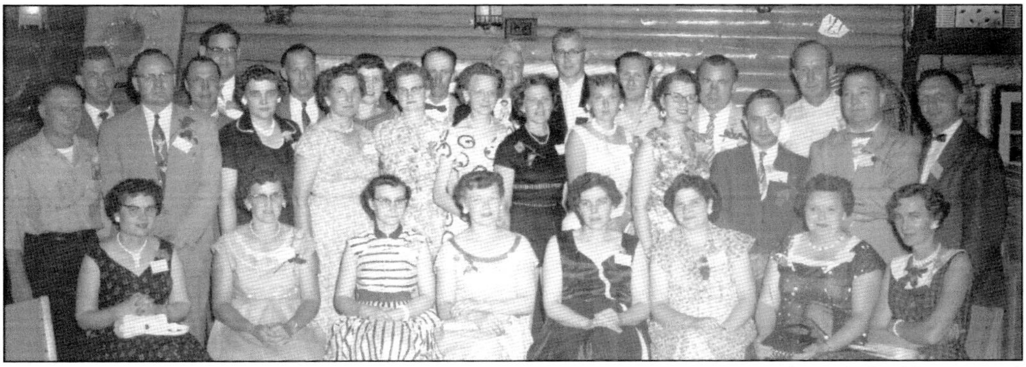

Members of the class of 1936 are pictured at their 20-year reunion, from left: (front row) Ione Dumars Murphy, Harriet Dunlap Kohlin, Ellen Anderson McCann, Betty Elstran Thornton, Lorraine Freese Forrester, Mary Jasper Liddell, Marcella Eaton Zempel, and Helen Ehlers Severn; (middle row) Wilson Ackley, Cecil Hanson, Georgina Goetz Peterson, Helen Dernovsek Kastner, Inez Henderson Beaudette, Dorothy Holtz, Doris Johnson Clark, Katheryn Bourgeois Wall, Dorothy Crain Porn, Leonard Bohnert, Jack Jasper, Stanley Clark; (back row) Robert Carr, Tom Joas, Robert Henneman, Robert Gelina, Mordella Dahl Shearer, Donald Hopkins, Lester Dodge, George Badman, William Greenwald, Winfred Gillett, and Charles Bejin. (Courtesy of Jim and Nancy Schuh.)

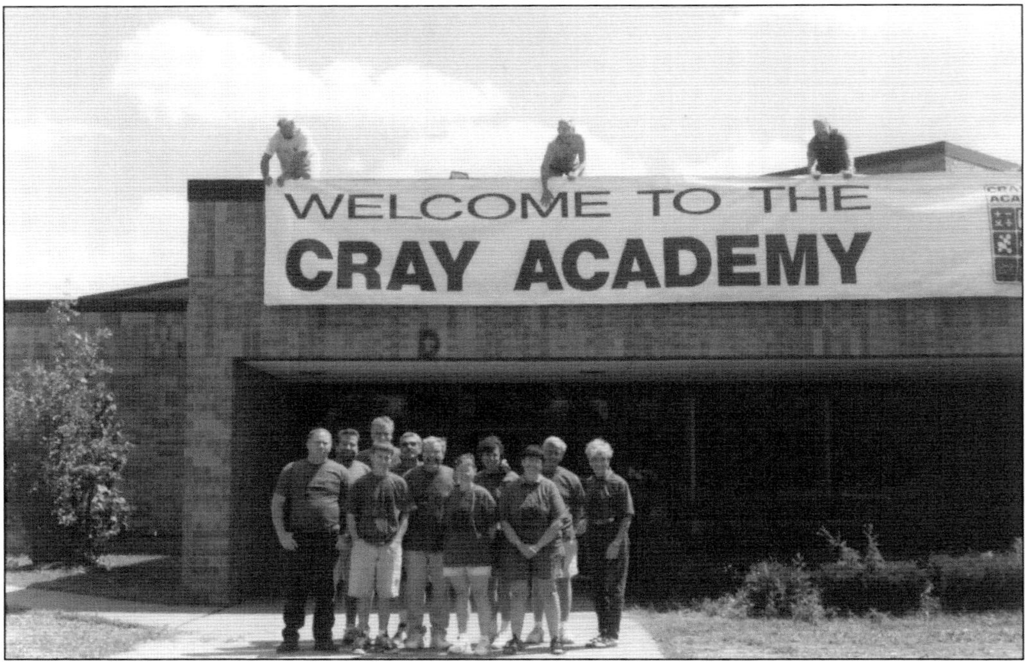

A cornerstone of the Cray Foundation's $500,000 educational initiative was the "Cray Academy." Headed by Dr. Julie Stafford, the academy, to be run for three weeks in the summer, offered teachers from Chippewa Falls, Eau Claire, and Rice Lake a place to expand their background in technology-related disciplines. (Courtesy of the *Chippewa Herald*.)

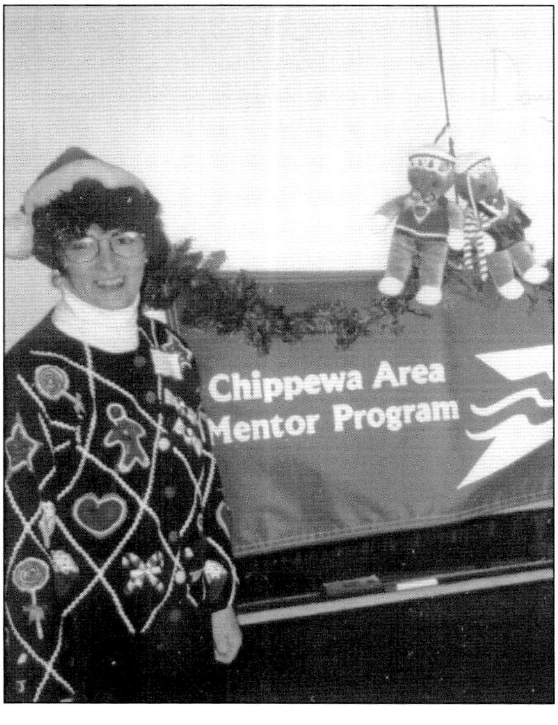

In 1989, the Deacons of Our Savior's Lutheran Church, wishing to make a real contribution to the City of Chippewa Falls, decided to help their "neighbors," students at the Chippewa Falls Middle School. The Mentor Program was born. The mission was to provide support to students by matching them one on one with a caring adult volunteer. Through the dedication of the first Director Carol Gienapp, the program has expanded to include all of the public schools and four Catholic schools. It has attracted hundreds of community volunteers who are committed to spending quality time with their students. (Courtesy of the Chippewa Area Mentor Program.)

Three

CELEBRATE! CELEBRATE!

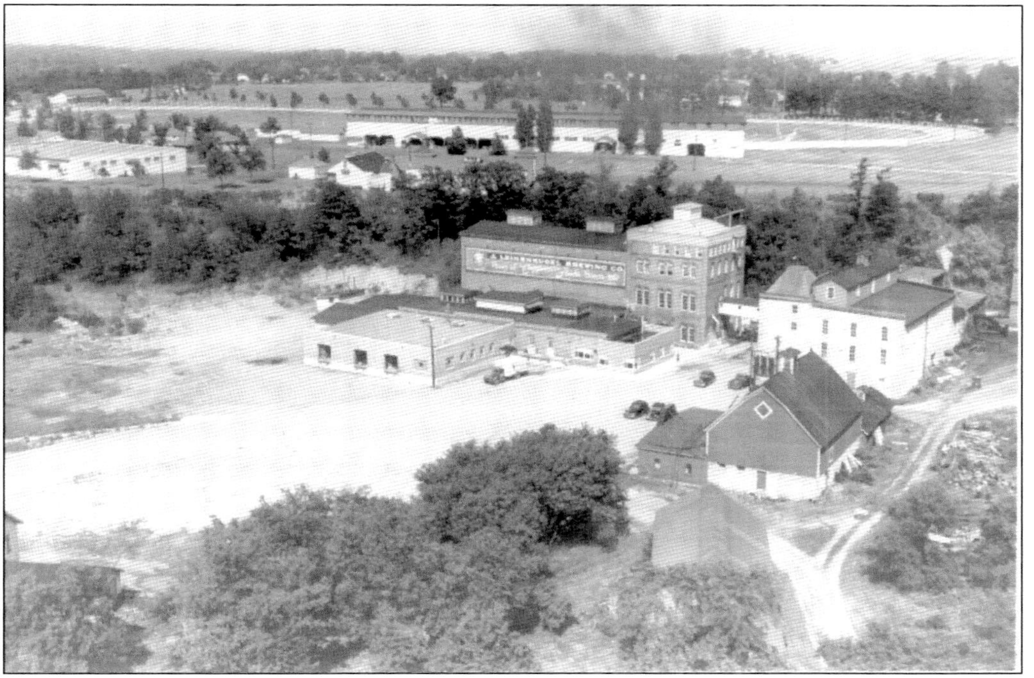

In 1897, all of Chippewa Falls turned out for the first annual meeting of the Northern Wisconsin State Fair. The streets, from the South Side to the fairgrounds, were decorated with bunting, floral arches, and lights. Jacob Leinenkugel and Alderman Nunke decorated the floral arch at the Star Mill while the city celebrated with speeches, parades, bicycle races, horse racing, and a circus. The proximity of the fairgrounds to Leinenkugel's Brewery was more than symbolic. According to William Casper, Leinenkugel's prided itself on maintaining good personal contact with its customers, so "when fair time came around, we'd invite the tavern owners in to see the plant. Then we'd go up to the fairgrounds and have a good time." (Courtesy of JLBC.)

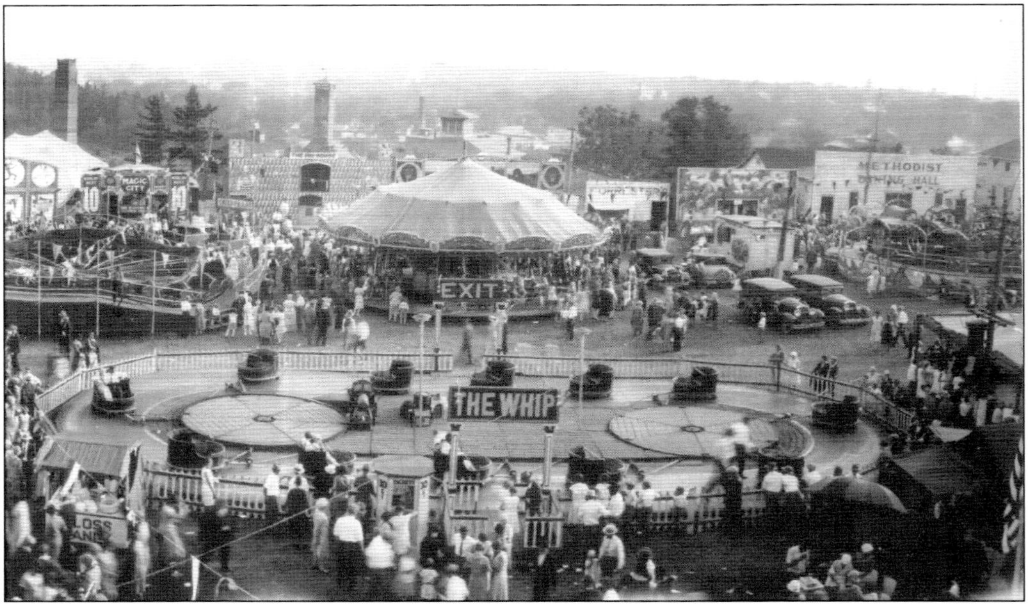

The midway of the Northern Wisconsin State Fair was filled with games, cotton candy and caramel apples, a roller coaster and bumper cars, the big and little Ferris wheels, carousels, and the Whip. The crowds were entertained in the grandstand while others toured the Fine Arts building, erected in 1904, and strolled through the agricultural exhibits. (Courtesy of CCHS.)

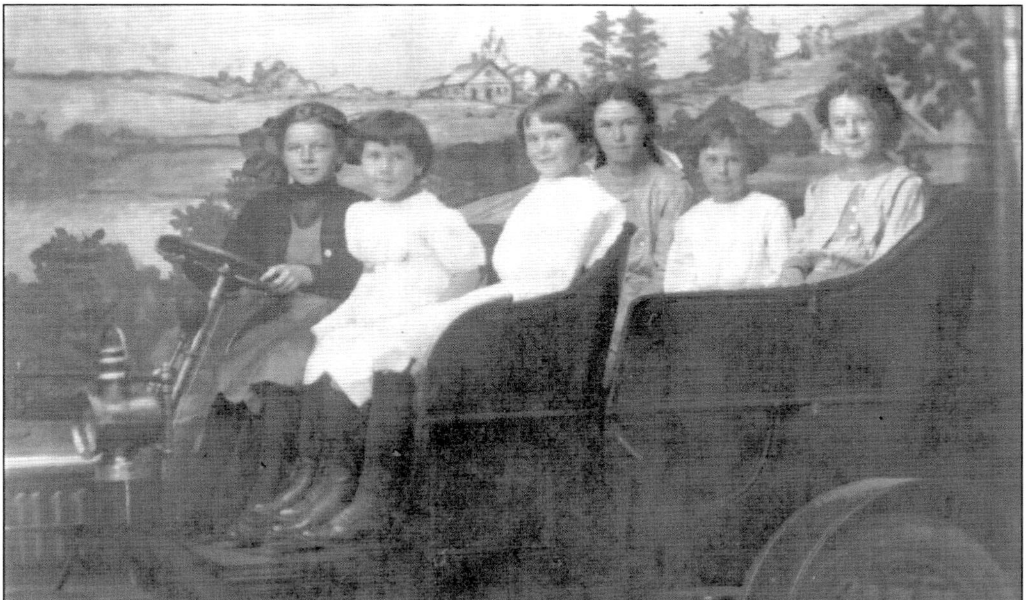

These young ladies sat for a picture during Fair Week in 1911. At the wheel of the car is Freda Johnson, who would later become a teacher and principal in the public school system. Next to her are Ruth McQuillan and Lucille McQuillan. In the second seat, from left to right, are Josephine, Frances, and Mary McQuillan. (Courtesy of Mary Kelly Anderson.)

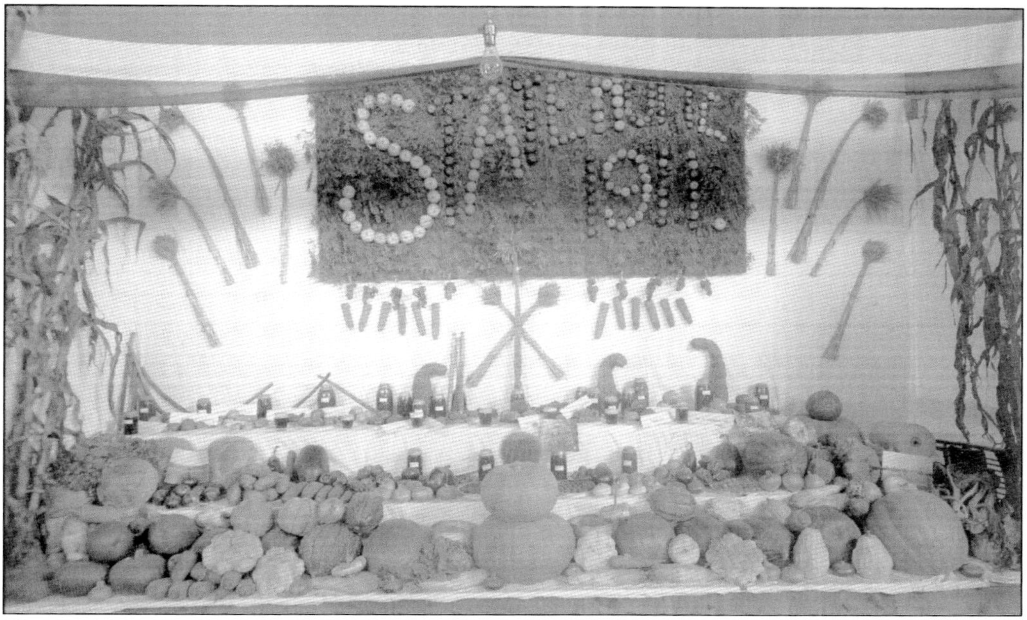

The children at the Wisconsin Home for the Feeble Minded, as part of the institution's philosophy of self-sufficiency, raised fruits and vegetables for the residents of the Home. In 1911, their display of fruits, vegetables, and grains was an attraction at the Northern Wisconsin State Fair. (Courtesy of CCHS.)

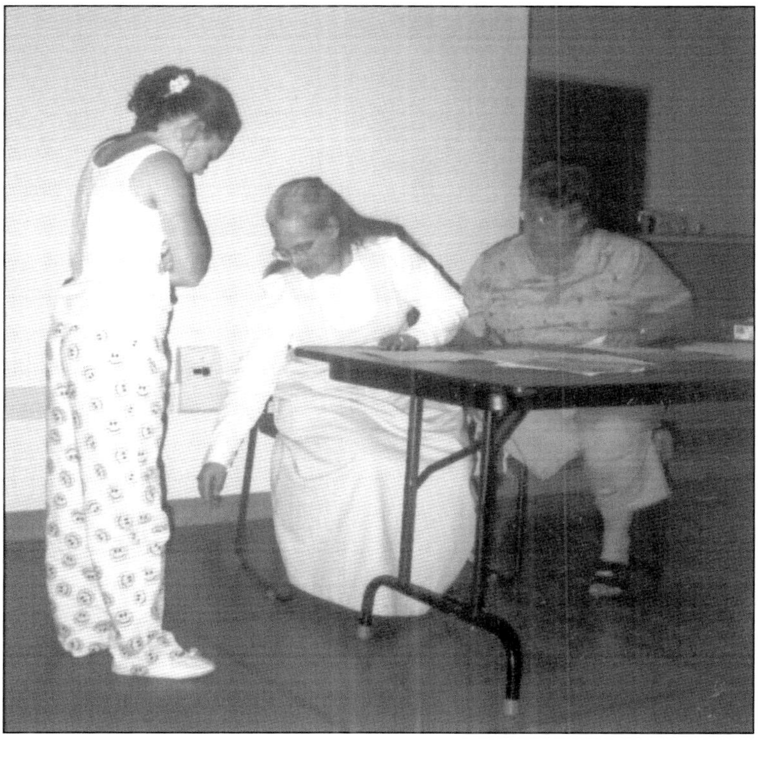

4-H Clubs have been an integral part of the Northern Wisconsin State Fair. 4-H members displayed their photographs, clothing, and cooking projects and many participated in the 4-H Clothing Revue. Pictured at the age of 11 is Alisha Bowe, a third-generation member of the Sunnyside 4-H club, discussing with the judges the construction and style of the pajamas she made for her 4-H sewing project. (Courtesy of Jean Bowe.)

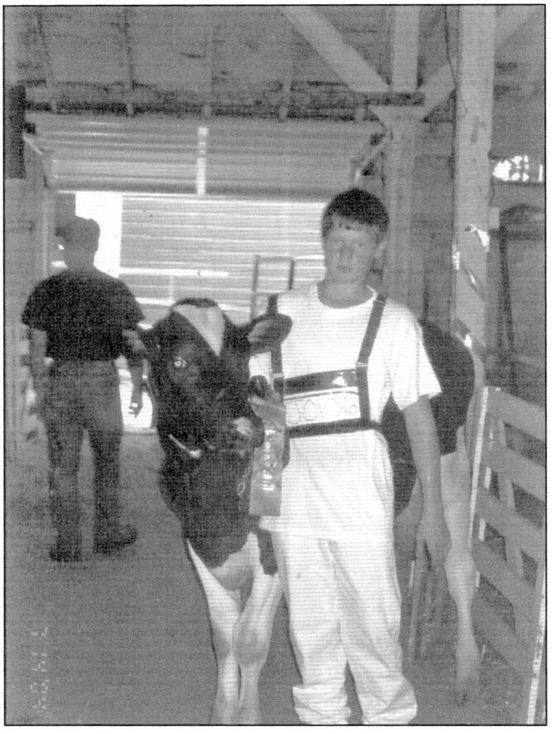

The Sunnyside 4-H Club was organized in 1930 and for years its members showed their prize cattle, pigs, horses, rabbits, and lambs at the Northern Wisconsin State Fair. Pictured in 2004 is Alex Bowe, a third-generation member of the Sunnyside 4-H club, getting ready to show his champion Holstein bull calf. (Courtesy of Jean Bowe.)

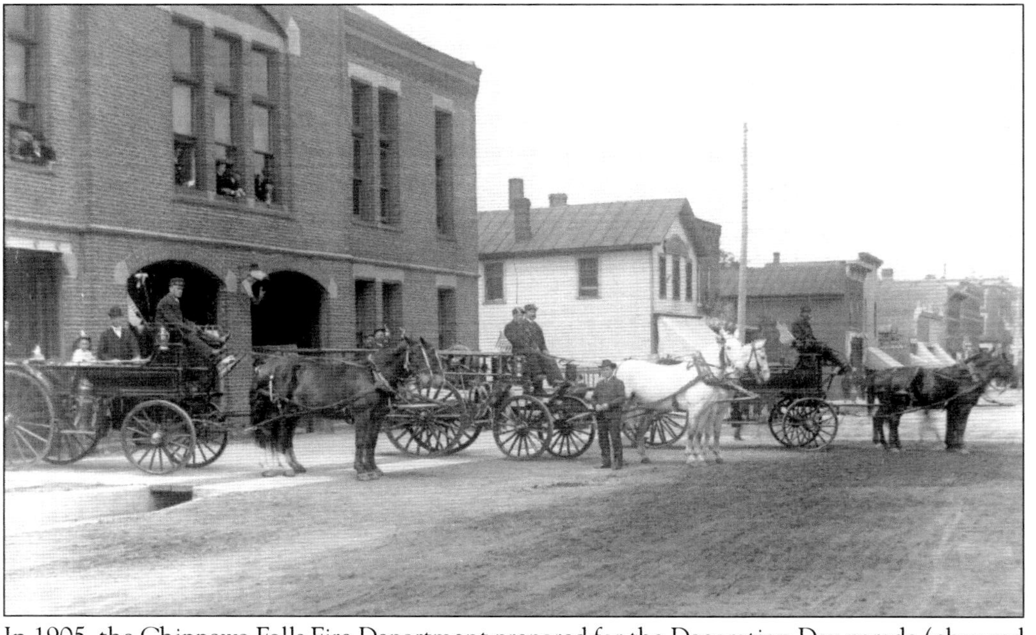

In 1905, the Chippewa Falls Fire Department prepared for the Decoration Day parade (changed to Memorial Day after World War I). On the first hose cart standing on the back are George Baker, Lee Boyd, Henry McAleer, and Driver Charles Ermatinger. On the Chemical Wagon standing on the back are Joe Meuli, Charles Brecke, Driver Al Pierce, and Fire Chief Orland Kibbie. On the Hook and Ladder truck is Driver Jack Bigler. (Courtesy of CFFD.)

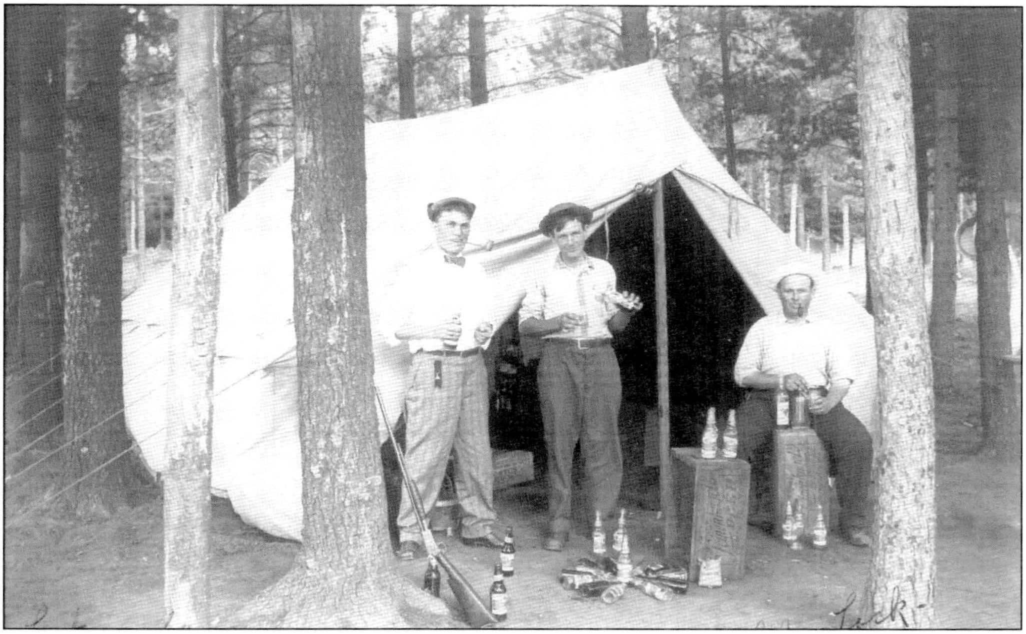

In 1912, Walter Lueck, Andrew Camastral, and Walter Schwaner pitched their tent in Irvine Park and celebrated the "last camping trip before we married" with plenty of artfully arranged Leinenkugel's beer. (Courtesy of the Carl Lueck Family.)

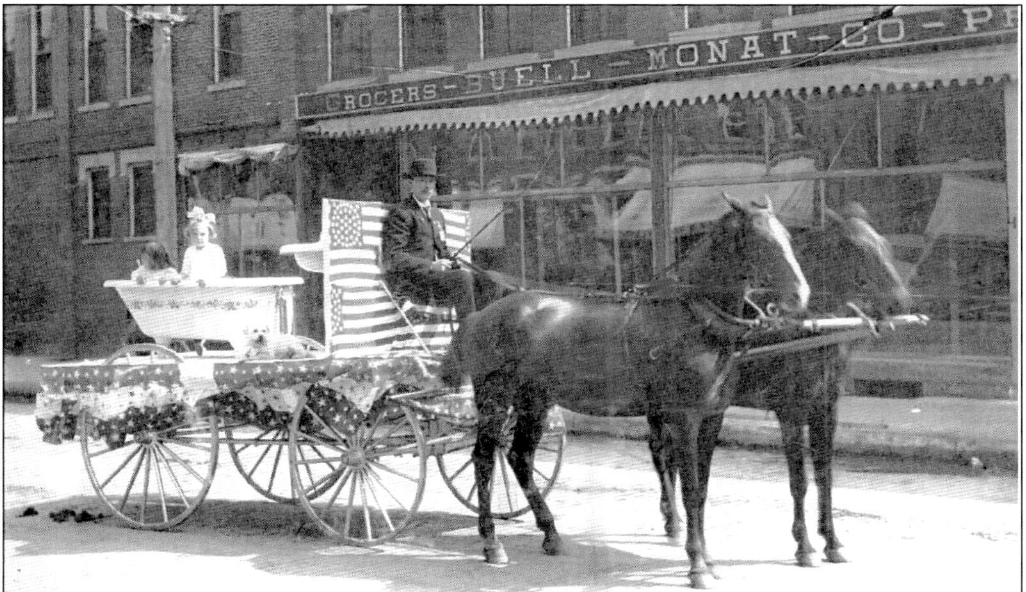

Phillip McQuillan, one of the early plumbing and heating engineers in Chippewa Falls, celebrated his Irish-American patriotism by participating in the 1907 Decoration Day Parade. Riding in the bathtub to advertise "Good Plumbing" were two of his 12 children, Ruth and Frances. (Courtesy of Mary Kelly Anderson.)

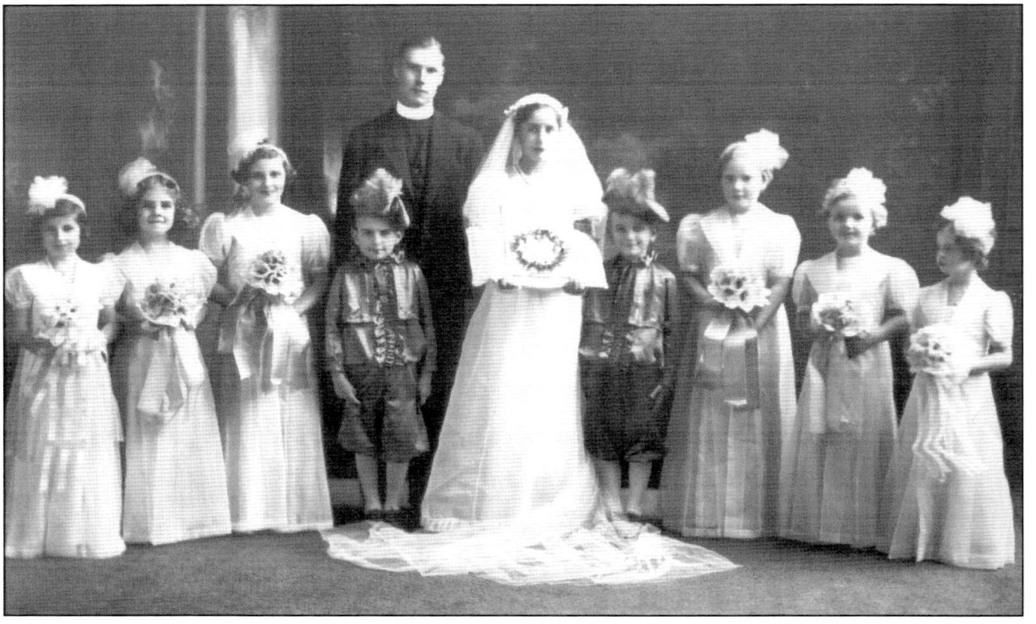

A native of Chippewa Falls, Father John S. Rondeau was ordained in 1938. On September 18, 1938, he celebrated his first Solemn High Mass at Notre Dame Catholic Church. The celebrants in his first mass were (left to right) Patty Pepin, Nancy Hub, Maripat McDowell, James Paul, Father John Rondeau, Mary Paquette, Donald Rada, Jean Haley, Audrey Krause, and Yvonne LeClaire. (Courtesy of Audrey Krause Mattison.)

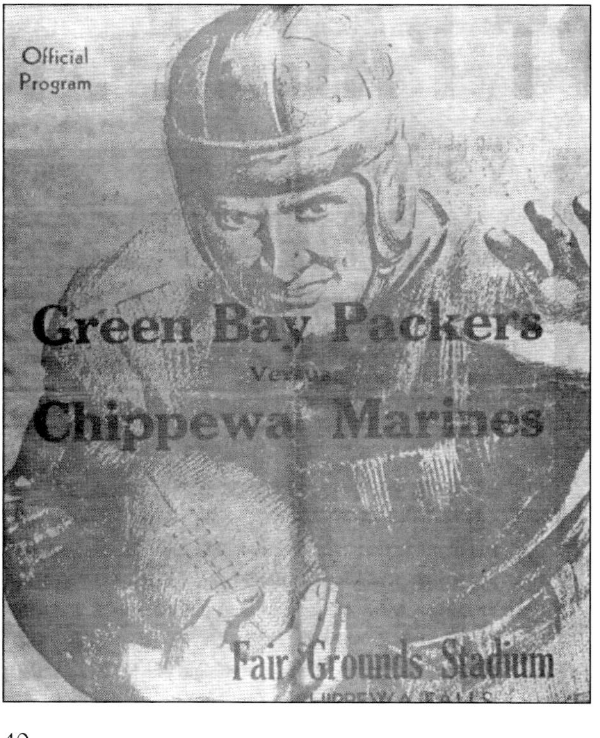

A city team, organized in 1918 and outfitted by a local company engaged in packing and shipping foodstuffs, entered the organized pro circuit in 1921 as the Green Bay Packers. From a struggling industrial league team, the Packers, coached by an employee of the packing company, Earl "Curly" Lambeau, rose to become one of the best in the country. On September 2, 1935, the Green Bay Packers played the Chippewa Marines on the new field at the fairgrounds in Chippewa Falls. The Packers won the football game 22–0. (Courtesy of CCHS.)

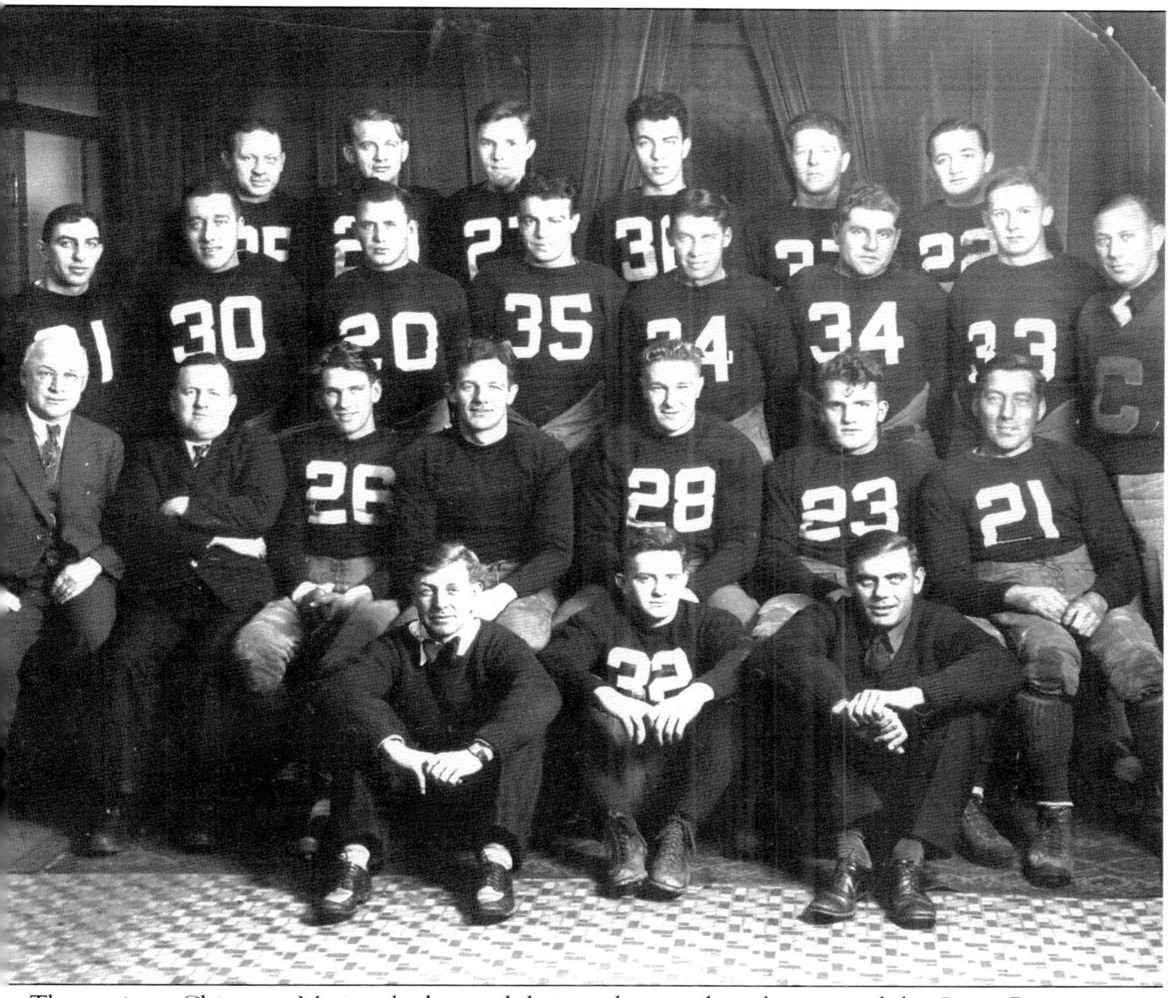

The semi-pro Chippewa Marines had started their sixth year when they invited the Green Bay Packers to Chippewa Falls for a game on Labor Day, 1935. The Marines held the Packers to 22 points. Members of the team are pictured here from left to right: (first row) Edwin Nyhus, manager, Red Dawson, and Mel Wang; (second row) Dr. Trinkle, Coach Bill O'Neil, R. Sallings, Eddie Kotal, Laddie LaDusire, Erv Gerhardt, and Ollie Claflin; (third row) Reinhold Hoppe, Wink Claflin, John Plenke, Kate Alphonse, Bill Lowe, Frank Kraut, Len Trinkle, and Chub Lund; (top row) Vern Anderson, Carl Mehls, Ben Weronke, Helixson, Dutch Bromeisl, and Jim Hart. (Courtesy of CCHS.)

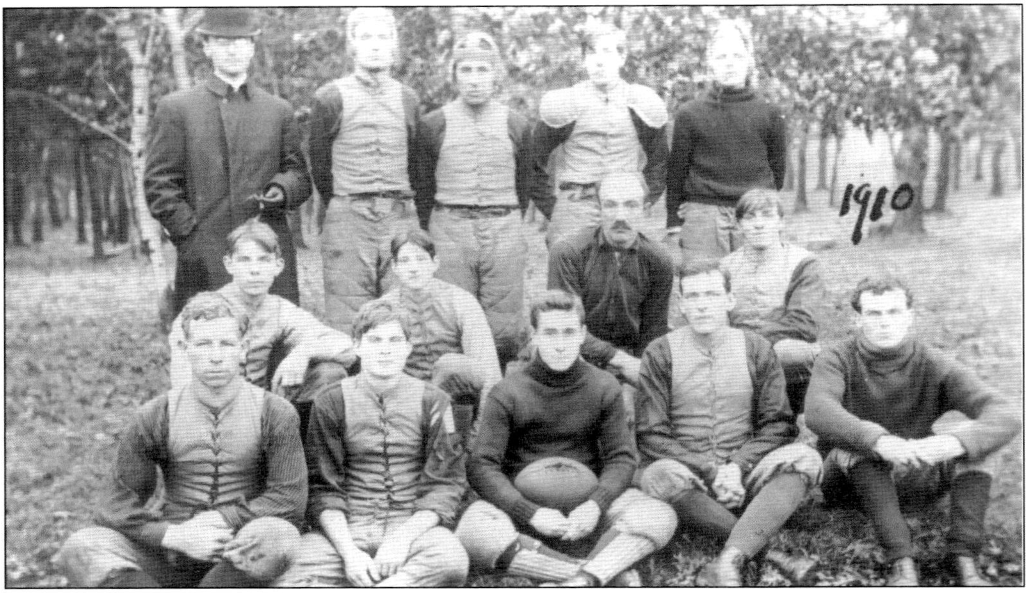

The Wisconsin Home for the Feeble Minded organized one of its first sports teams in 1910. The football players pictured here performed off the Home grounds, competing against other high school teams in the Chippewa area. In 1922, the institution's name was changed to the Northern Wisconsin Colony and Training School, the same year the school's basketball and baseball teams were organized to compete with area sports teams. (Courtesy of CCHS.)

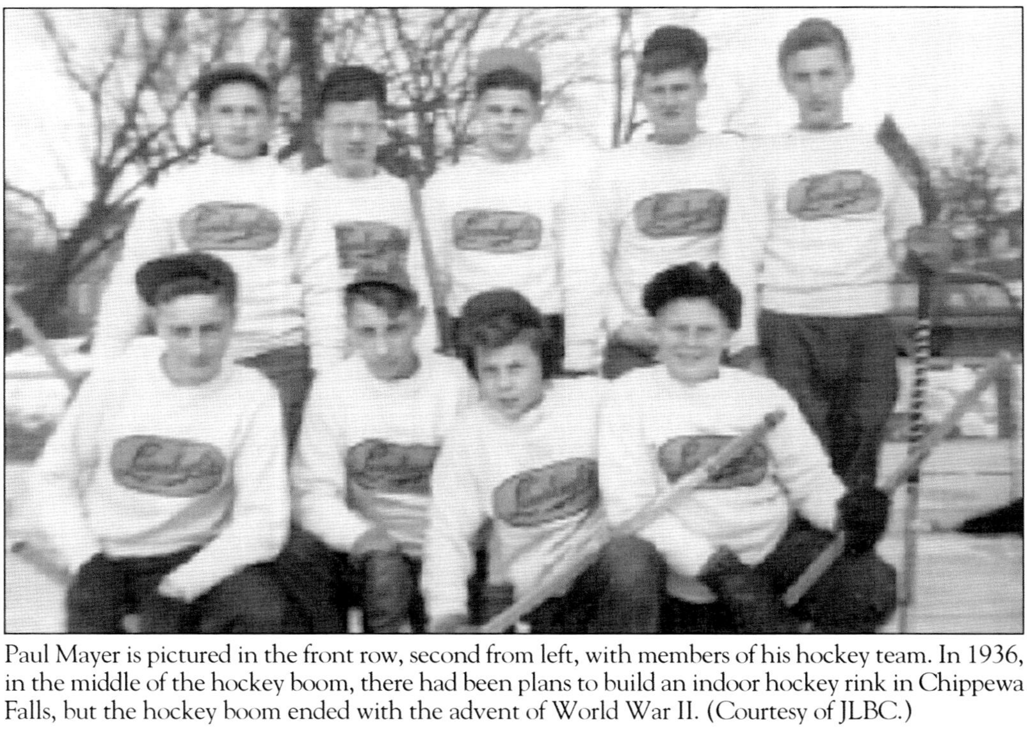

Paul Mayer is pictured in the front row, second from left, with members of his hockey team. In 1936, in the middle of the hockey boom, there had been plans to build an indoor hockey rink in Chippewa Falls, but the hockey boom ended with the advent of World War II. (Courtesy of JLBC.)

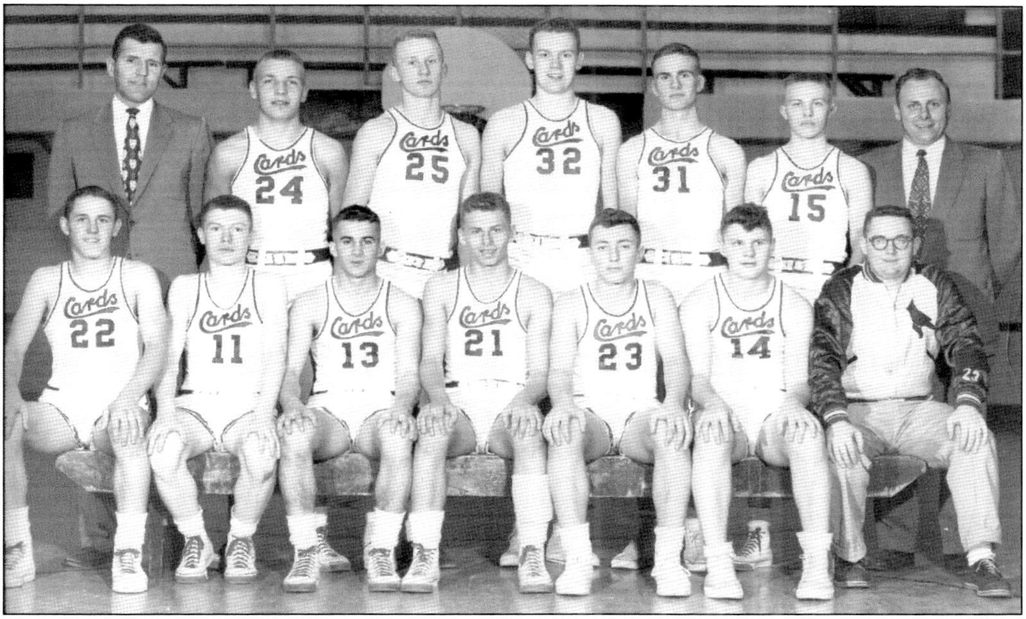

Players on the 1954–1955 Chi-Hi Basketball team are pictured from left to right: (front row) John Abrams, Emery Crowley, Bill Hanzlik, Don Zutter, Dave Gutkneckt, Julian Olson, and Manager C. Roder; (second row) Head Coach Tom Lehman, Bill Larson, Ray Holte, Dennis Krause, Jim Meyer, Lynn Mellen, and Coach Orrie Boettcher. (Courtesy of Don and Mona Zutter.)

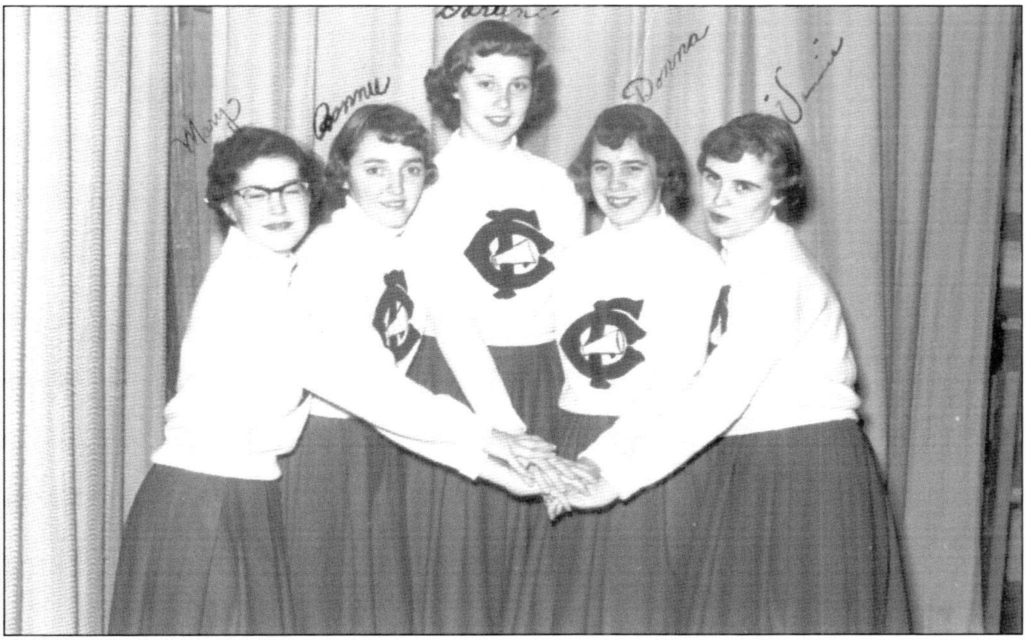

Chippewa Falls Senior High School cheerleaders in 1954–1955 who were responsible for elevating school spirit and planning pep rallies were, from left, Mary Peloquin, Bonnie Hedrington, Darlene Bollom, Donna Cahoon, and Vonnie Jensen. (Courtesy of Don and Mona Zutter.)

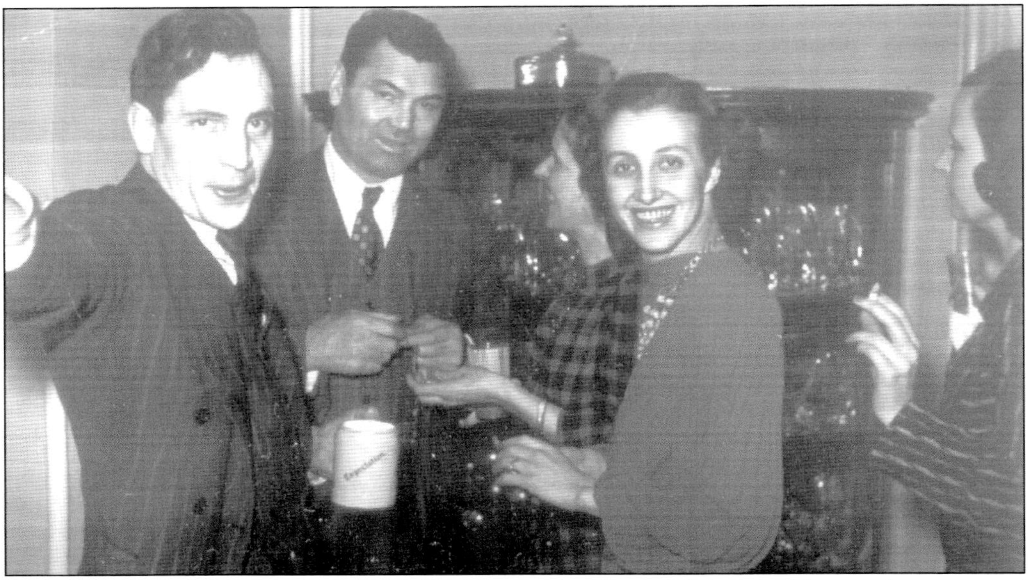

Jack Dempsey, the former heavyweight boxing champion of the world, was the center of attention at a party given in the 1940s at the Carl Leinenkugel home at 821 North Bridge Street. Pictured (from left to right) are Carl Leinenkugel, Jack Dempsey, Marion Murphy, and Ruth (Mrs. Carl) Leinenkugel. (Courtesy of CCHS.)

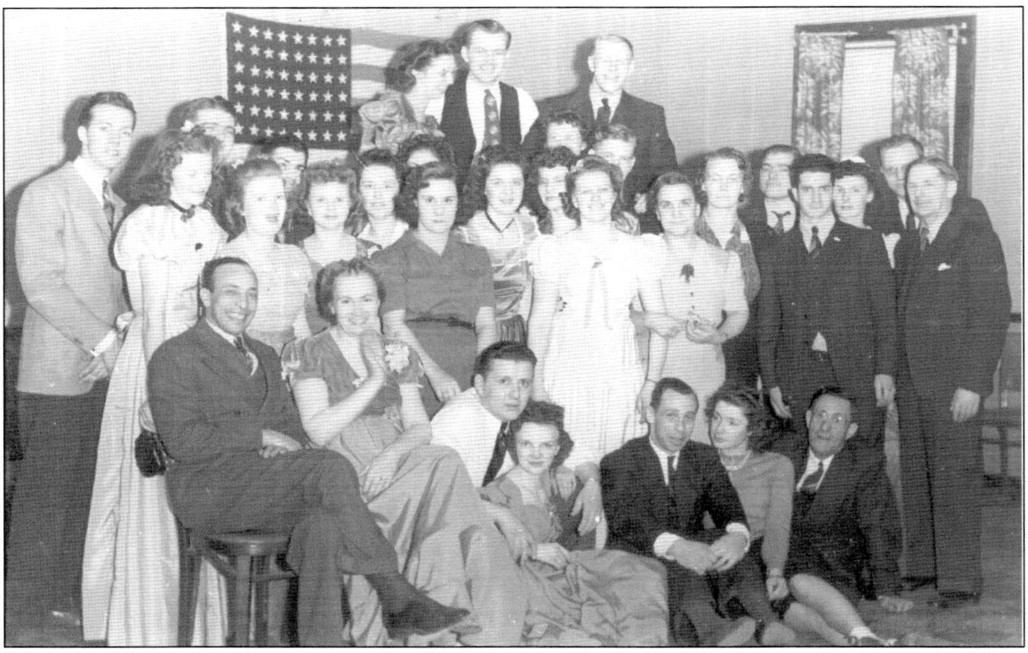

Mary and Alvin Krause, owners of Krause's Café at 207 N. Bridge Street, celebrated with their employees at a formal party. Pictured (seated, from left) are Juan Hart and Mary Krause. In the center kneeling on the floor are Gilbert Reiter and Bobbie Reiter, who would eventually own and operate their own restaurant, Reiters, on Lake Wissota. (Courtesy of Audrey Krause Mattison.)

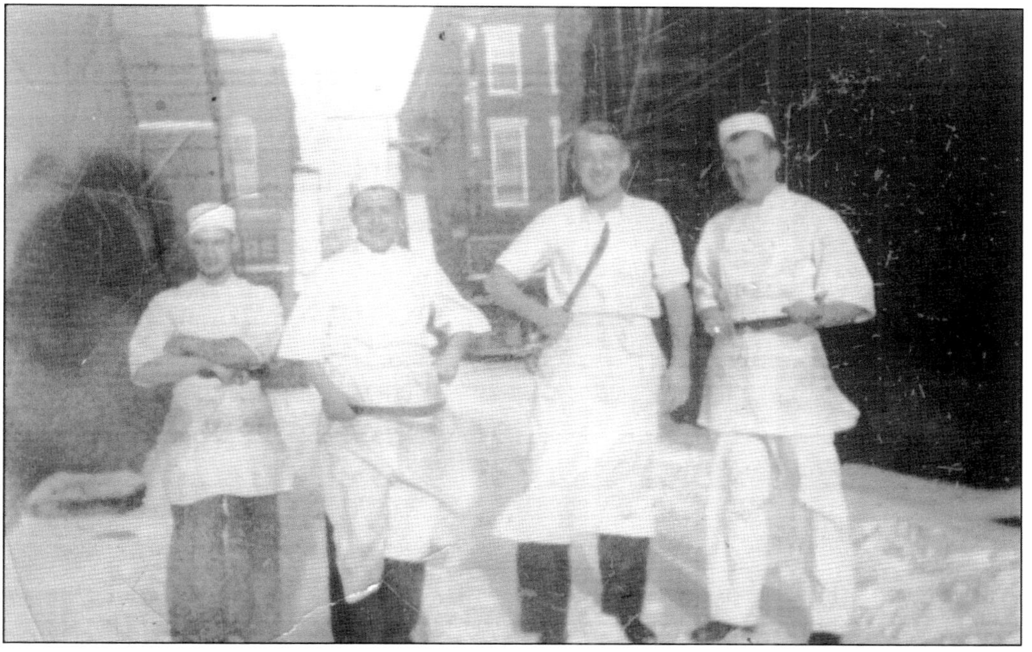

In 1938, Krause's Café was located at 207 N. Bridge Street. Standing in the alley between Central Street and West Grand Avenue are the cooks at Krause's (from left to right) Terp Hall, Gib Reiter, Howard Reiter, and Gil Gilbertson. If one of the cooks wanted a day off, the other cook had to work a 24-hour shift to fill in for the absent cook. (Courtesy of Maureen Gilbertson Roach.)

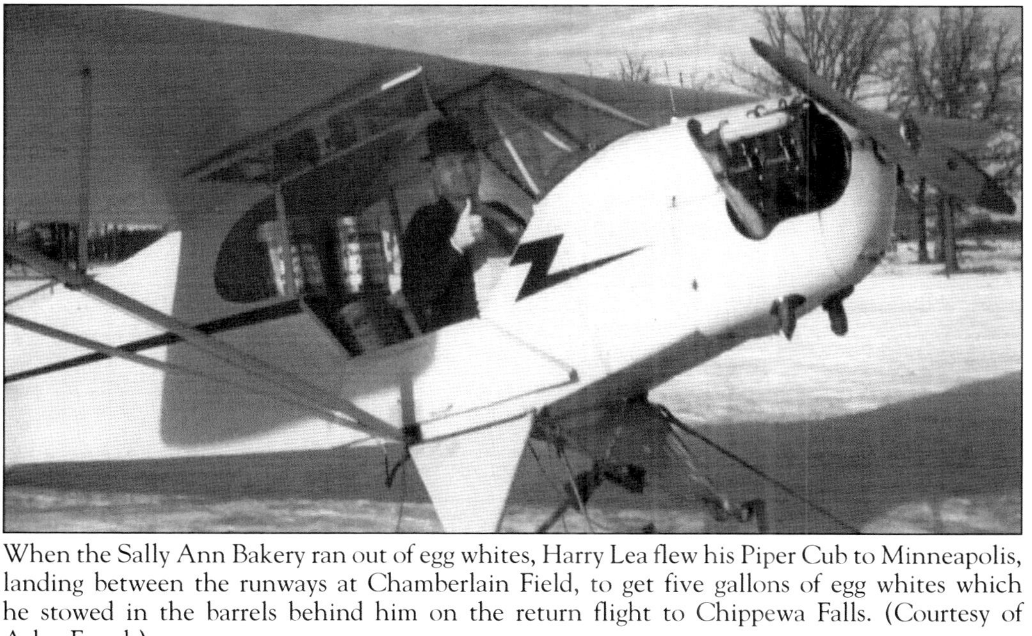

When the Sally Ann Bakery ran out of egg whites, Harry Lea flew his Piper Cub to Minneapolis, landing between the runways at Chamberlain Field, to get five gallons of egg whites which he stowed in the barrels behind him on the return flight to Chippewa Falls. (Courtesy of Arley Engel.)

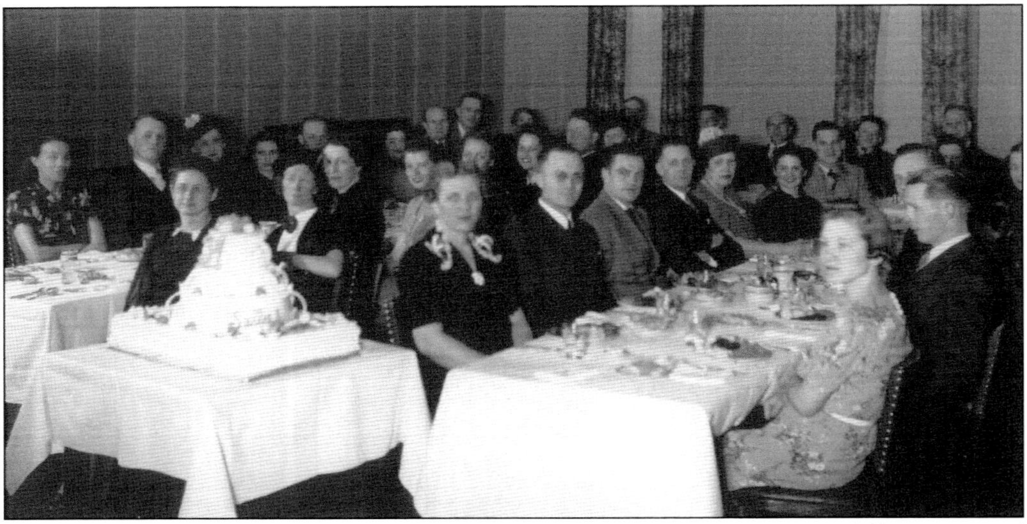

On August 31, 1961, after 57 years of serving the community, Harry Lea regretfully announced the closing of the Sally Ann Bakery in Chippewa Falls. The Steam Bakery, established in 1904 by C.O. Lea, and carried forward by Harry Lea and his family, prided itself on quality Sally Ann Bakery products. Harry Lea hosted a farewell dinner in 1961 which was held on the second floor of Skogmo Café. (Courtesy of Arley Engel.)

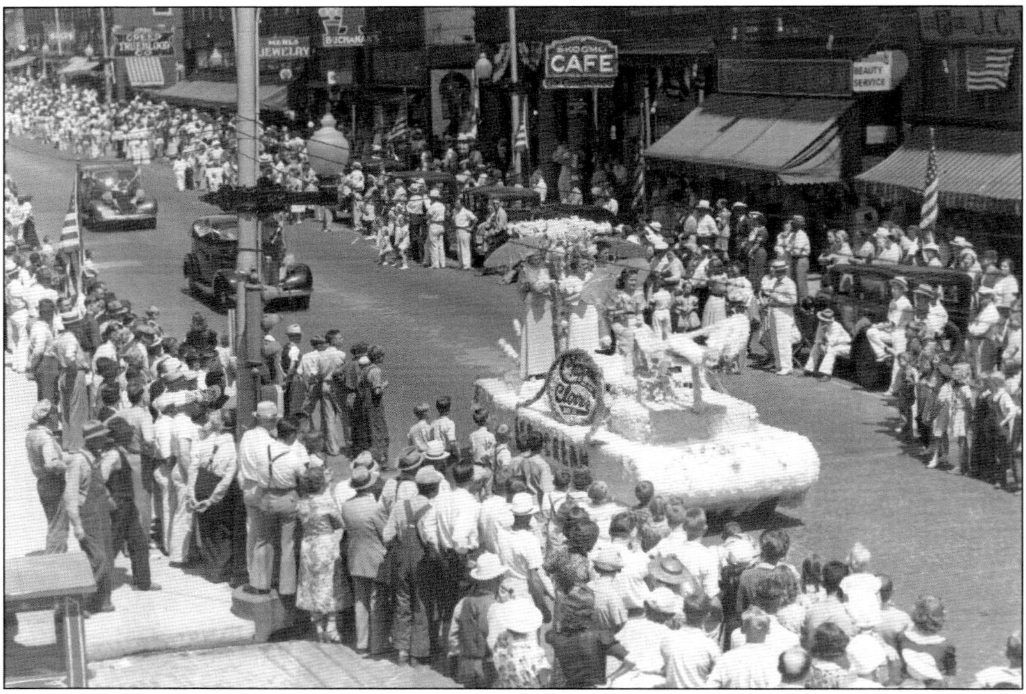

The Chippewa Valley Centennial and Home-Coming Exposition in 1937 was one of the biggest events in Chippewa Falls. Parades, bands, dances, and "entertainment and acts" were all free. Children enjoyed merry-go-rounds, the Ferris wheel, kiddie car rides and pony rides, and thousands gathered to view the parade down Bridge Street. (Courtesy of CCHS.)

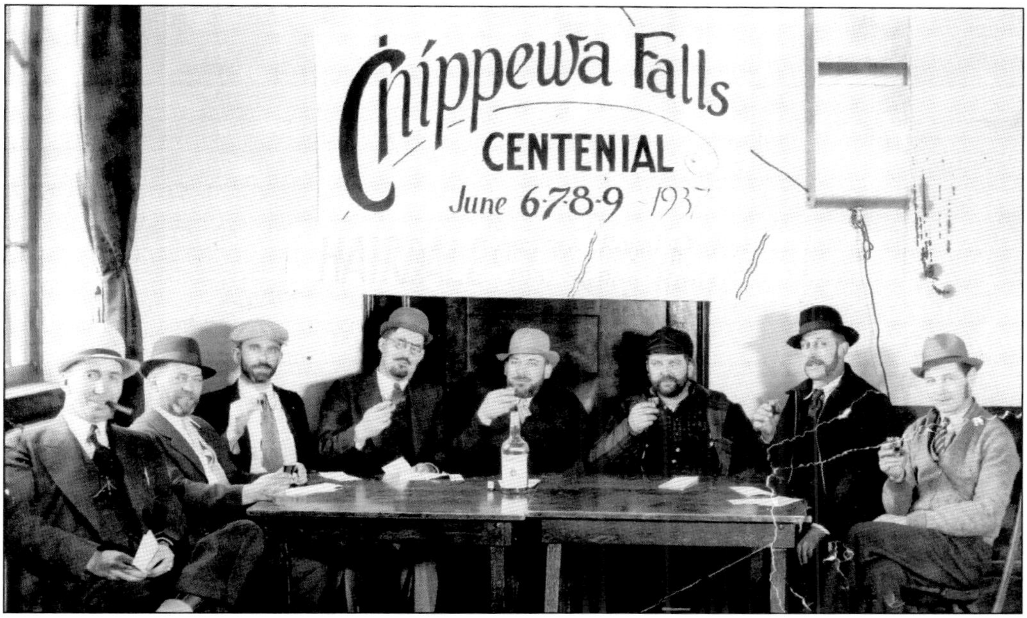

Despite the fact that in 1901 King Camp Gillette invented the safety razor, members of the Royal Order of the Dog House, whose name came from the wives whose husbands were "in the dog house" while growing scratchy whiskers, set their razors aside to boost the centennial in June 1937. Prizes were given for the longest, most unique, and fullest beards. Pictured sporting their whiskers are (from left to right) unknown, unknown, Oscar Huber, Alvin Krause, unknown, John Steinmetz, unknown, and H. Jasper. (Courtesy of Audrey Krause Mattison.)

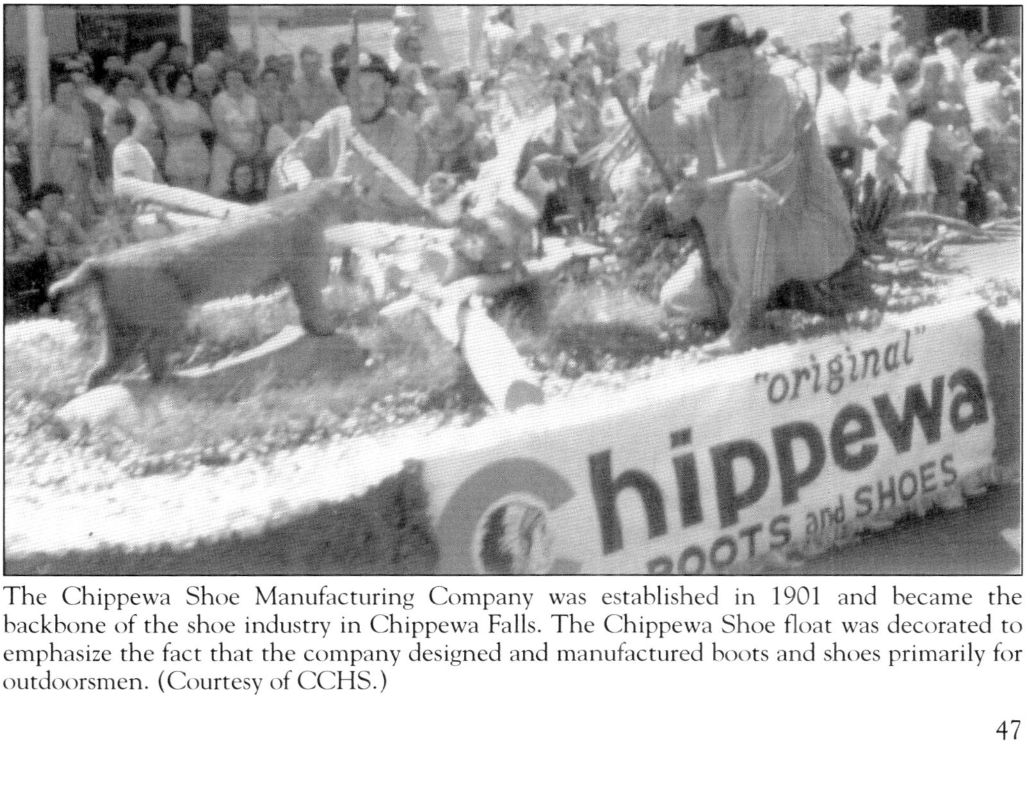

The Chippewa Shoe Manufacturing Company was established in 1901 and became the backbone of the shoe industry in Chippewa Falls. The Chippewa Shoe float was decorated to emphasize the fact that the company designed and manufactured boots and shoes primarily for outdoorsmen. (Courtesy of CCHS.)

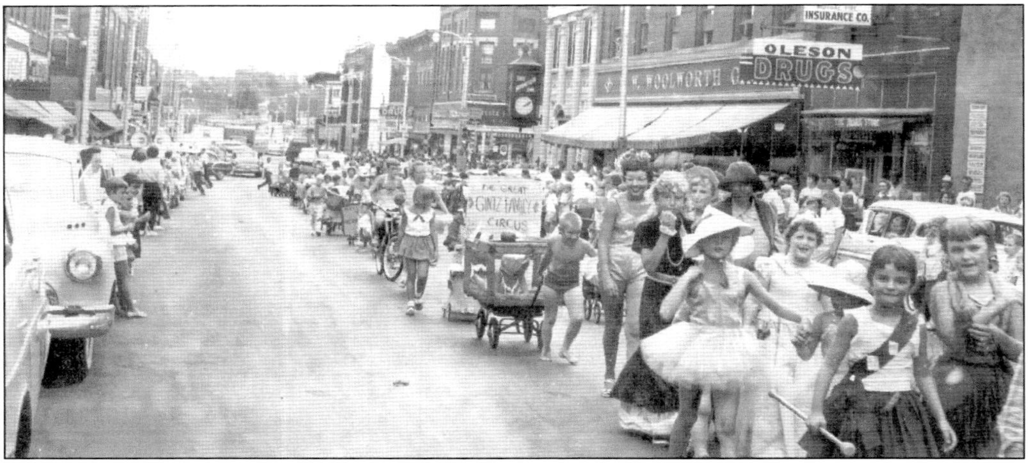

The Doll and Pet Parade, sponsored by the Chamber of Commerce, was a popular event for children in the Chippewa Falls area. In this *c.* 1950 parade, costumed children and their pets stretched the length of Bridge Street. After the parade, thirsty participants and onlookers could enjoy a malted milk at Oleson Drug Store or french fries and a cherry Coke at Woolworth's lunch counter. (Courtesy of CFACC.)

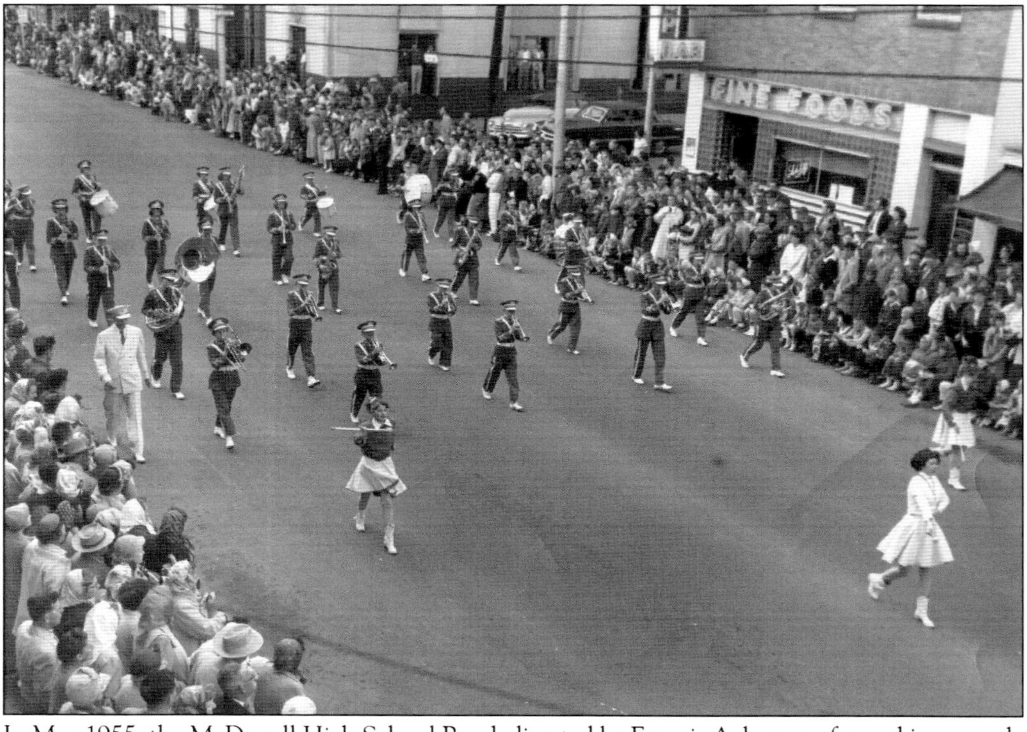

In May 1955, the McDonell High School Band, directed by Francis Ackert, performed in a parade on Barstow Street in Eau Claire, Wisconsin. The band was led up the street by majorettes Geraldine Bergevin, Mary Lu Kelly, and Sally Rushman. (Courtesy of Mary Kelly Anderson.)

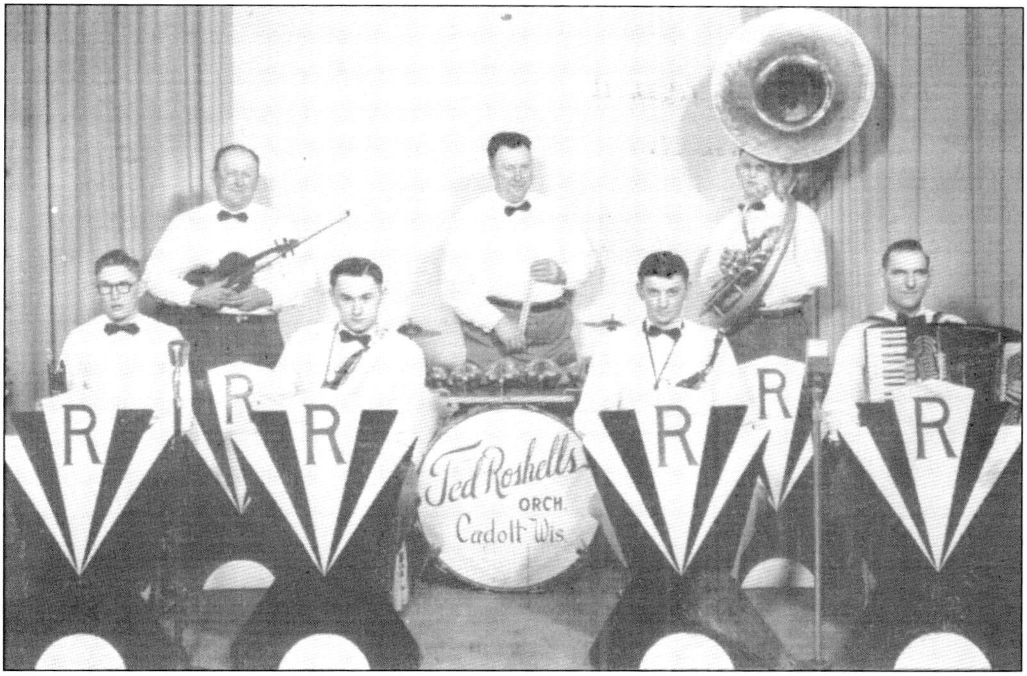

The Ted Roshell Orchestra, founded by Bill and Joe Roshell, was available for dances and offered "Old Time Music of the Best and Modern by Request." Pictured from left to right are band members: (seated) Bill Roshell Jr., Gene Roshell, Marvin Roshell, and George Loew; (back row) Bill Roshell Sr., Joe Roshell, and Jim Larker. (Courtesy of Roshell Electric.)

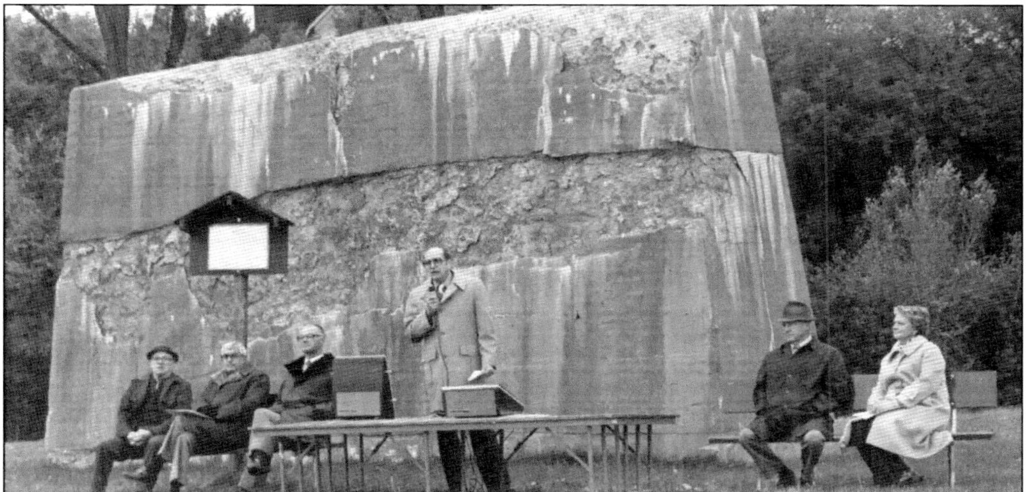

The dedication of the Hiram S. Allen Park was held October 7, 1978. Hiram Allen, considered the "father" of the city he generously supported his entire life, contributed significantly toward the growth of Chippewa Falls. Those who participated in the dedication ceremony were (from left to right) Poet Laureate Tony Vincent, Mayor Jeremiah Cashman, master of ceremonies Cal Kraemer, City Attorney David Raihle Sr., attorney Marshall Wiley, and local historian Ruth Willut. (Courtesy of the *Chippewa Herald*.)

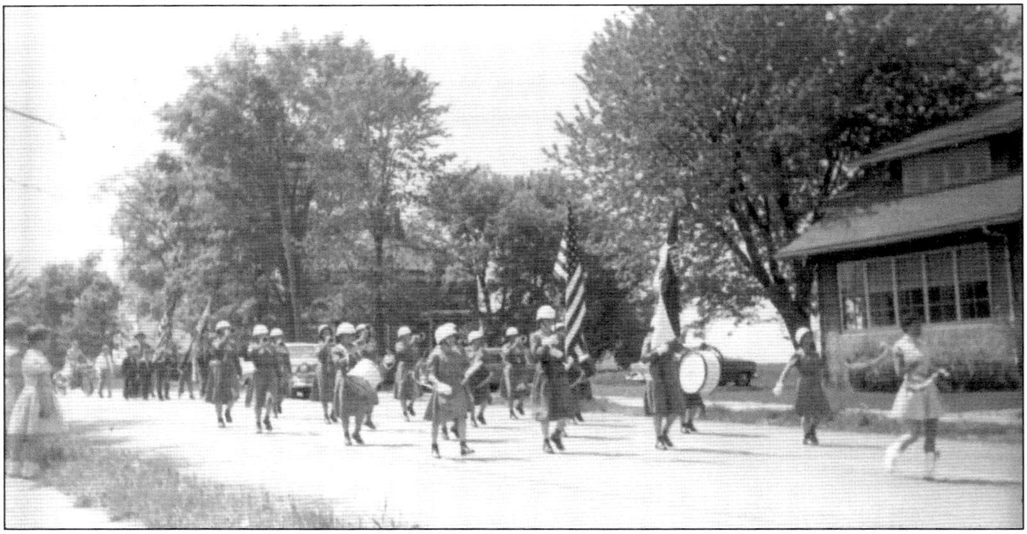

In 1967, the Wisconsin Colony and Training School's talented Drum and Bugle Corps performed in 15 parades within a 60-mile radius of Chippewa Falls. The Wisconsin Colony and Training School's orchestra and band presented several outdoor concerts during the summers that were open to the public. (Courtesy of CCHS.)

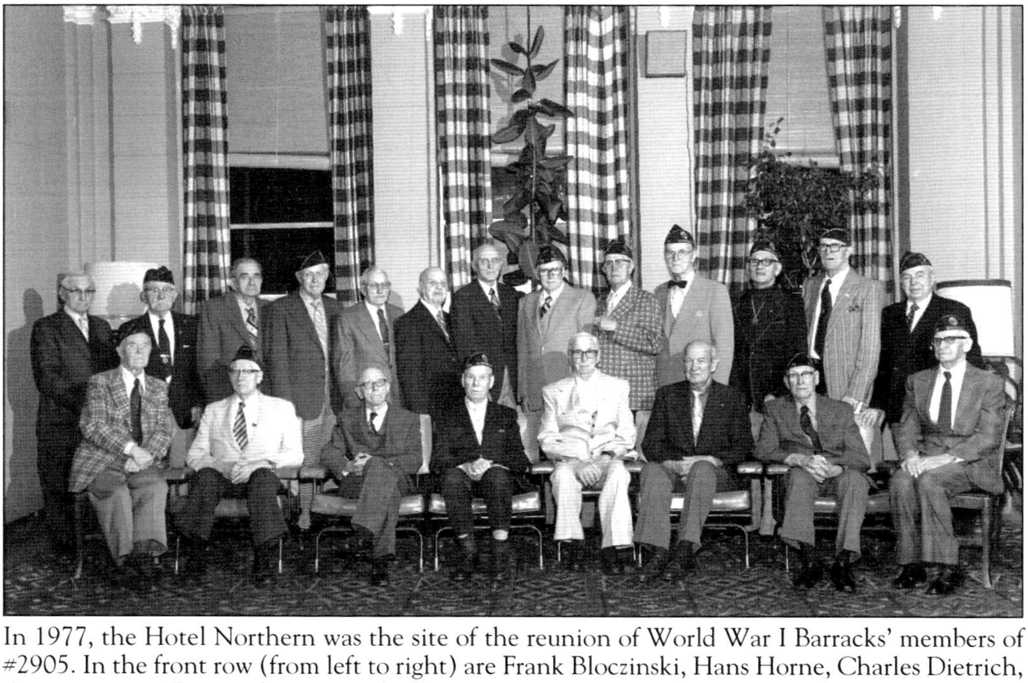

In 1977, the Hotel Northern was the site of the reunion of World War I Barracks' members of #2905. In the front row (from left to right) are Frank Bloczinski, Hans Horne, Charles Dietrich, George Pevan, Dan Farley, Conrad Thronson, unknown, and Andrew Elbert. Standing (from left to right) are unknown, Irvin Frederich, George Borgenheimer, Eric Forrest, unknown, Louis Greenwood, Art Lunde, unknown, unknown, Leo Harris, Ed Rada, Sever Remol, and Homer Hebert. (Courtesy of CCHS.)

Four

Water Makes the Falls

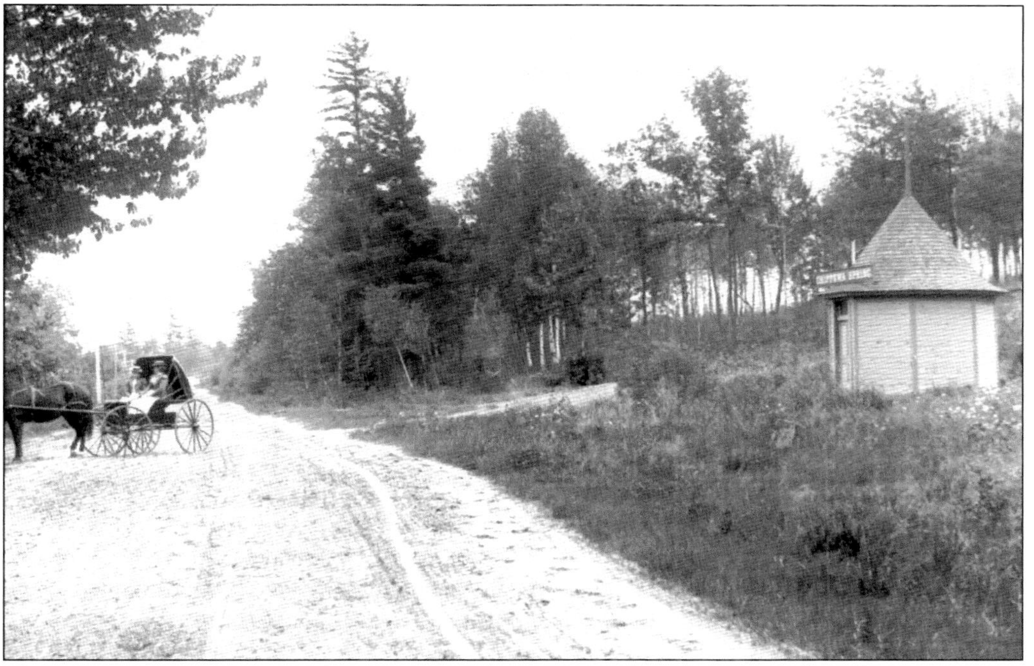

The history of Chippewa Falls is inextricably intertwined with water. The Chippewa River, Duncan Creek, and the springs attracted Native Americans, French and British fur traders, lumbermen, and those seeking another chance at life. The river transported logs from upstream, the creek helped mills produce flour, and the springs provided pure drinking water to a growing population. In 1885, under the administration of Mayor T.J. Cunningham, the water works were built and the purest water in the world ran through the wooden pipes. When his rheumatism disappeared, Thaddeus Pound believed the health-giving properties of the spring water cured him and he incorporated Chippewa Springs Company in 1894. The original Spring House was dedicated in 1893 and completely restored and rededicated in 1993. (Courtesy of CCHS.)

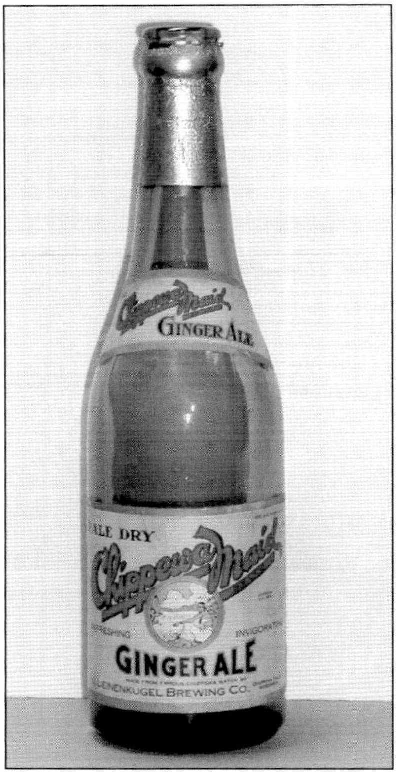

The passage of the Volstead Act in 1919 making the production and sale of intoxicating beverages illegal occurred just as Leinenkugel's beer sales mushroomed. For a short time, Leinenkugel's manufactured "near beer," then moved into the production of soda water. When the 21st Amendment was ratified in 1933 marking the end of Prohibition, Leinenkugel's was the largest manufacturer of bottled soda water in northwestern Wisconsin. (Courtesy of JLBC.)

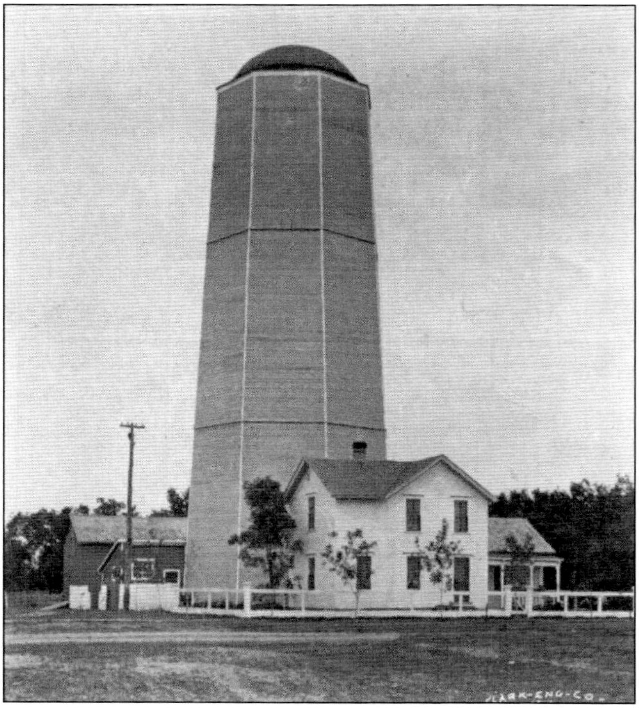

The 365,000-gallon vertical standpipe, constructed between 1880 and 1885 and located on a lot off East Grand Avenue, was the only water tower in the city. Eight artesian wells and one deep well, installed in 1953 at the city's east well field, were the only sources of water for the entire city. (Courtesy of David R. Redard.)

Homes at the far end of the water works system in Chippewa Falls often experienced low water pressure. The growing population necessitated the addition of other water towers. In 1962, towers were built on the West Hill and on the South Side, shown here. The East Hill tower was built in 1972. (Courtesy of Dave Gordon.)

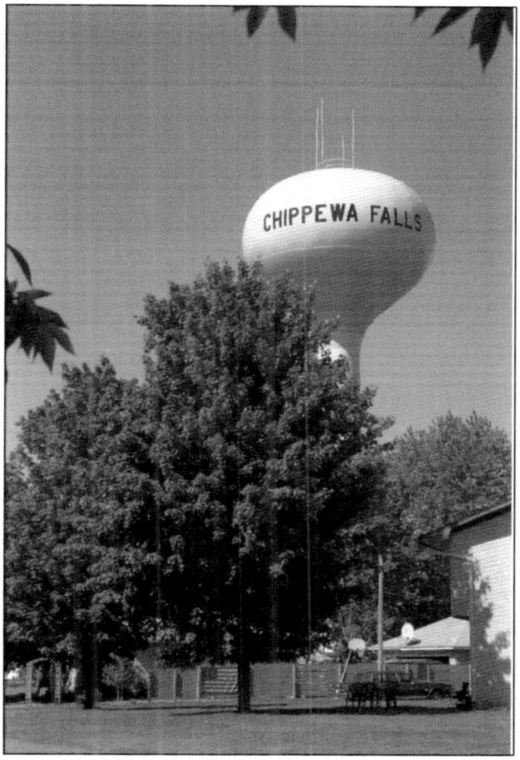

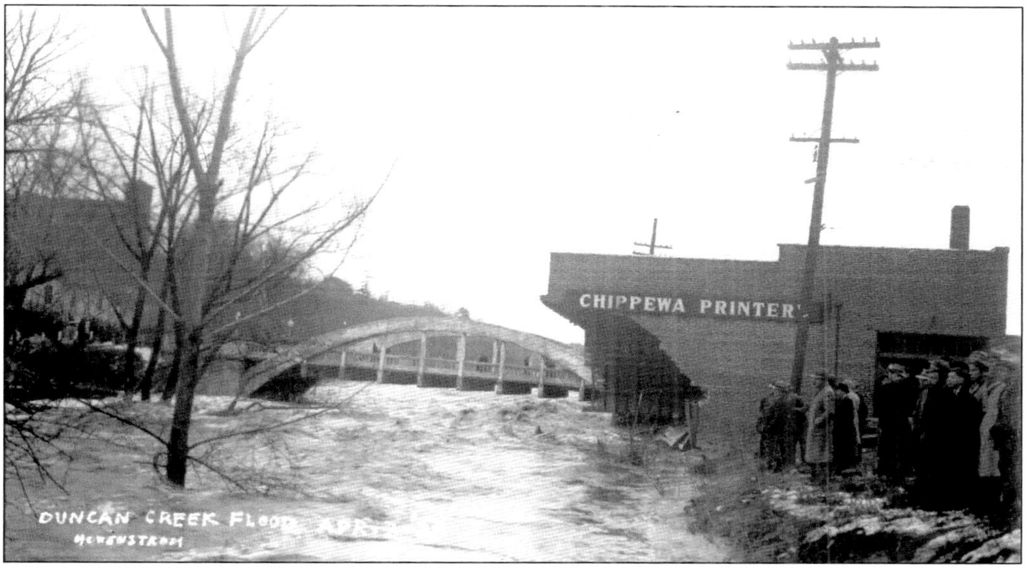

On April 3, 1934, Duncan Creek went on a rampage, sweeping away bridges and buildings. Irvine Park was completely flooded and schools were dismissed so students living on the East Hill could get home. Staff members of the 1934 *Chi-Hi Monocle* were horrified to see part of the Chippewa Printery structure, where the school annual was being prepared, collapsing into the flood waters. (Courtesy of Kris and Dave Martineau.)

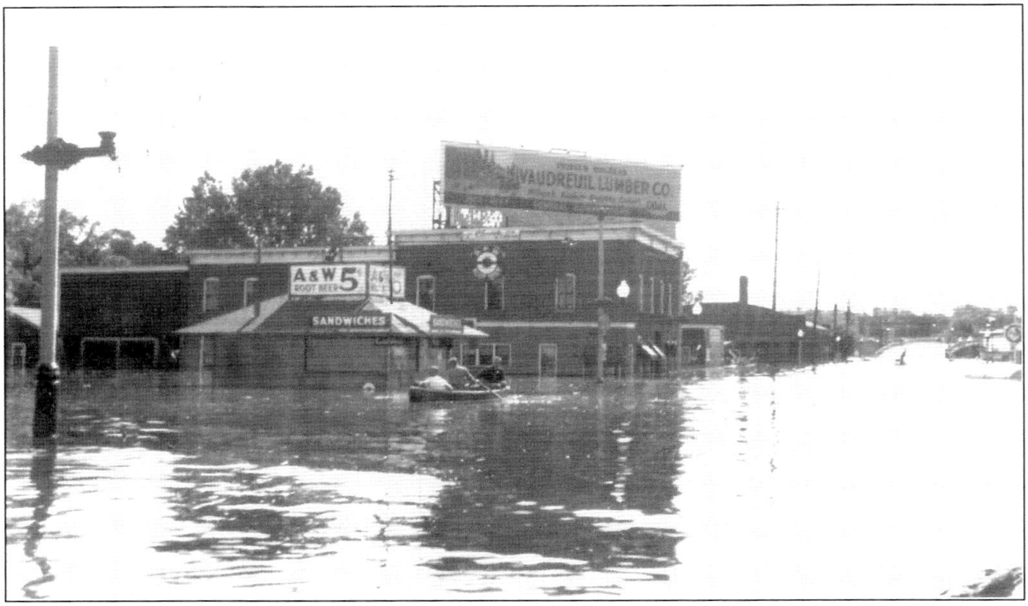

The 1941 Labor Day Flood, caused by heavy rains north of Chippewa Falls, flooded many streets and businesses. Three men in a boat rowed past the inundated Vaudreuil Lumber Company and the A&W Root Beer stand pictured at its original location at the corner of River and Bridge Streets. (Courtesy of Kris and Dave Martineau.)

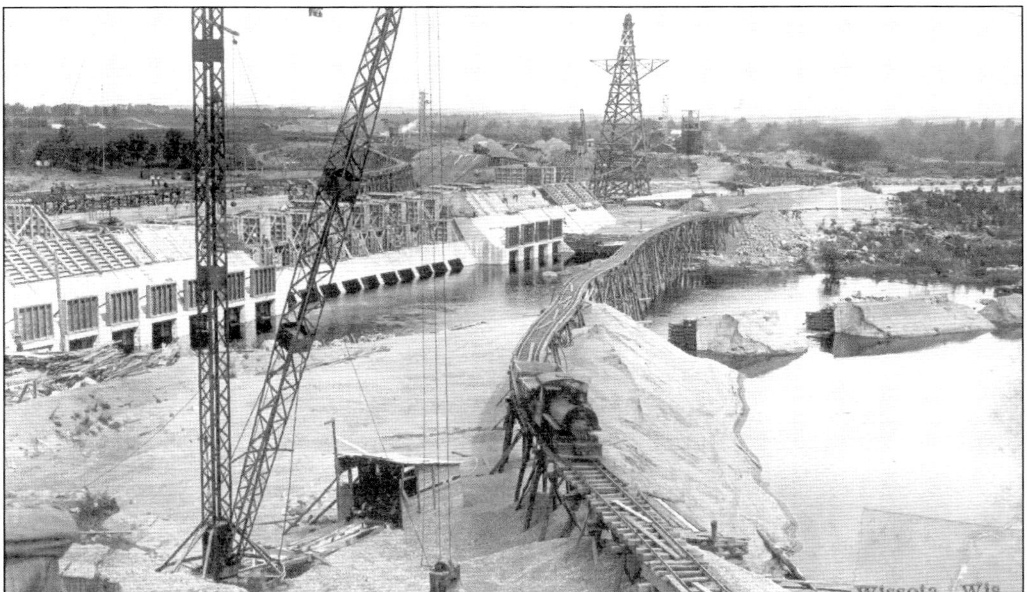

The Wisconsin-Minnesota Power and Light Company hydropower dam, built from 1916–1918, with a height of 67 feet and a total length of 4,290 feet, was the largest of all earth dams in the world at the time. It became the chief source of power for Chippewa Falls and created Lake Wissota, which promoters noted with time "will be lined with summer homes." (Courtesy of Wendy Mittermeyer.)

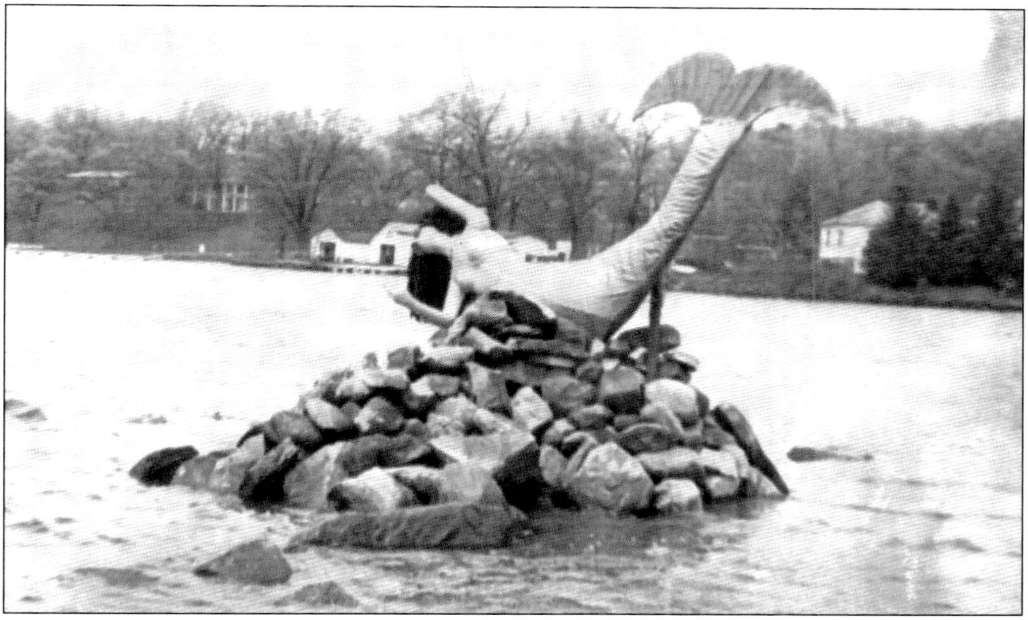

For a few months in the summer of 1984, a mermaid perched on a pile of rocks in Little Lake Wissota. Built of plywood, chicken wire, a mop head dyed green, and green clothes, the mermaid was set up very early one spring morning so the builders could remain anonymous. The mermaid caused traffic jams on County X as people slowed to get a better look at the life-sized mannequin created by Bob Leidholdt, family members, and friends. (Courtesy of the *Chippewa Herald.*)

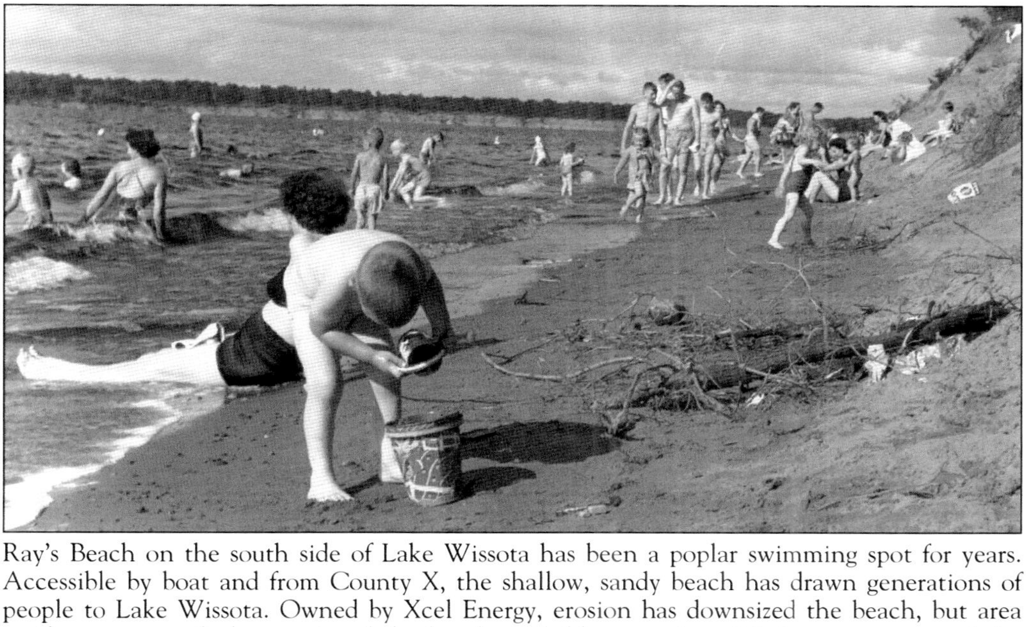

Ray's Beach on the south side of Lake Wissota has been a poplar swimming spot for years. Accessible by boat and from County X, the shallow, sandy beach has drawn generations of people to Lake Wissota. Owned by Xcel Energy, erosion has downsized the beach, but area residents, many of whom enjoyed the beach as children, are hopeful the great asset to Lake Wissota can be maintained. (Courtesy of CFACC.)

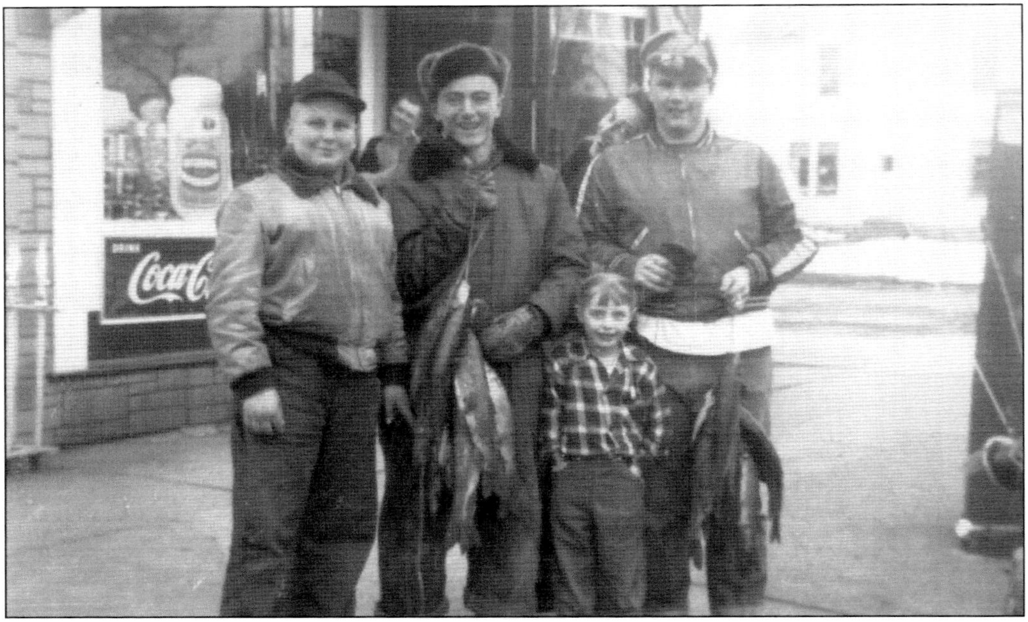

Standing in front of Krueger's store c. 1947, proudly displaying their fish caught in Duncan Creek, are (from left to right) Larry "Tiny" White, Roger Meyer, and Don Stratton. John LeCleir, standing in the screen door, admired the catch. (Courtesy of Arley Engel.)

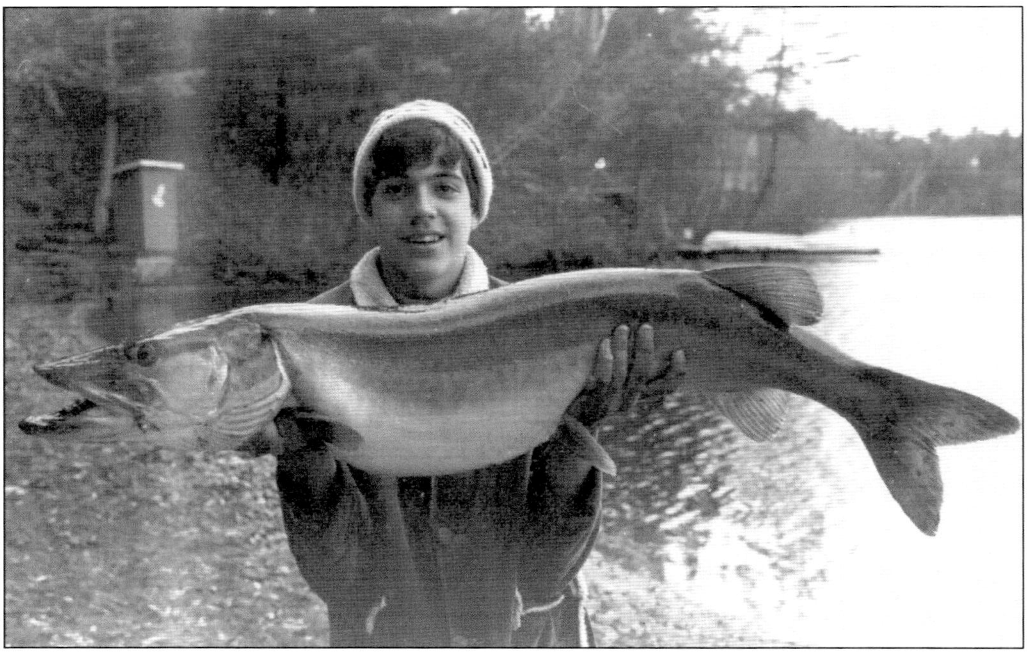

In May of 1936, 30 cans of baby muskellunge and 70 cans of walleyed pike were planted in Lake Wissota. The fry were brought from the Island Lake hatchery that was supported by local fishermen. Pictured is Mike Henry with the 32-pound, 48 1/2-inch-long muskellunge he caught October 21, 1972, in Lake Wissota. (Courtesy of CFACC.)

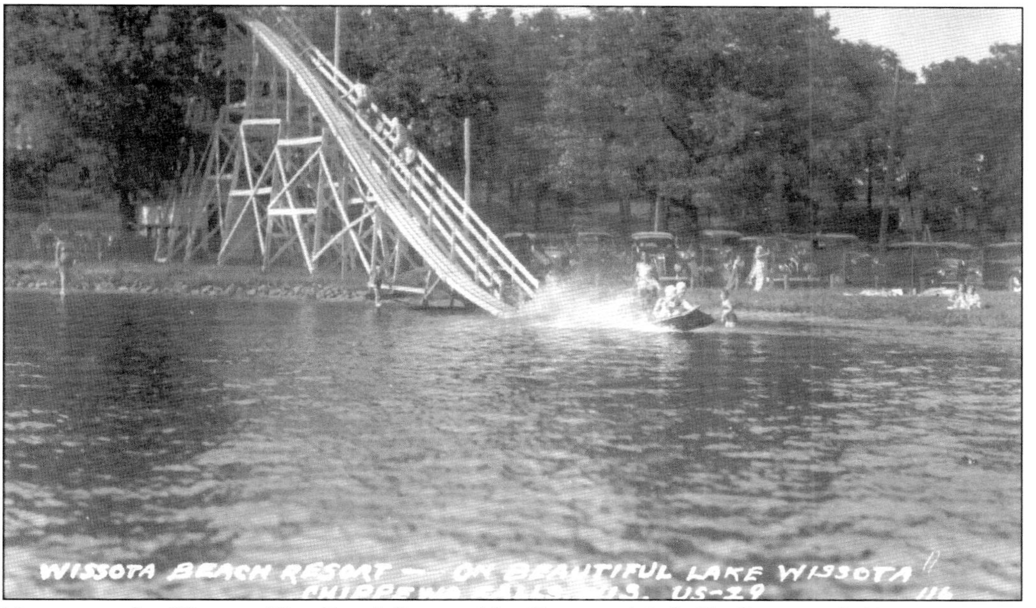

Visitors to the Wissota "Pay Beach," owned by Ernie and Isabelle Cote, paid 10¢ to swim at the beach and take trips down the wood toboggan slide. Built in 1946, liability insurance rates eventually forced the family to remove the slide. (Courtesy of Bill and Lou Nagle.)

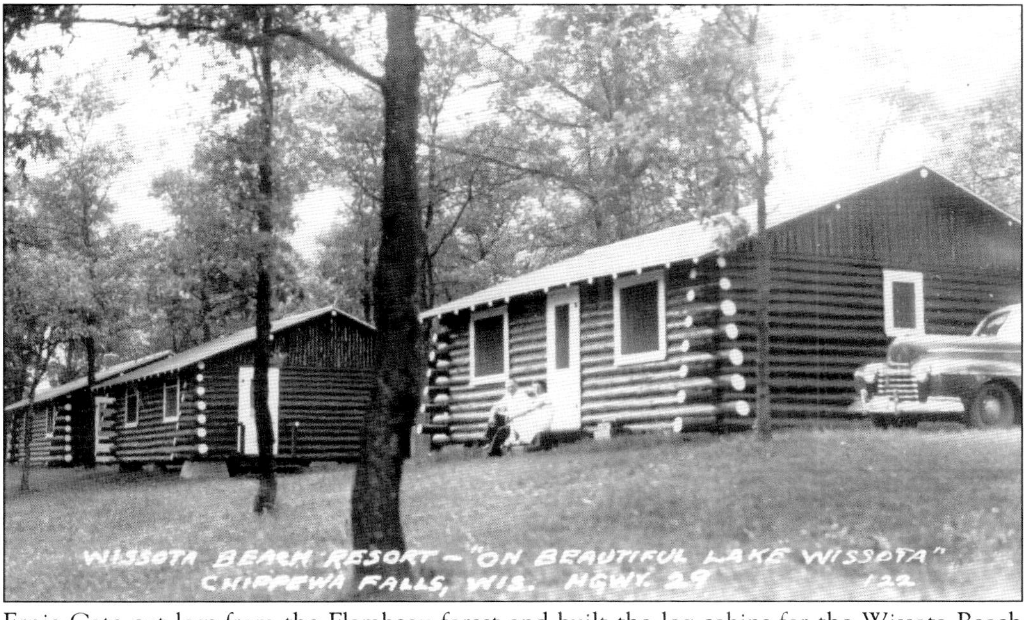

Ernie Cote cut logs from the Flambeau forest and built the log cabins for the Wissota Beach Resort. For $1.50 per night, visitors could stay in a cabin furnished with beds and a wood stove. The resort consisted of the cabins, small white cottages along the lakeshore, two bath houses, and a concession stand where, on Sundays, four workers could make $100 a day in nickels. (Courtesy of Bill and Lou Nagle.)

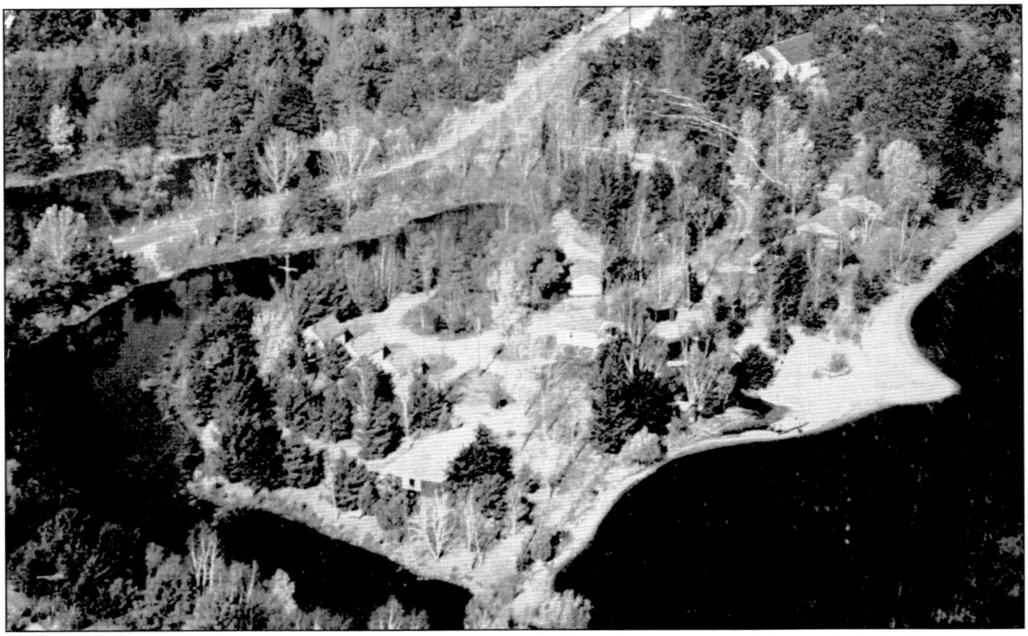

The Hideaway Resort, located at 77 Hydro Lane, was established by Harry and Blanche Frenette Lea in the early 1950s. Still in the family today, operated by Matt and Rhonda Elstran, the Hideaway Resort hosts over 100 descendants of Harry and Blanche each year on the Fourth of July. (Courtesy of Ron Lea.)

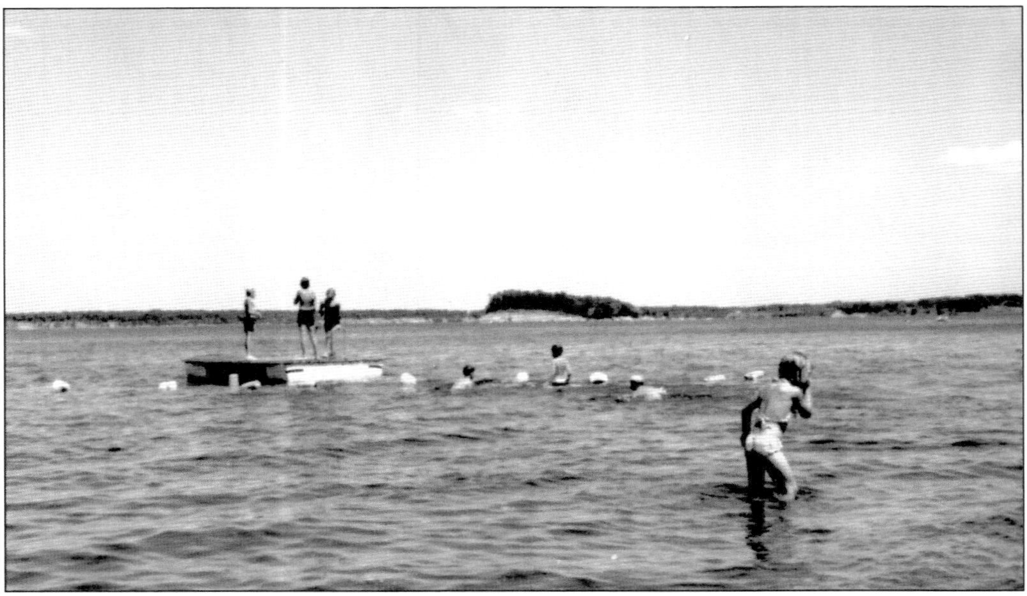

Children staying at the Hideaway Resort could swing from a rope in a tree into the waters of this sandy beach on Lake Wissota. In the background, once a hill near the Lester Dodge farm, is the famous island created by the waters of Lake Wissota. It became a popular destination for boaters and sometimes campers. (Courtesy of Ron Lea.)

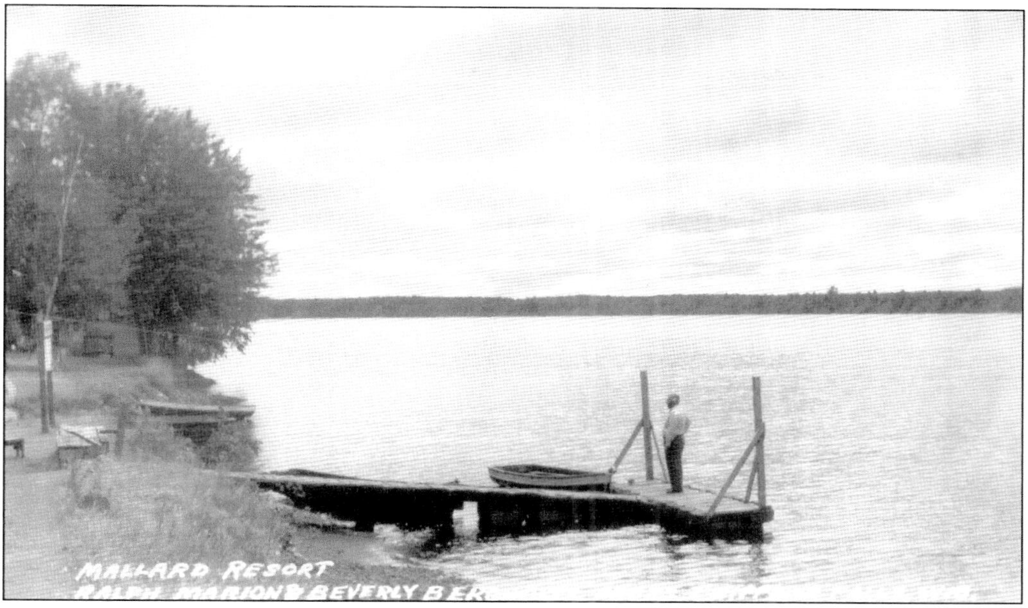

Mallard Resort, purchased in 1946 by Ralph and Marion Bergholtz, has been a favorite destination for generations of families. Bev Chartier, who was 10 years old when her parents bought Mallard's, has witnessed the growth of the resort. From one dock in 1946 to 17 docks presently, the resort continues to attract boaters cruising along the Chippewa River and campers seeking the peace and beauty of the northwoods. (Courtesy of Bev Chartier.)

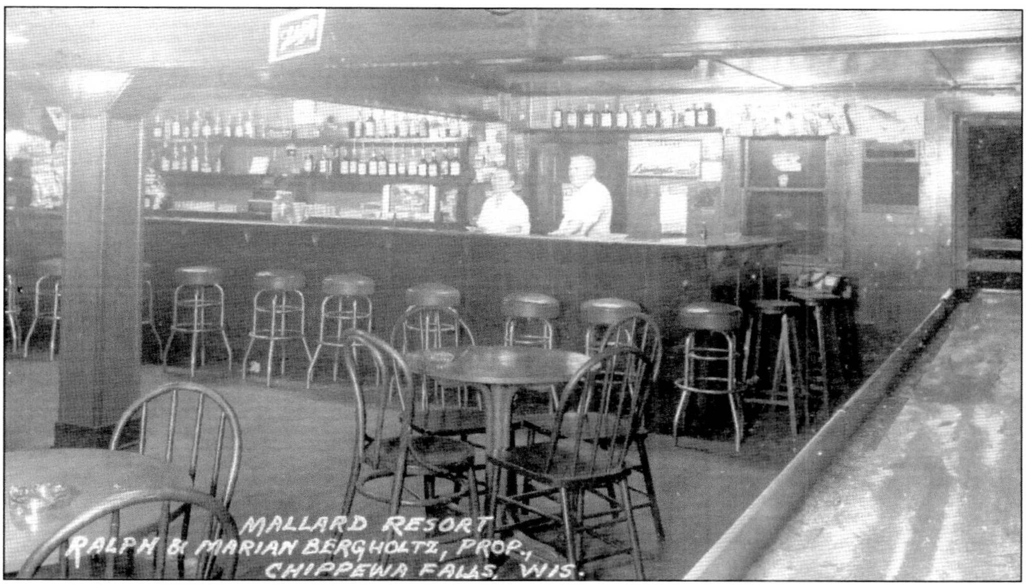

Bev Chartier, the daughter of Ralph and Marion Bergholtz (pictured behind the bar), returned to Chippewa Falls in 1966 to help her mother run Mallard Resort. Four generations of families have enjoyed their friendships with the Chartiers. In 1983, Frank Vroblosky joined in that legacy of friendship and became part of the Mallard Resort family until his death in 2000. A favorite toast at the resort is "God bless the Mallard." (Courtesy of Bev Chartier.)

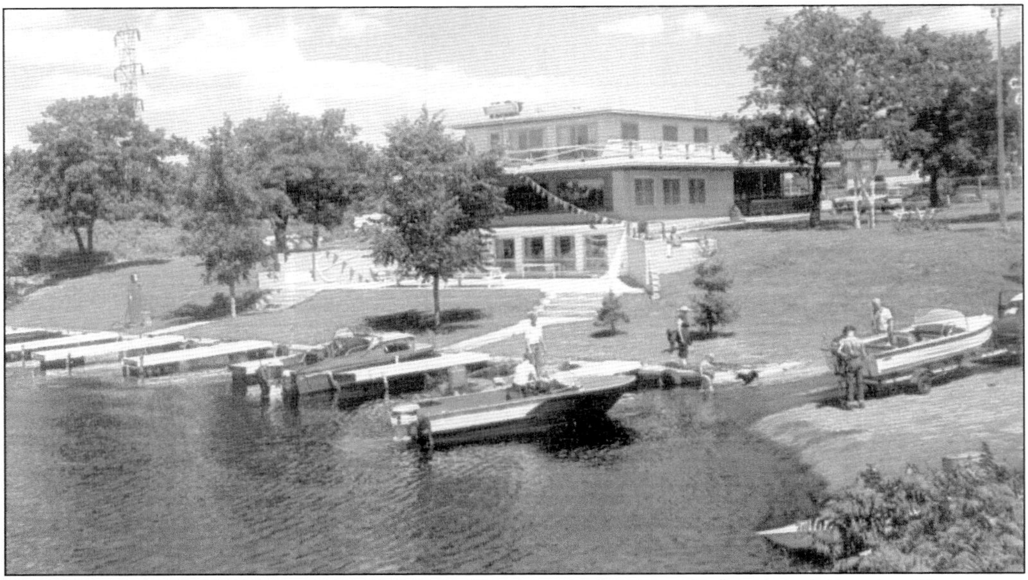

LeQue's Supper Club became Water's Edge Supper Club when Richard and Carolyn Horstman purchased the business on Lake Wissota in 1969. The popular Water's Edge hosted boating parties and class reunions on its deck. The Horstmans sold the restaurant in 1991 and now, after several changes in ownership, it is called The Docks On Wissota. (Courtesy of Bev Chartier.)

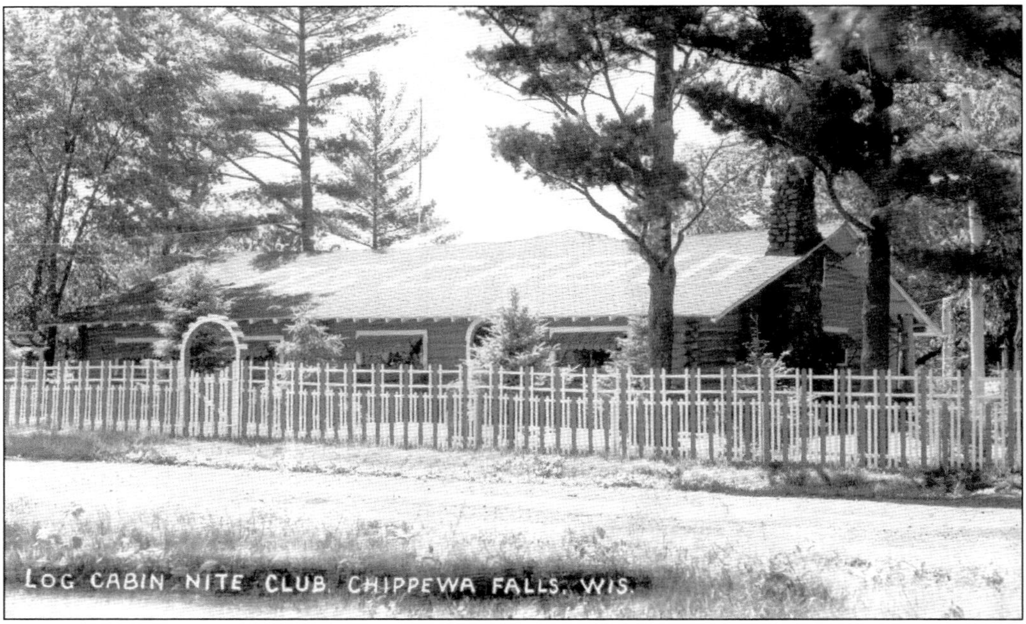

Located on Duncan Creek below Eagleton and Klinger's farm, the Log Cabin Night Club provided good food and dancing for its patrons. It had a cook who knew how to prepare catfish in a palatable manner, according to Ralph Christoffersen. (Courtesy of Bev Chartier.)

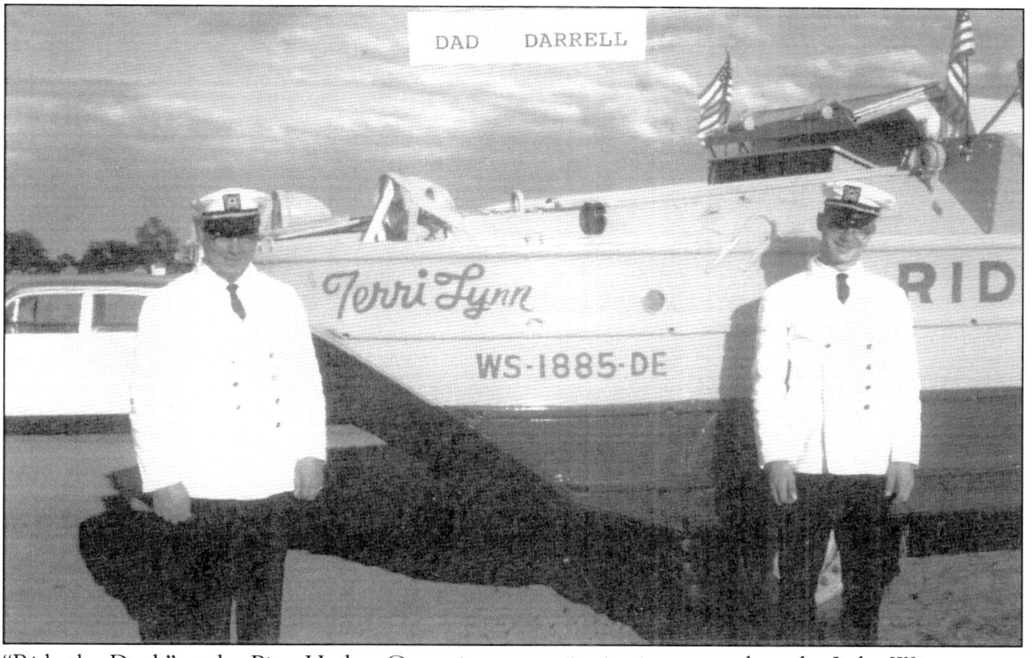

"Ride the Duck" at the Pine Harbor Campsite was an invitation to explore the Lake Wissota area during a one-hour excursion on land and water. During the 1960s, Mr. and Mrs. Lester Dodge offered the amphibious boat rides to children for $1.25 and to adults for $1.75. Pictured are Lester Dodge on left and his son, Darrel Dodge, who also piloted the Duck. (Courtesy of Arley Engel.)

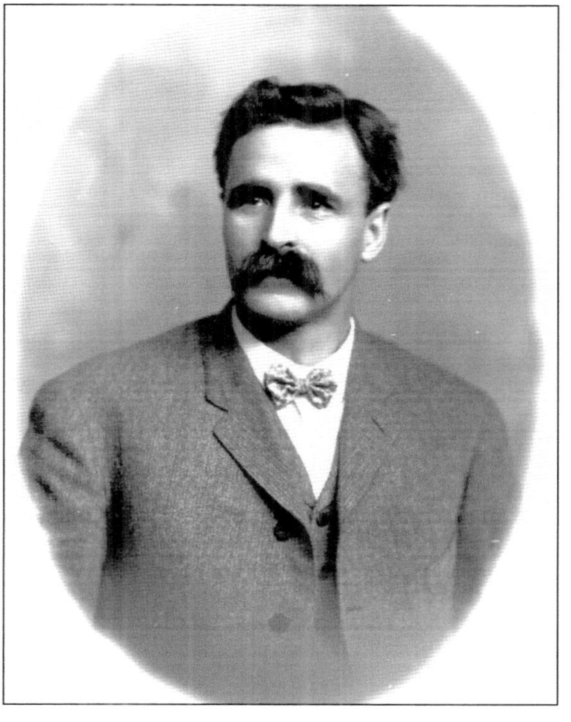

Walking along Duncan Creek below the Glen Mills, the setting was described in 1900 as a "beautiful little trout stream" where children swim and picnic along the banks. In June 1909, several cans of trout fry arrived from the Madison hatchery and T.W. Sugars consigned seven cans to Duncan Creek and the rest to Stillson Creek, ensuring the future of those trout streams. (Courtesy of Dolores Beaudette.)

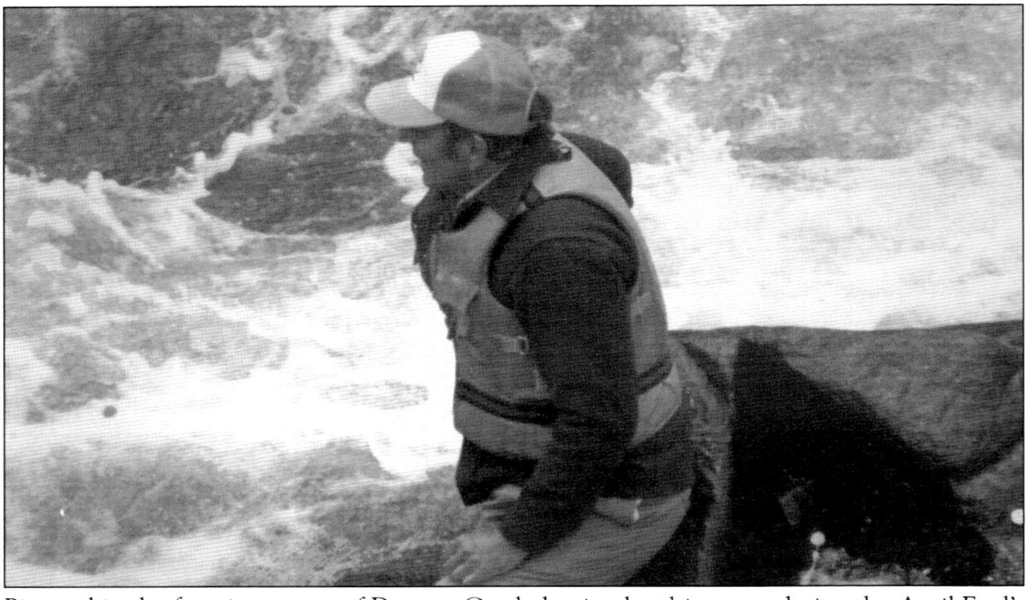

Pictured in the foaming waters of Duncan Creek, having lost his canoe during the April Fool's Day canoe race, Jack Barney contemplated his options. As the founder of Extrusion Dies who encouraged the entrepreneurial spirit, he also believed in mentoring new employees. When John "Jack" Barney died in May 1984, a provision of his will generously stipulated that trout fry be placed in Duncan Creek each spring for the enjoyment of the children of the area. (Courtesy of Harry Lippert.)

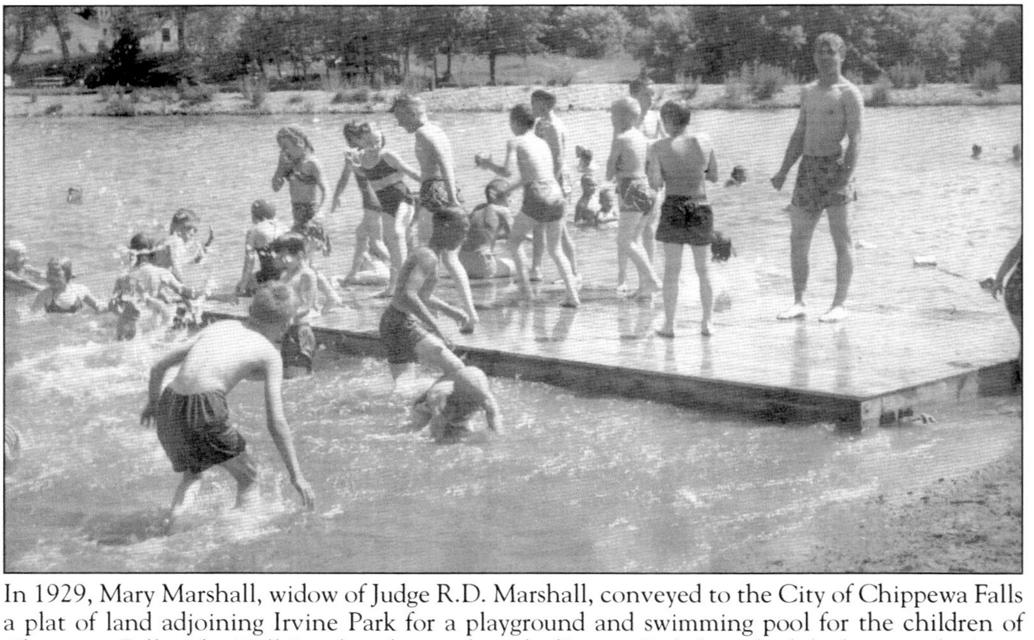

In 1929, Mary Marshall, widow of Judge R.D. Marshall, conveyed to the City of Chippewa Falls a plat of land adjoining Irvine Park for a playground and swimming pool for the children of Chippewa Falls. The Mill Pond at the south end of Irvine Park furnished dual season facilities for swimming and ice skating and was filled with water supplied by the diversion of Duncan Creek. (Courtesy of CFACC.)

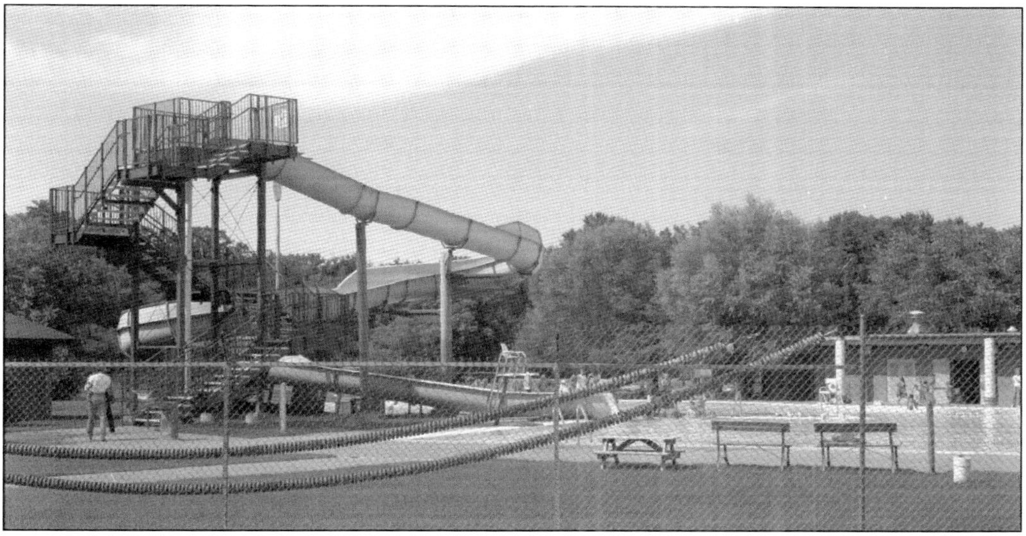

In 1967, the Chippewa Foundation announced that a new outdoor pool would be constructed at the Mill Pond site. Robert Halbleib chaired the planning committee, Seymour Cray Jr. donated 100 shares of Control Data stock, and 700 volunteers collected pledges for the new pool which opened in 1969. Area residents and visitors swam in the 178-square-foot concrete and gravel pool until it was replaced by the Bernard F. Willi pool in 1991, pictured above with a water slide and 85 degree water. (Courtesy of Dave Gordon.)

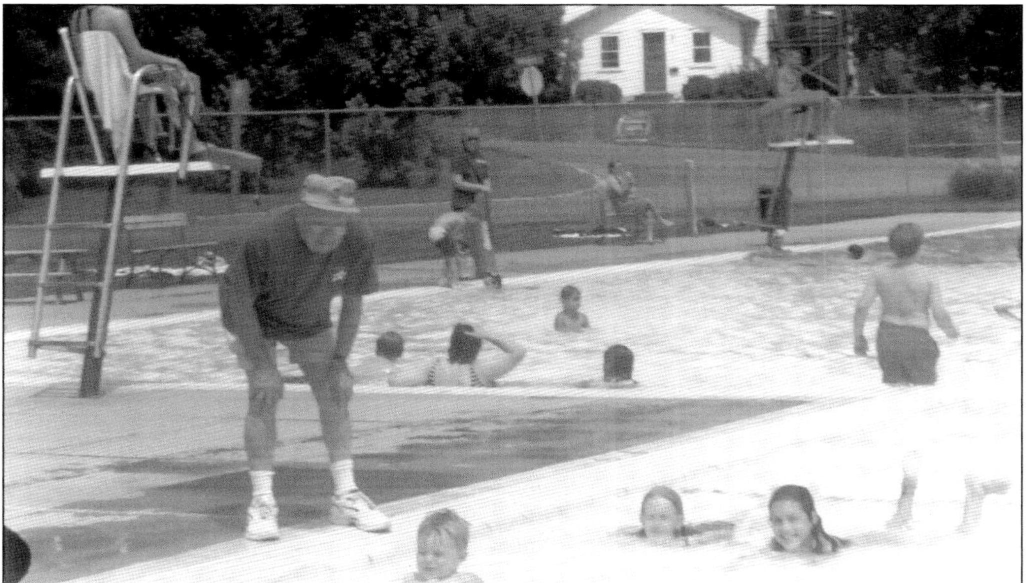

The Bernard Willi zero depth pool holds approximately 200,000 gallons of water. Former Mayor Bernard Willi declared on June 27, 1991, "Yesterday was one of the most wonderful days of my life. Little kids were taking my hand and trying to get me in the water, and I thought that was great." (Courtesy of the *Chippewa Herald*.)

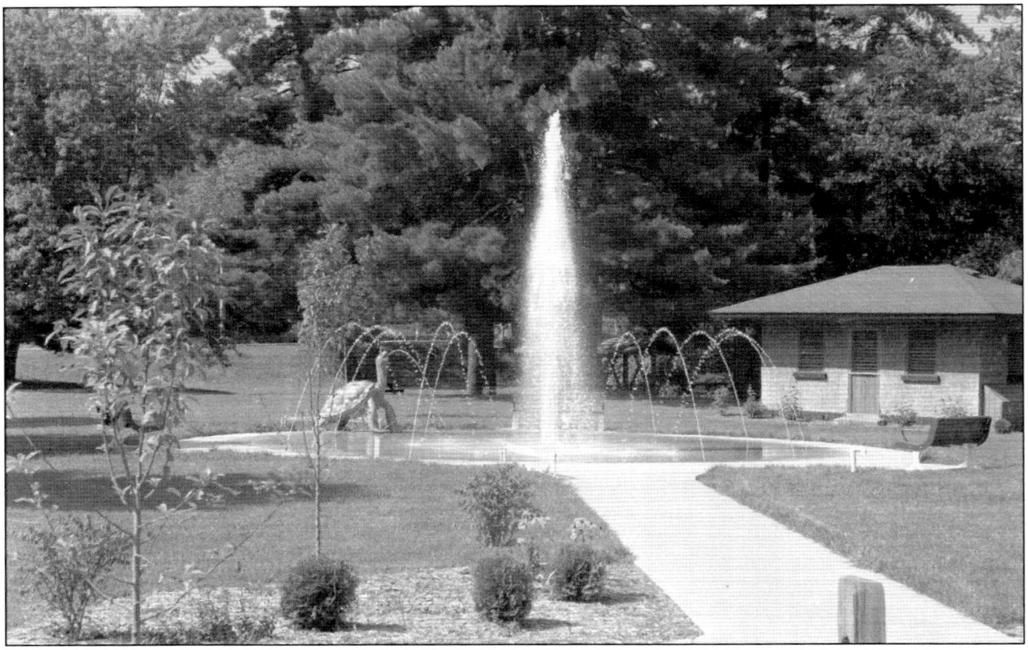

The Northwestern Bank and the Mason Companies have a history of philanthropy in Chippewa Falls. To celebrate their 100th anniversaries in 2004, the two businesses donated the monies to build this new fountain in Irvine Park. (Courtesy of Dave Gordon.)

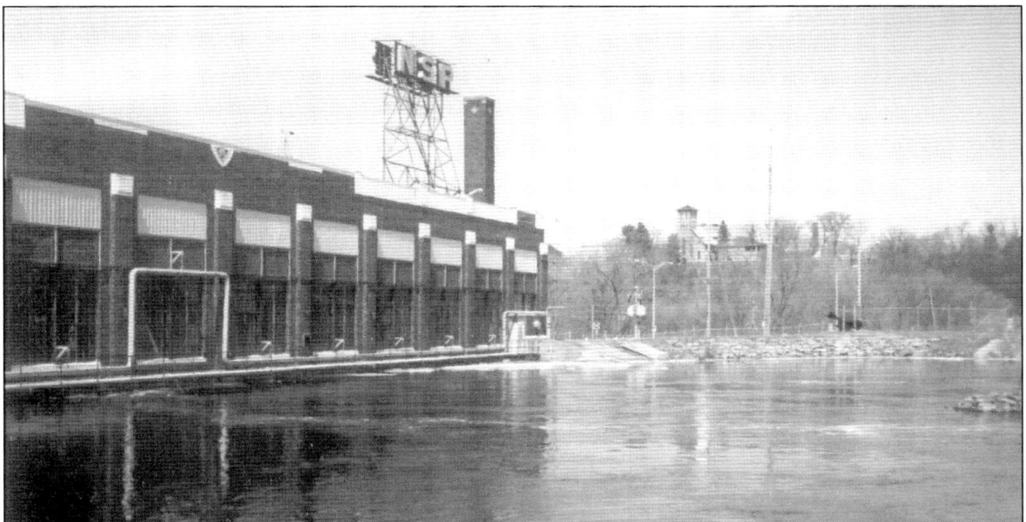

The Northern States Power Company purchased the Wisconsin-Minnesota Light and Power Company in 1923 and constructed its first hydropower plant in Chippewa Falls. It was built in 1927–1928 at the site where the first lumber mill was located 90 years earlier. Using construction methods that relied on muscle as well as machinery, crews completed the $35 million project in ten months. The brightly-lit NSP sign became a Chippewa Falls landmark. (Courtesy of CFMIT.)

Five

Earth, Wind, & Fire

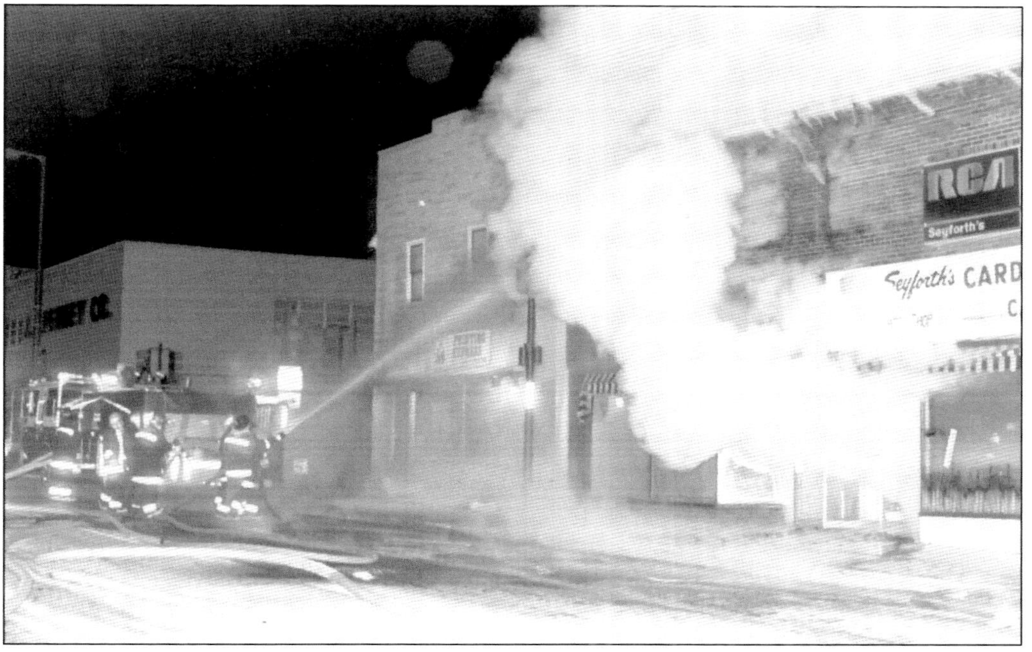

The forces of nature have always challenged Chippewa Falls. The earliest account of the impact of weather in the area is that of a devastating storm, noted by Jonathon Carver in 1767. The city of Chippewa Falls was incorporated in 1869, the same year a fire destroyed most of the buildings in the fledgling commercial district. A volunteer fire department was organized the following year. In 1874, the magnificent Tremont House vanished in a blaze of flames, despite the efforts of the fire department. Floods were a constant threat, even after dams were built to control the Chippewa River. A devastating tornado in 1958 killed nine people and destroyed Irvine Park, but the tenacious community of Chippewa Falls regrouped and rebuilt. On January 6, 1988, at approximately 4:25 in the morning, police officer Bob Adams noticed smoke coming from Seyforth's Card and Gift Shop at 219 N. Bridge Street. Area firefighters fought the blaze in sub-freezing temperatures, but the building was destroyed. Glen Seyforth regrouped and moved his business to Spring Street. (Courtesy of CFFD.)

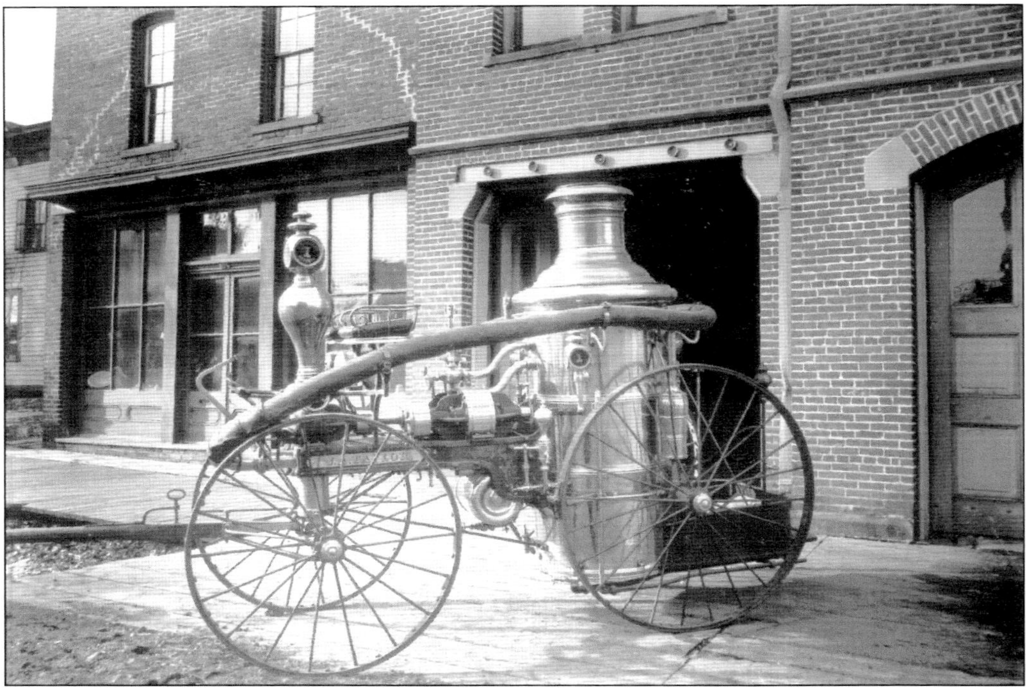

The destructive fires that occurred inevitably in the lumbering town of Chippewa Falls prompted 25 men to form a volunteer fire department in 1870. City bonds were issued to purchase the $5,000 Silsby steam rotary engine which was named after James Taylor, the chief engineer in the department and the mayor. At first pulled to fires by the volunteers and bystanders, horses were later purchased for that difficult task. (Courtesy of CFFD.)

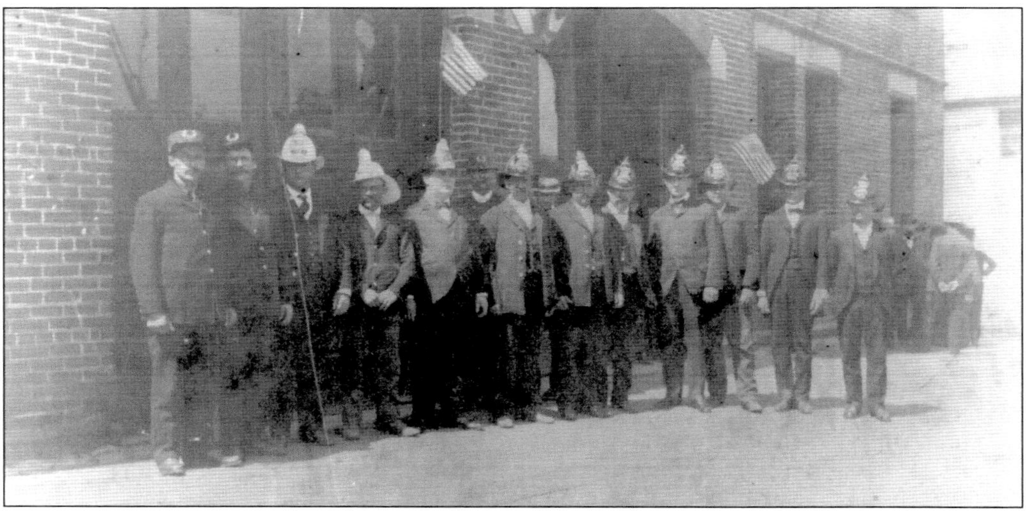

The Chippewa Falls Fire Station and City Hall were located on the northwest corner of Bay and Central Streets. Pictured in 1902 are (from left to right) Albert Huber, Roderick McPhee, John Anglum, Joe Meuli, Jim Tracey, Chippewa Falls policeman John Thornton, Tom Duffy, Chippewa Falls Mayor George McCall, Charles Brecke, August Schaller, Otto Groetzinger, Al Olson, Henry McClaire, and Frank Leslie. (Courtesy of CFFD.)

As the city grew, so did the demands on the fire department and its equipment. Pictured in 1915, when Ed Brecke was Fire Chief, members of the department test their hoses to assure their capacity to reach the three- and four-story buildings in Chippewa Falls such as the Rutledge Home, pictured in the distance. (Courtesy of CFFD.)

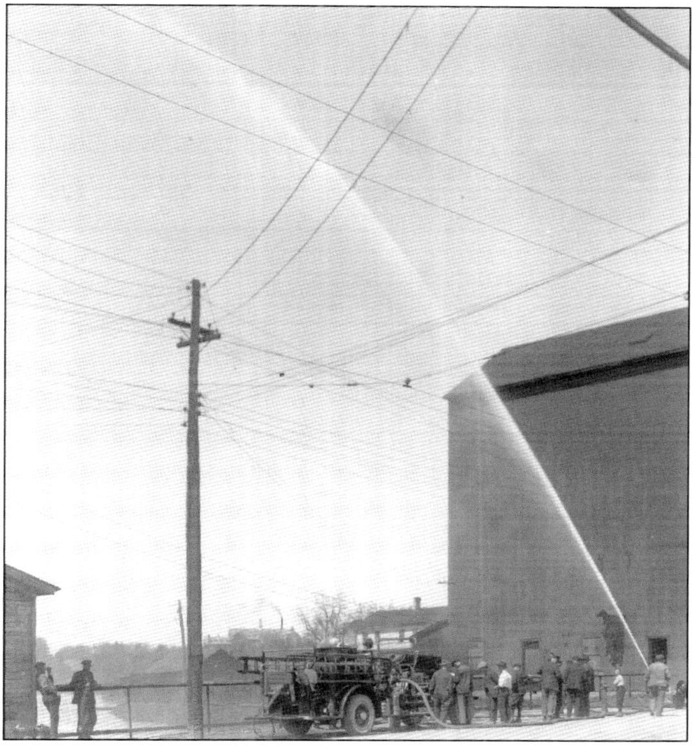

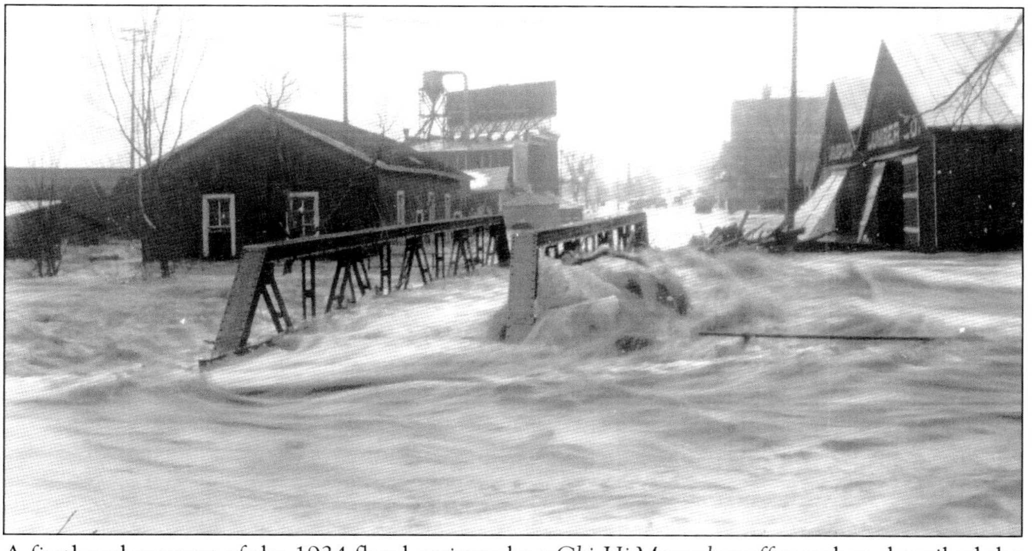

A firsthand account of the 1934 flood, written by a *Chi-Hi Monocle* staff member, described the progress of the turbulent waters through Chippewa Falls. "At twelve o'clock the large bridge across Duncan Creek at East Central Street was washed away and swept down the creek as hundreds of people gasped in awe, expecting that it would strike the Spring Street bridge and sweep it away also." (Courtesy of Marlys Ostby.)

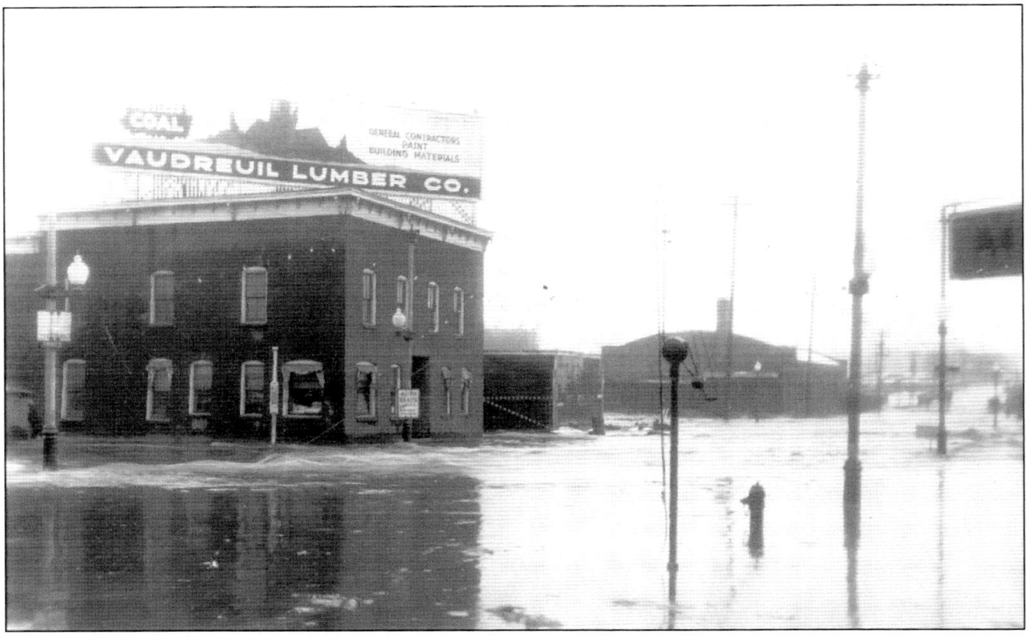

The entire Vaudreuil Lumberyard was under water and parts of the warehouse and much of its valuable lumber were washed away in the 1934 flood. After the water subsided, some of the lumber was salvaged from along the banks of the Chippewa River, but the damaged sheds were demolished. (Courtesy of Kris and Dave Martineau.)

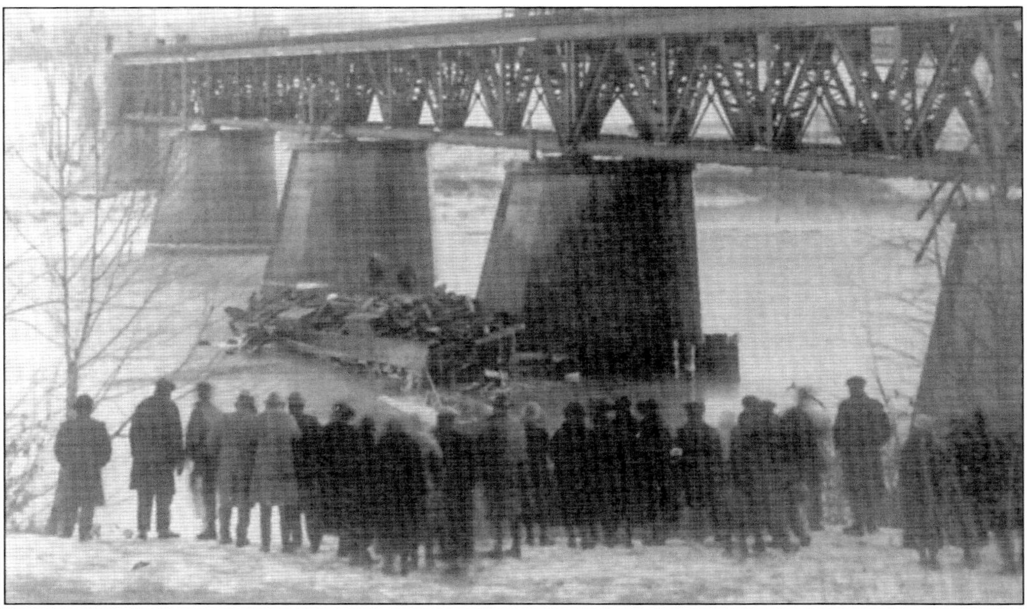

The most serious railroad accident in the Chippewa Falls area occurred on December 20, 1924, when a dining car of the eastbound Soo Line passenger train No. 2 went over the side of the Soo Line bridge in Chippewa Falls and plunged into the river, killing eight people. Seven others survived by crawling out the windows (Courtesy of CCHS.)

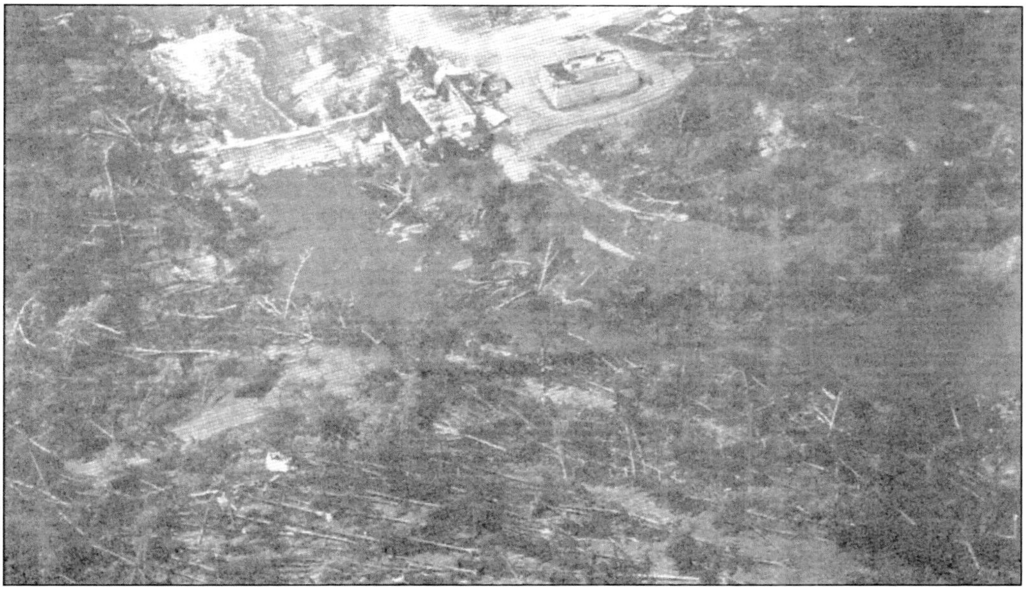

On June 4, 1958, an incredibly destructive tornado pummeled northwestern Wisconsin and struck parts of Chippewa Falls. Irvine Park was described as a tangled mass. Thousands of trees, mostly white pines, were uprooted, and elk and buffalo escaped their enclosures. Park Superintendent Charles Ermatinger retired shortly after the tornado and Ralph Wolfe began the difficult job of rebuilding Irvine Park. (Courtesy of CCHS)

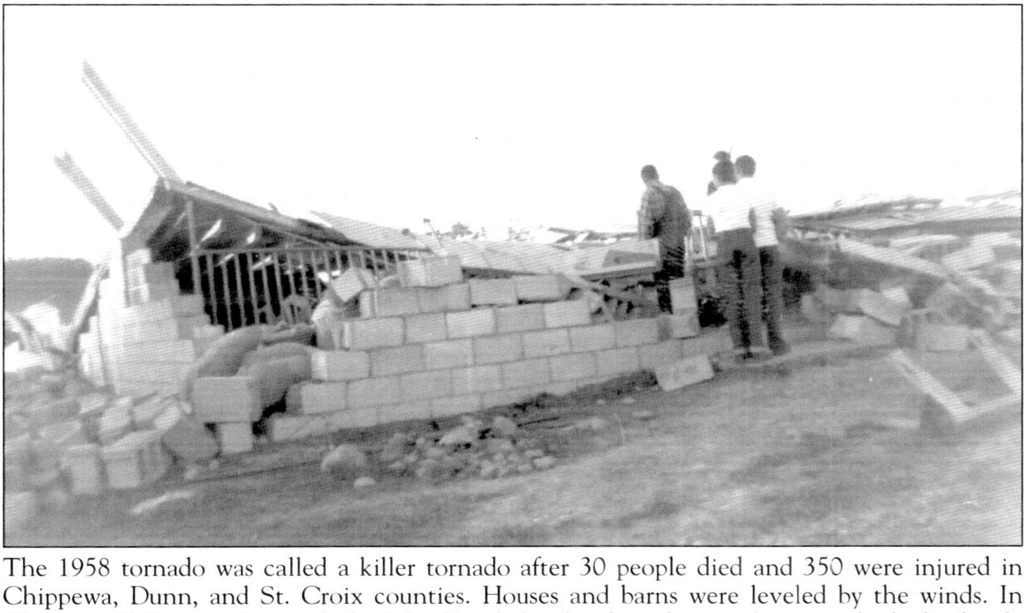

The 1958 tornado was called a killer tornado after 30 people died and 350 were injured in Chippewa, Dunn, and St. Croix counties. Houses and barns were leveled by the winds. In Chippewa Falls, tragedy struck the John Butak family when the new barn in which the family had taken refuge collapsed. This scattered mess of metal and new lumber marked the scene where Lillian Butak, her son John Jr., and daughter, Irene, became victims of the destructive tornado. (Courtesy of CCHS.)

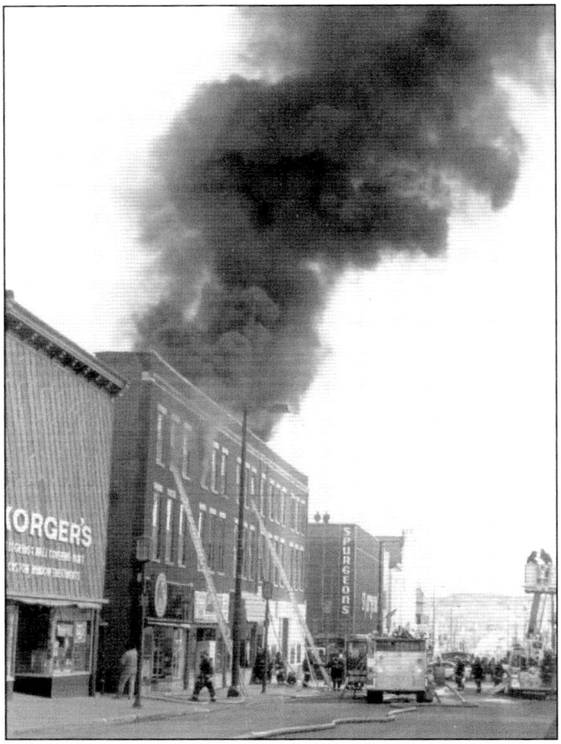

On March 14, 1991, the historic Cobban Block building on Bridge Street burned. Nearly 40 firefighters fought the blaze which roared through the upper two stories of the three story building. The heavy smoke and flames, visible for miles away, severely damaged the F&S TV and Appliance store, Treptow's Appliance, Ann's Decorating, and the Salvation Army, as well as the upper level apartments. (Courtesy of CFFD.)

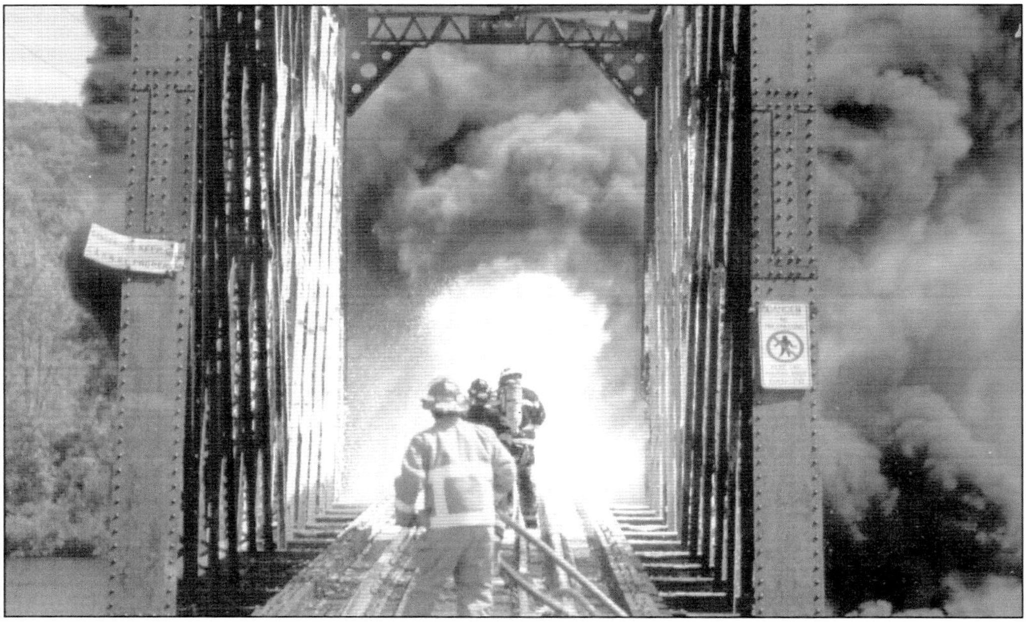

Despite the dangerous situation after an arsonist set fire to the Chicago and Northwestern Railroad Bridge in July 1993, firemen tried to get to the fire but had to retreat when the bridge began to collapse. In 2005, the Chippewa Falls Fire Department will be 135 years old. In all those years, the department has not lost a fireman in the line of duty. (Courtesy of CFFD.)

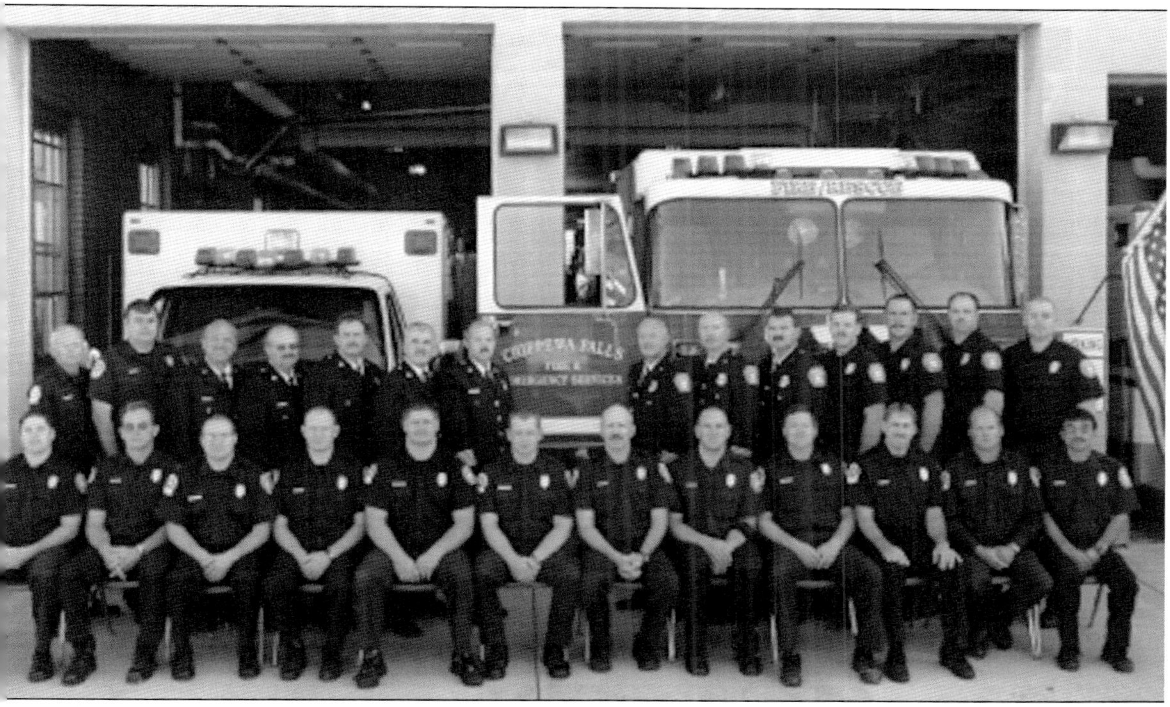

Established in 1870, the Chippewa Falls Fire Department will celebrate 135 years of service in 2005. Pictured are, from left to right: (seated) Kyle Schimmel, Darrel Vajgart, Dan Boos, Lee Douglas, Jim Speath, John Bowe, Bruce Krejci, Keith Ziehr, Steve Leahy, Bill Schulz, Joe Przybylski, and Merve Hanson; (standing) Tom Brick, Ian Turner, Randy Pederson, Tony Bowe, Mike Hepfler, Dan Meagher, Fire Chief Tom Larson, Randy Missfeldt, Jon Taylor, Joseph See, Chuck Geottl, Jason Thom, Dan Loschko, and Trevor Weiland. (Courtesy of CFFD.)

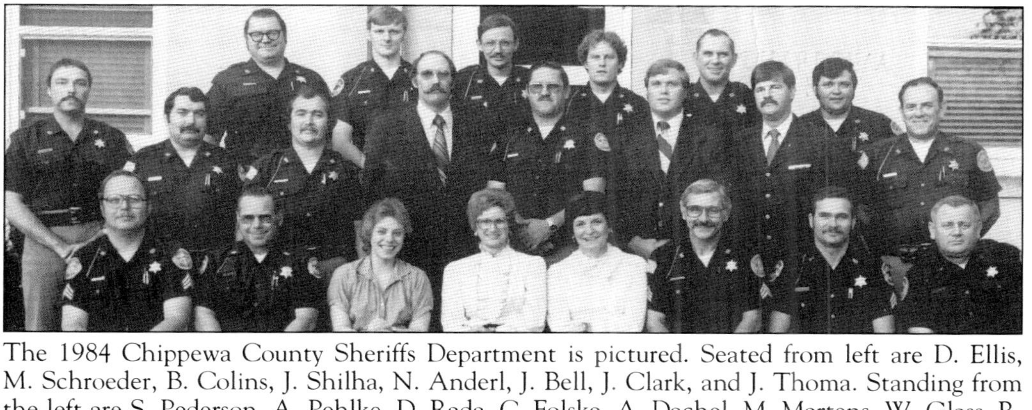

The 1984 Chippewa County Sheriffs Department is pictured. Seated from left are D. Ellis, M. Schroeder, B. Colins, J. Shilha, N. Anderl, J. Bell, J. Clark, and J. Thoma. Standing from the left are S. Pederson, A. Pehlke, D. Rada, C. Folska, A. Dachel, M. Martens, W. Glass, R. Sorensen, F. Froberf, K. Oemig, W. Kelly, J. Kowalczyk, M. Gerrits, and R. Wanish.

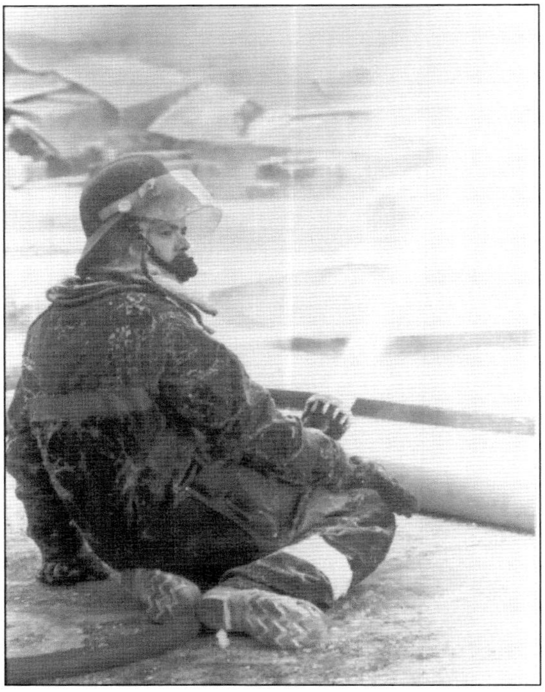

While a student at University of Wisconsin-Eau Claire in 1974, Tom Larson became a reserve fireman with the Chippewa Falls Fire Department and discovered his true calling. After attending the Chippewa Valley Technical College's new Fire Science program, Tom was hired full-time in 1980. Promoted to Lieutenant in 1990, he became Fire Chief in 2002. (Courtesy of CFFD.)

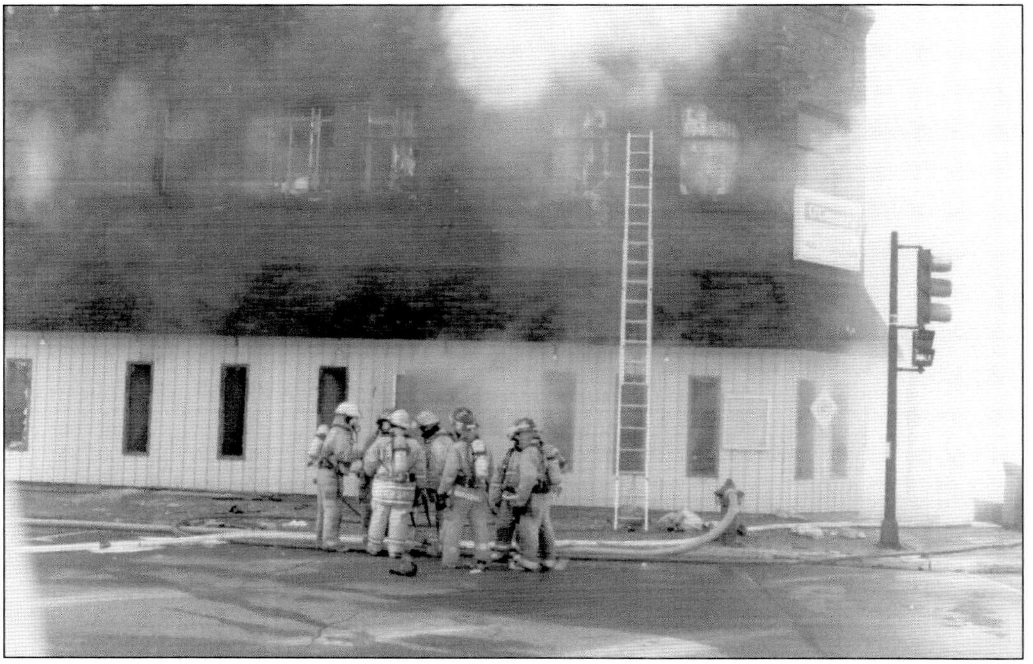

A city ordinance was passed in 1885 prohibiting the construction of wooden buildings. However, even an ordinance could not completely prevent fires in downtown Chippewa Falls. On May 7, 2002, on the Empire Block, the firefighters battled a blaze at O'Connor's Sports Bar at 3 E. Spring Street. (Courtesy of CFFD.)

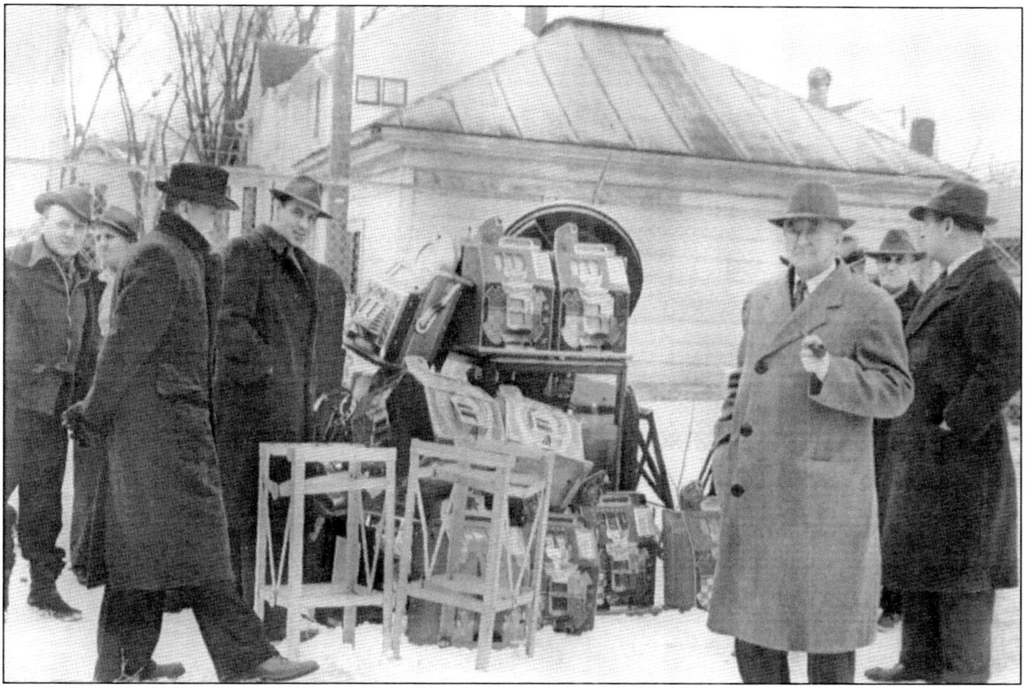

In April of 1906, District Attorney Dayton Cook ordered city saloons to remove slot machines and the "saloonkeepers were not at all pleased over it." As Judge Dayton Cook, he again confronted the slot machine controversy. Judge Cook, in the light coat with his pipe, is pictured with Sheriff Conrad Thronson behind him after a slot machine raid designed to rid the city of "these illegal devices." (Courtesy of Chippewa County Sheriffs Dept.)

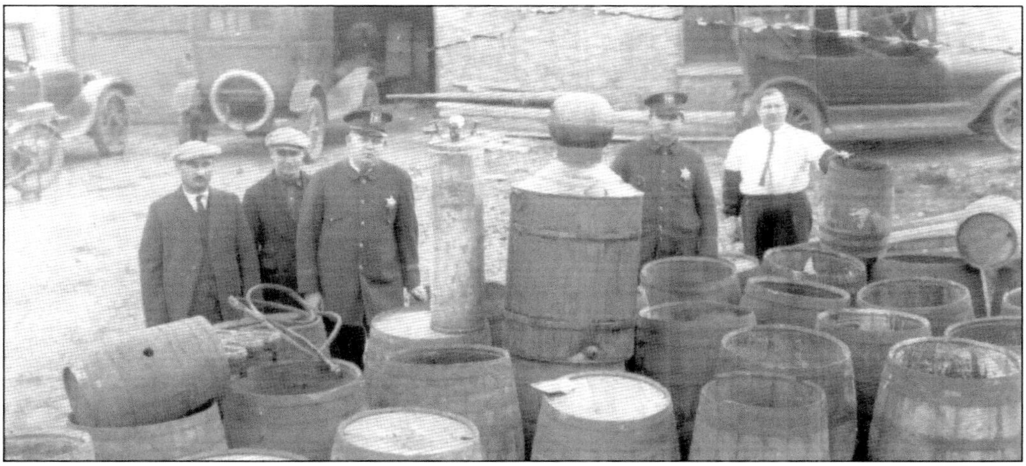

Temperance leaders equated winning the Great War with national sobriety. By December of 1917, Congress had enough votes to pass a Prohibition amendment that was ratified in 1919. Speakeasies and illegal distilleries flourished. In December of 1931, at the height of Prohibition when a half-barrel of beer sold locally and unlawfully for $12 to $14, Federal Prohibition Officer John McCullum and his agents destroyed 429 barrels of "wort beer" in Chippewa County. (Courtesy of CCHS.)

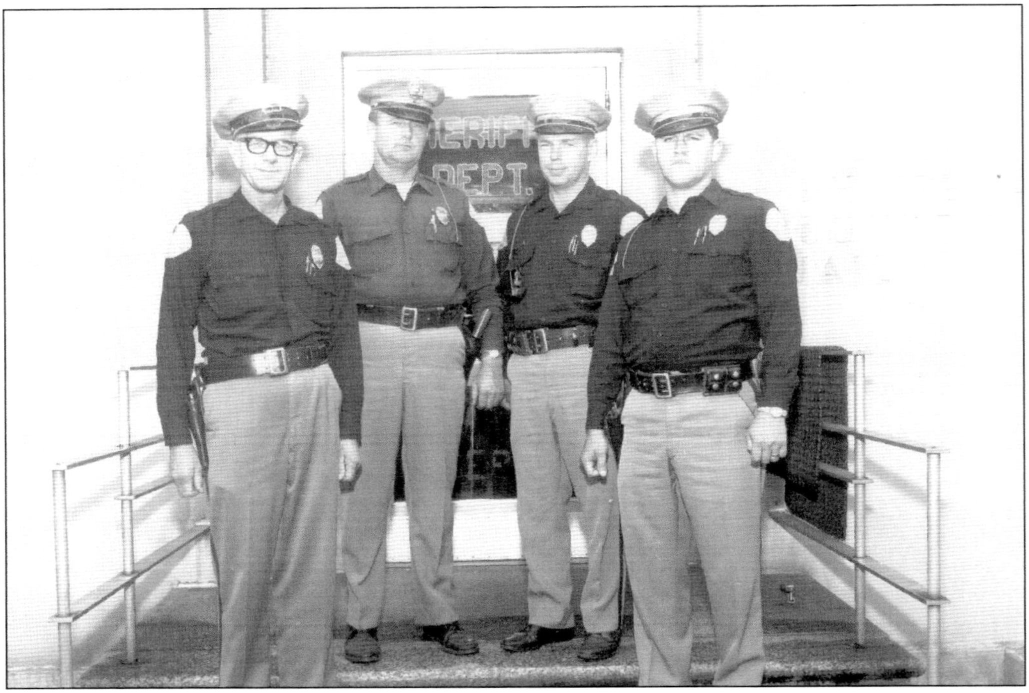

At its inception in 1968, the Traffic Department was part of the County Highway Department and each patrolman was responsible for providing his own squad car. In 1980, the Chippewa County Traffic Department became part of the County Sheriffs Department. Pictured (from left to right) are Chief Max Brookshaw, Patrolmen James Revoir, Marvin Schroeder, and Alfred Dachel. (Courtesy of Marvin Schroeder.)

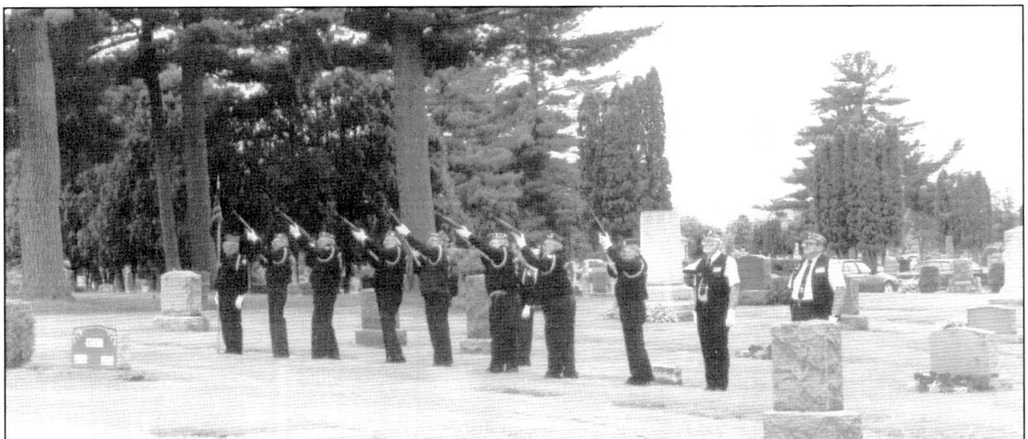

On March 15, 1919, delegates from 1,000 units of the American Expeditionary Force met in Paris to form an organization of veterans called the American Legion. Its purpose was to help with rehabilitation, to promote national security and Americanism, and to help with child welfare. In 1958, the Chippewa Falls Patriotic Council, comprised of the American Legion and the Veterans of Foreign Wars, was organized to honor those who have served their country, which it does each time members appear at a veteran's funeral. (Courtesy of Clarence Fagner.)

Six

WOMEN OF THE FALLS

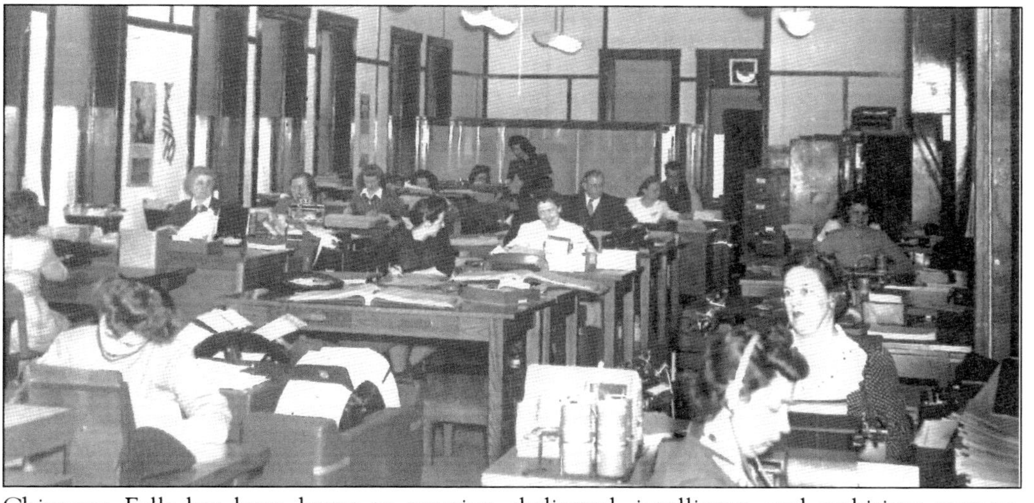

Chippewa Falls has been home to creative, dedicated, intelligent, and ambitious women. Historically, women's responsibilities ranged from nurturing and educating their children to working alongside their husbands on farms, to working outside the home in order to supplement the family income. Women expected to work hard and they were respected for it.

Angeline Demarais, for many years known as the area's first physician, used herbal remedies to heal the illnesses and broken bones of the lumbermen. Miss Mandane Buzell, the first teacher, taught from 1854 until 1856 when she married James Taylor, superintendent of schools. In 1907, Mrs. Ellen Richards, one of America's first women chemists, suggested that "women have done nearly everything, and the skies have not fallen." Phone companies had offered women one of the few jobs for which they were "suited" in 1907, the position of telephone operator.

During World War I, 1.4 million women replaced men at their jobs, doing everything from assembly-line work to steeple jacking.

Women had almost always worked at Mason Shoe, in the office and doing the detail sewing and finer work. The reputation of the craftsmanship of Mason shoemakers spread and soon Mason Shoes were being sold all over the country. Women telephone operators, pictured above, took orders from the salesmen for shoes and boots in the precise size and width desired by their customers. (Courtesy of CFMIT.)

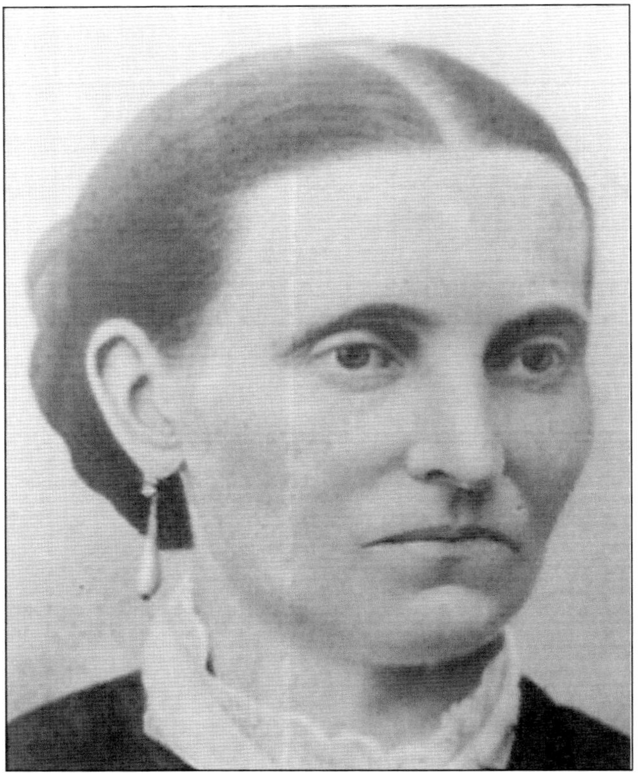

Josephine Imhoff married Jacob Leinenkugel in 1865 in Sauk City, Wisconsin. When Jacob decided to establish his own brewery, she moved with him and their young son, Mathias, to Chippewa Falls. She worked beside him as they struggled to build up their brewery. She prepared three meals a day for brewery workers, while caring for the four Leinenkugel children. Josephine died at the relatively early age of 44. (Courtesy of JLBC.)

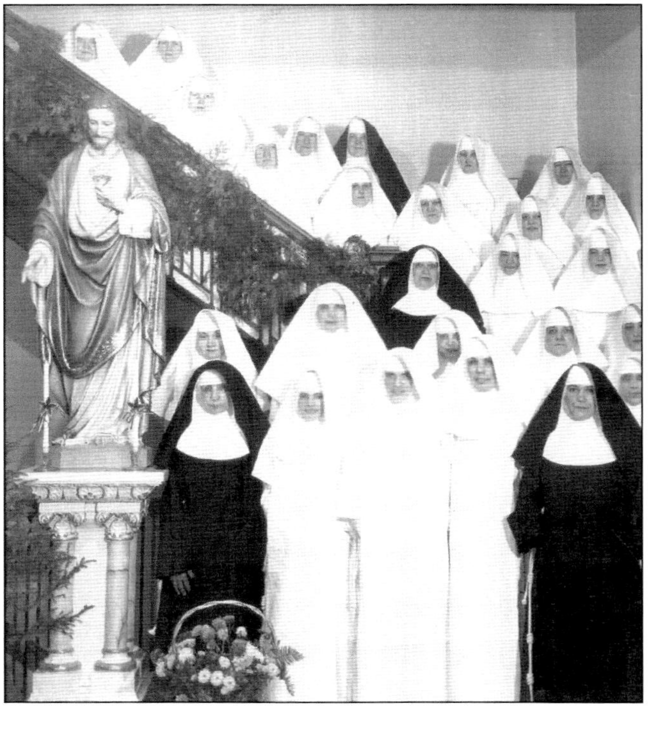

In 1885, Father Goldsmith—concerned about the illnesses and injuries in the lumbering camps—summoned the Hospital Sisters of the third Order of St. Francis, led by Sister Rosa Walzer, to Chippewa Falls. The sisters did not charge for their services and would often care for patients in their homes, doing the cooking and laundry, in addition to nursing duties. In 1888, Edward Rutledge sold property on Pearl Street to the Sisters on which a three-story hospital was built. (Courtesy of St. Joseph Hospital.)

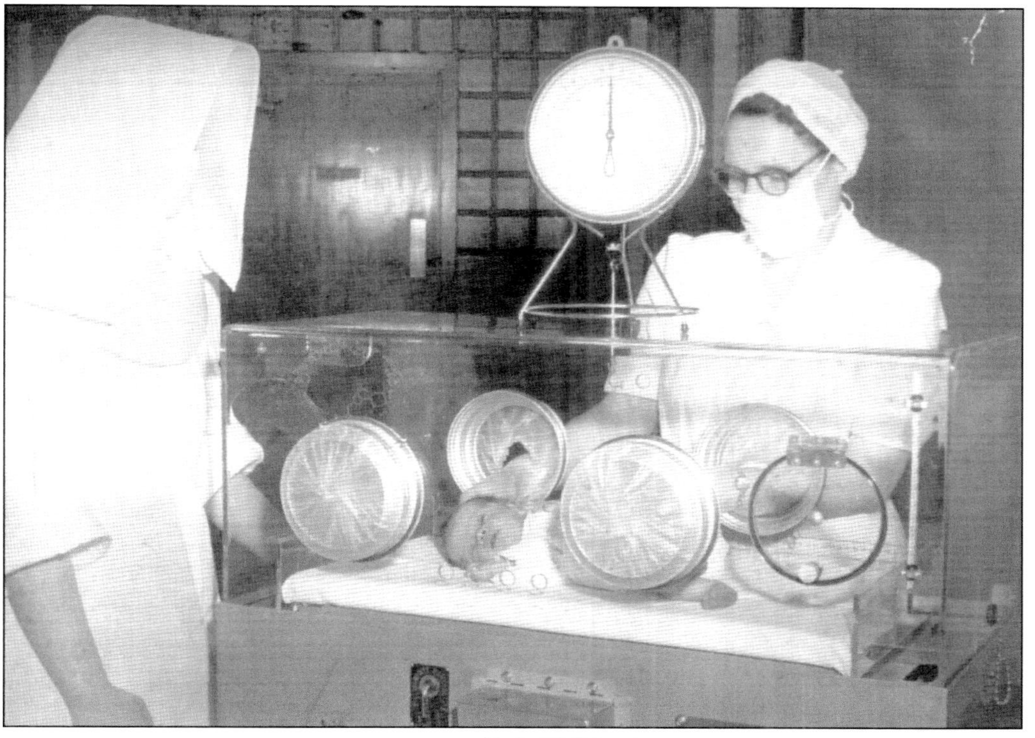

The Hospital Sisters carried their patients up the stairs until 1902 when an Eaton-Prince elevator was installed for $1,725. Women who came to the hospital to have babies were cared for by a private nurse in a private room until a maternity ward was opened in 1915. (Courtesy of St. Joseph Hospital.)

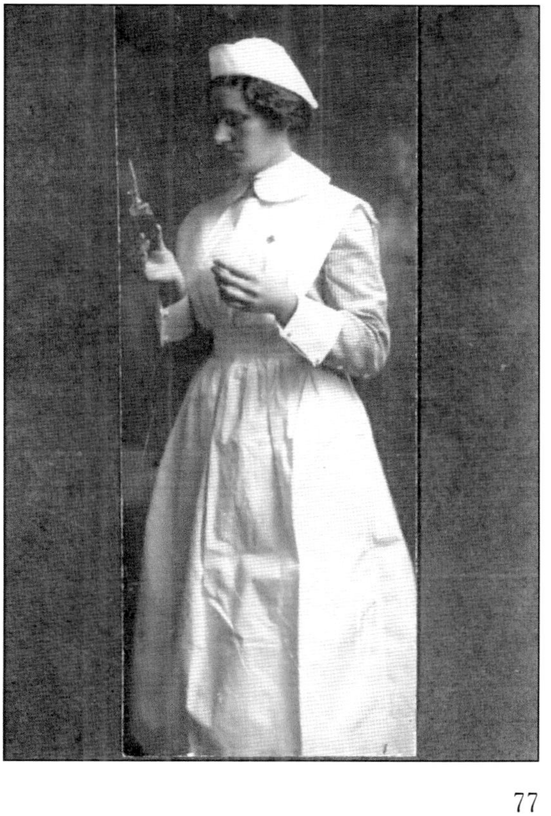

The Maternity Department at St. Joseph's Hospital became a reality in 1915 when the Hospital Sisters arranged for Caroline Meinen's nursing education through a correspondence course. After completing her nursing education, Carrie Meinen, who attended daily Mass in Tilden, took over full-time supervision of the new maternity ward at St. Joseph's Hospital. (Courtesy of St. Joseph Hospital.)

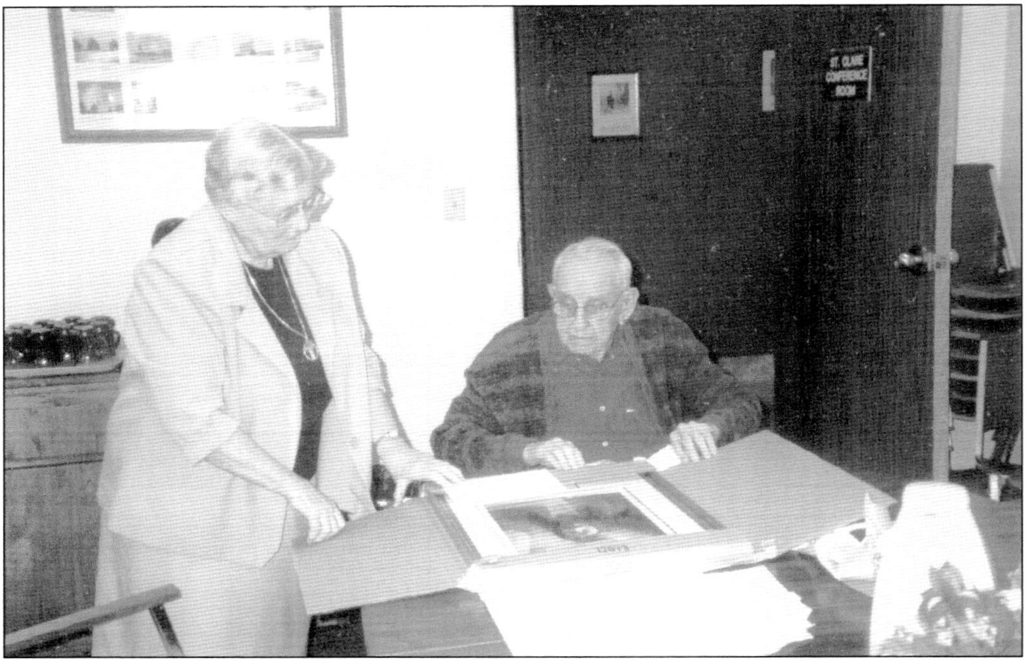

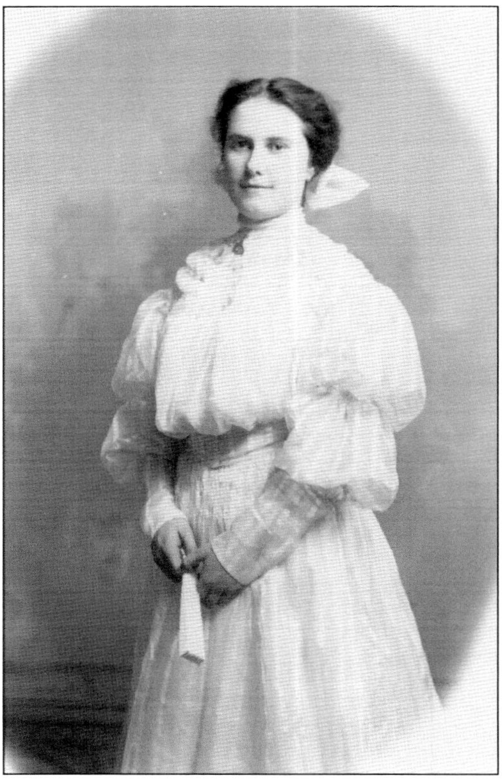

The three-story hospital built in 1888 served the community for 90 years before the Hospital Sisters turned to the community for help in constructing a new facility. Sister Francis Elizabeth Schmitz, the hospital administrator from 1969 to 1982, began the process of securing funds for the project. In 1975, the $10 million hospital on County I was completed. Dr. John Sazama, who practiced in Chippewa Falls for 40 years before retiring in 1983, and Sister Francis Elizabeth Schmitz continued the Hospital Sisters' tradition of compassionate care in the new hospital. (Courtesy of Sister Francis.)

Juliana Coleman was born in 1887 in Chippewa Falls and attended Notre Dame grade school and high school. After graduating in 1905, she entered the Congregation of the School Sisters of Notre Dame, pronouncing her vows as Sister Mary Hilaria in 1908. A teacher, principal, and religious superior, in 1956 she was elected Commissary General and placed at the head of all the Notre Dame nuns in the United States, Puerto Rico, Japan, Guam, and Honduras. (Courtesy of Dolores Beaudette.)

The church and related activities were central to the upbringing of children in the fledgling community of Chippewa Falls. Catherine and Elizabeth O'Neil were the daughters of Eugene O'Neil, a former mayor, one of the organizers of the Lumberman's Bank, and an associate of the Chippewa Lumber and Boom Company. For Catherine O'Neil's first communion, her sister Elizabeth, on the left, was her candle bearer. (Courtesy of Dolores Beaudette.)

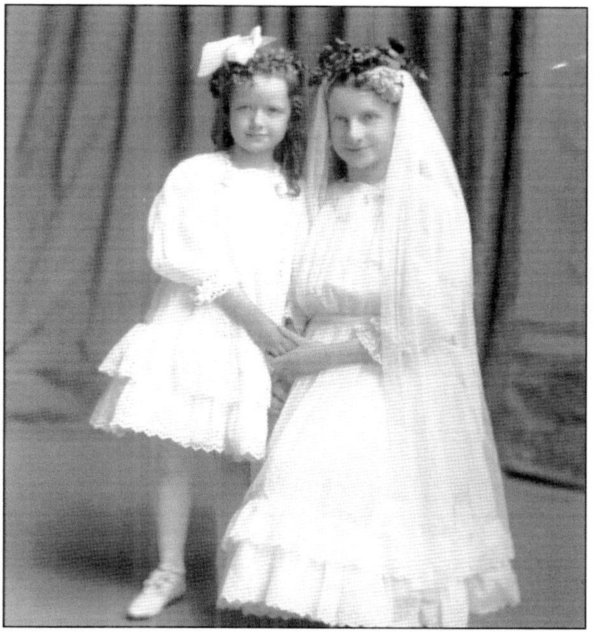

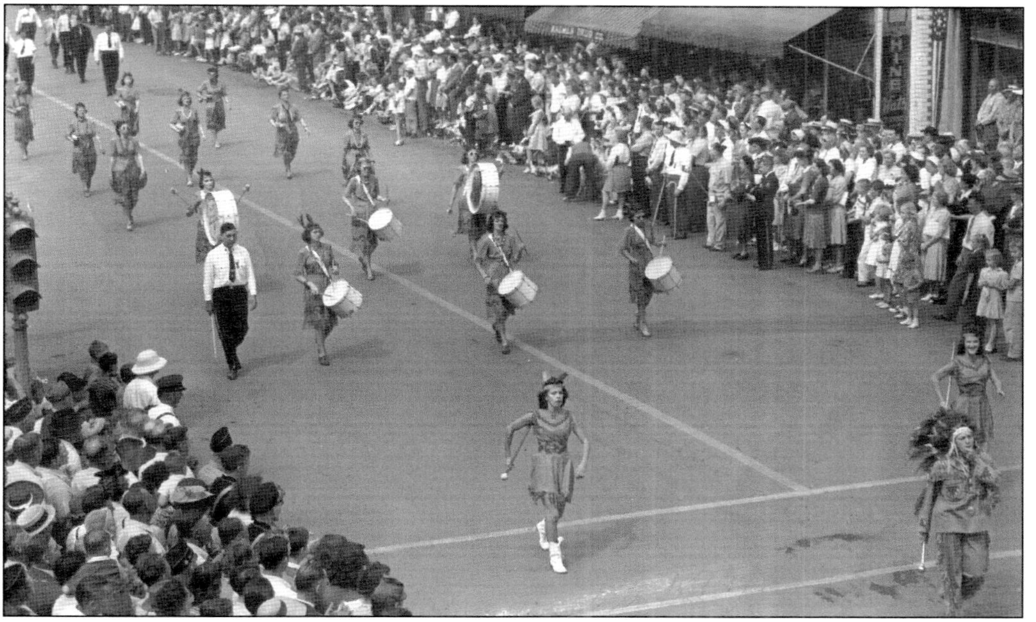

American Legion Auxiliary Drum & Bugle Corp members all had a close family member in the military. Shown marching in this photo are the following: (in front) Drum Major Margaret Hanson, Majorette Sue Felber Cherrier, and Majorette Sis Greenwood McCarthy; (first row) Otto Berg, commander, Mary Ann Murphy Durand, Delores Myre Globensky, and ? Mauer; (second row) Rose Greenwood, Evelyn Gardner, and Pat Carlson Birch; (third row) Mary Holland and Beverly Roberg; (fourth row) Marie Davis, Winnie Bowe, and Alice Eystad; (fifth row) Rita Peterson, Kathleen LeaVesseur, and Margaret Rasmus, followed by the American Legion members of Post 77, World War I Veterans. (Courtesy of Paul Rasmus.)

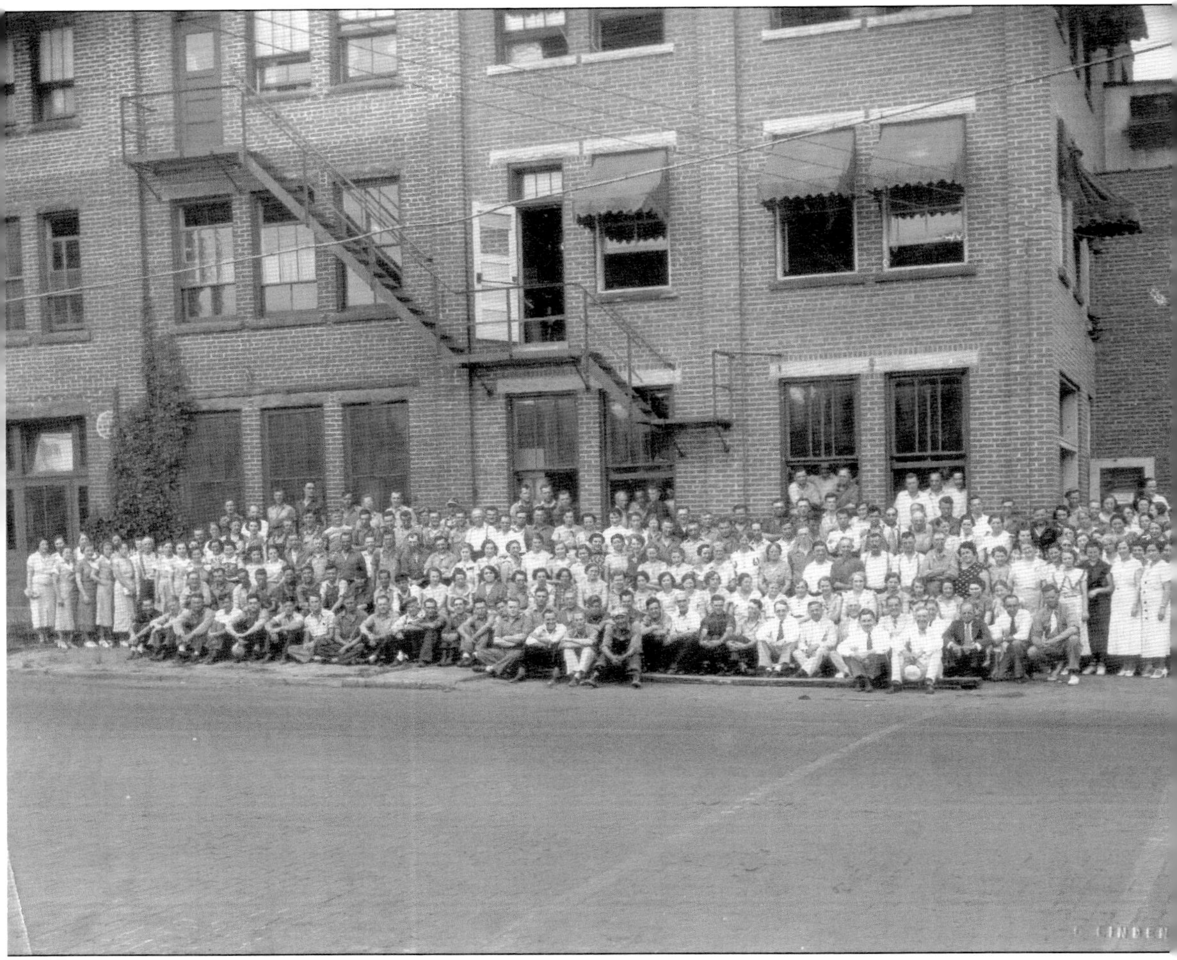

The beginnings of the city's manufacturing sector produced goods for the growing lumbering industry. In the Chippewa Woolen Mill, pictured above, begun by Charles Mandelert and operated for 60 years by members of the Mandelert family, women had a substantial presence making the "All Wool" woolens. When the mill closed in 1962, many longtime friends who had worked side by side for 30 or 40 years were separated. However, Chippewa Woolen Mill workers held reunions for over 30 years, with their last party at Connell's Supper Club in 1986. (Courtesy of CCHS.)

In 1916, Gertrude Ederle swam the English Channel. In 1932, Amelia Earhart flew solo across the Atlantic. In 1937, Kathryn Johnson was the first city woman to make a solo airplane flight over Chippewa Falls, thereby earning her private pilot's license. Sitting on a 1935 Harley-Davidson motorcycle in front of Lueck's Cycle Shop at 7 E. Spring Street, Dot Erdman waited for members of the motorcycle club who gathered on Sundays for rides, picnics, and fishing at their clubhouse on Lake Wissota. (Courtesy of the Carl Lueck Family.)

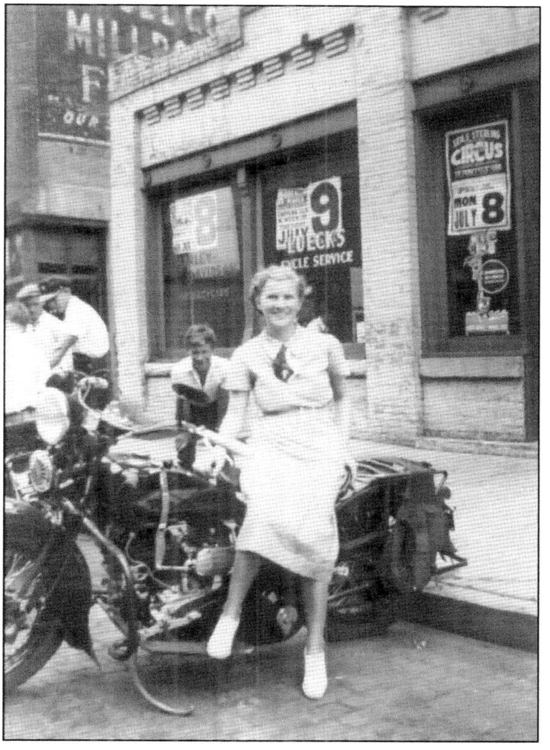

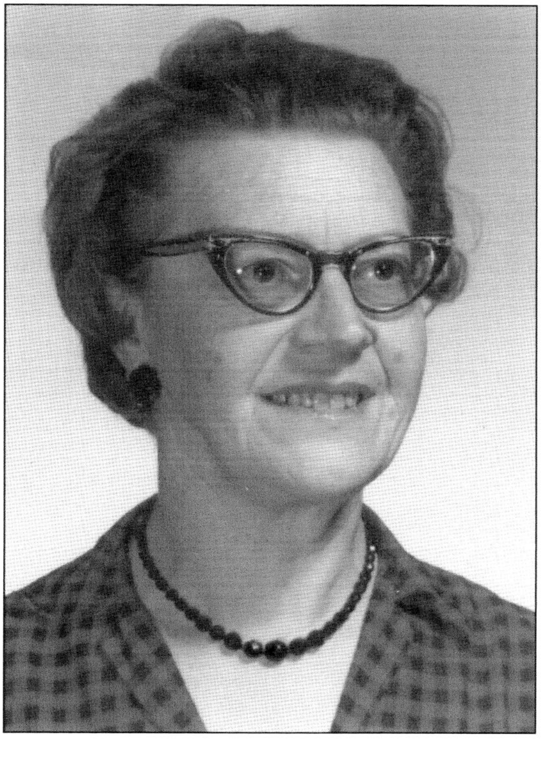

Women have played an important role in education, whether nurturing their children in the home or teaching in a classroom. Elementary children were always Gertrude Korger's forte and for 50 years she challenged their minds as their teacher and principal. Describing her life as "very fulfilling," when she retired in 1978, over 400 people attended a reception in her honor at Korger-Chestnut School, renamed to honor this dedicated teacher. (Courtesy of Gertrude Korger.)

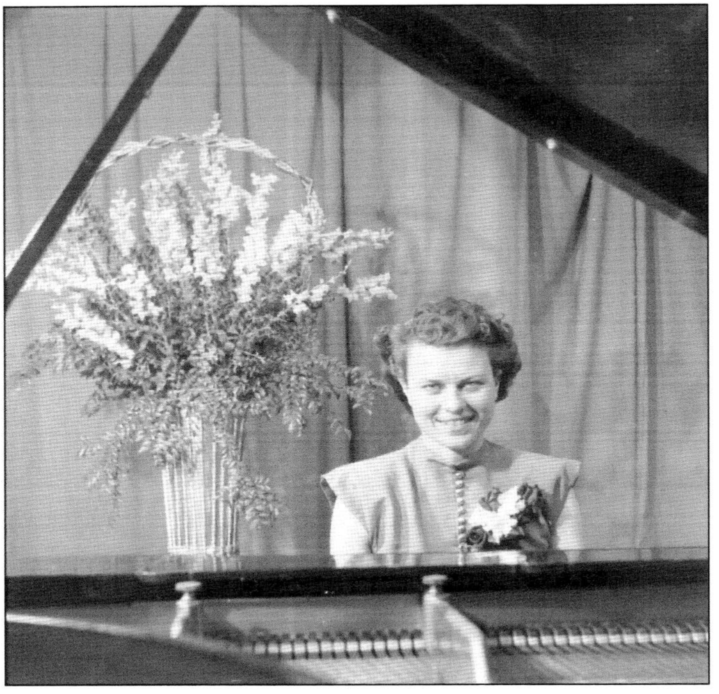

Devoting 31 years to teaching music should have been enough of a career for Dolores Beaudette, but upon her retirement in 1980, she began the business, Research Service. Her lifelong interest in history has produced numerous works, including a series of interviews with older citizens, a collection of photographs by Bish, and well-researched books on the boot and shoe industry and the springs of Chippewa Falls. (Courtesy of Dolores Beaudette.)

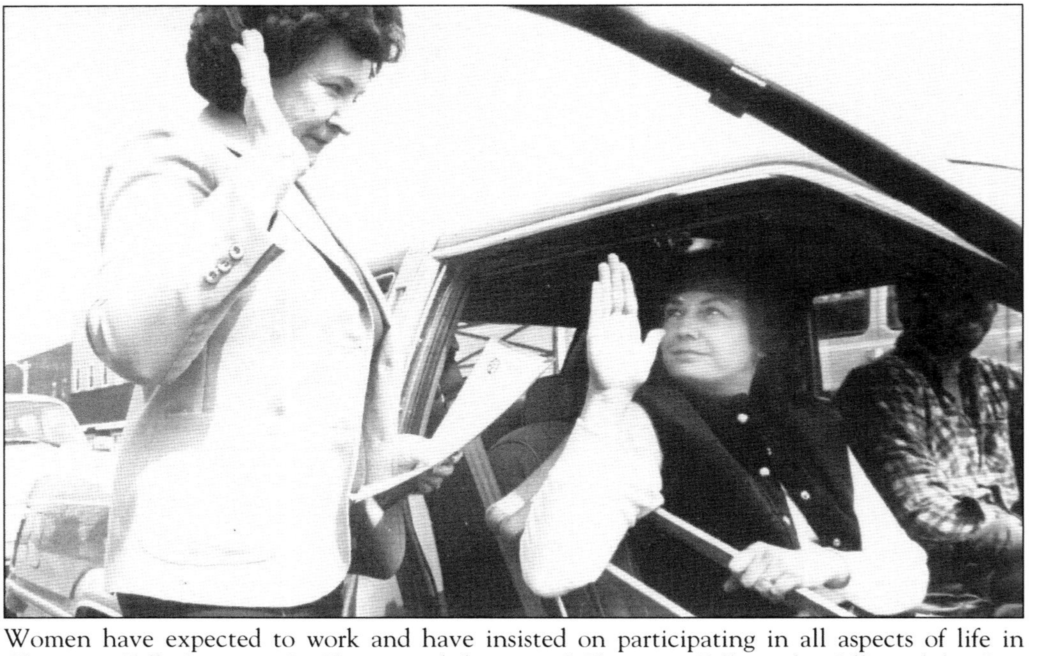

Women have expected to work and have insisted on participating in all aspects of life in Chippewa Falls. Lucyann LeCleir served the city of Chippewa Falls in the Office of the City Clerk from April of 1960 until her retirement in July of 1996. When newly elected 3rd Ward Alderman Judith Loiselle injured her leg and was unable to climb the stairs to the second floor Council Room to be sworn into office, City Clerk Lucyann LeCleir administered the oath of office to Ms. Loiselle in her car. (Courtesy of the *Chippewa Herald*.)

The Register of Deeds office records all legal documents for Chippewa County. In June of 1967, Register of Deeds Agnes Peloquin hired Beatrice Roycraft to be Deputy Register of Deeds. When Agnes Peloquin retired in 1977, Bea Roycraft was appointed by Governor Schreiber to complete her term. For eight terms thereafter, until her retirement in 1995, Beatrice Roycraft served Chippewa County with grace and competence. (Courtesy of Bea Roycraft.)

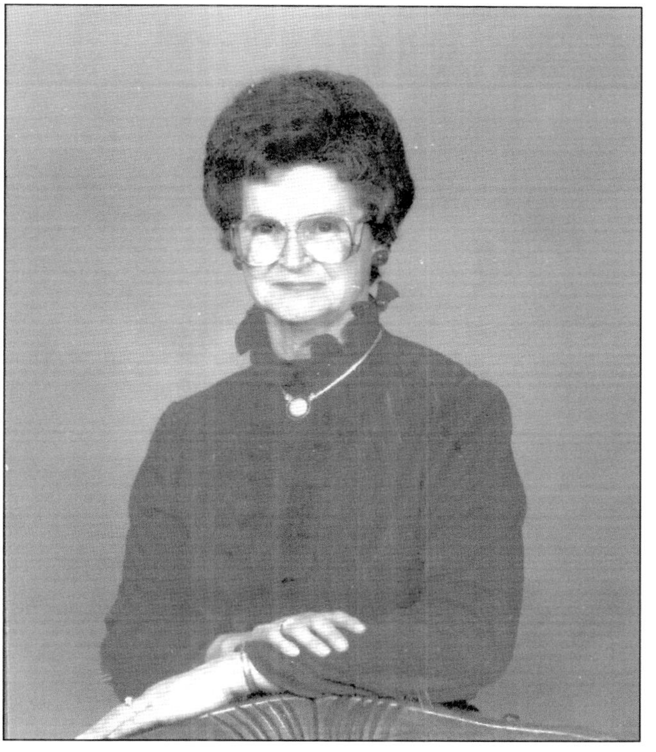

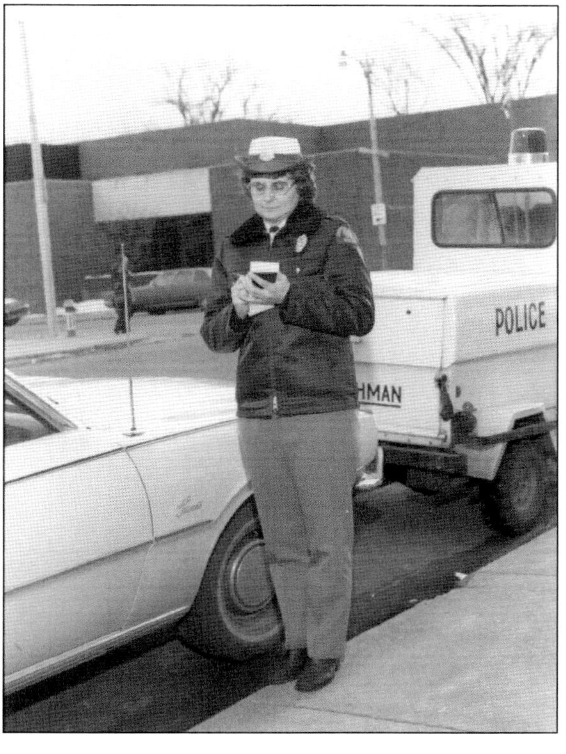

For years, downtown parking has allowed individuals convenient access to stores and businesses. Historically, the City Council created parking lots, set parking fees, and eventually hired meter maids to enforce the parking limits. Darlene Culbert was hired in 1969 as the city's meter maid and for 24 years she patrolled the streets of Chippewa Falls, leaving reminders on the windshields of cars. On March 18, 1981, Mayor Howard Olson declared it the "end of an era" when the city council voted to remove the remaining parking meters in the city. Darlene Culbert retired in 1993. (Courtesy of Darlene Culbert.)

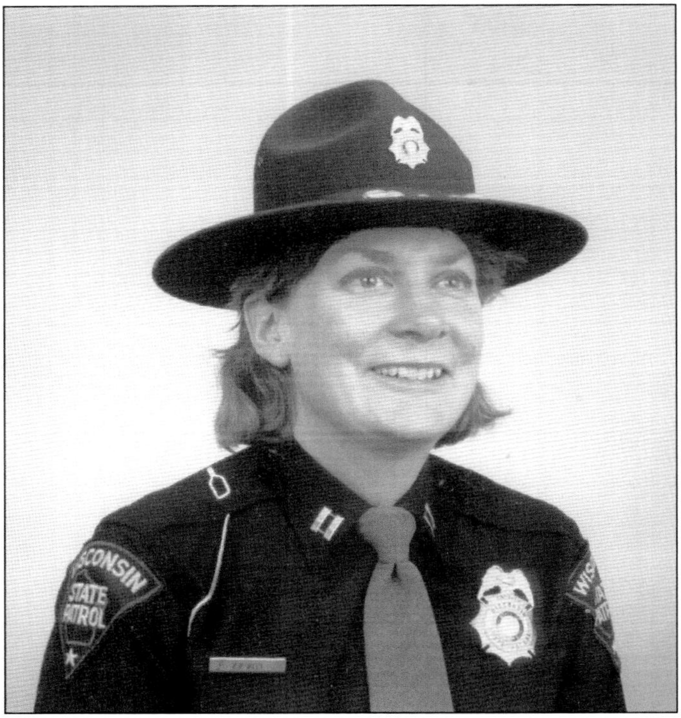

For five years, Marsha Wiley taught foreign languages in Colorado and Wisconsin. However, when the Wisconsin State Patrol opened its recruit classes to women, Wiley enrolled, completed training, and was assigned as a motor carrier inspector, before becoming the second female trooper in the history of Wisconsin. Eventually, she became the first female to attain the rank of Captain. She was the first female District Commander in Madison and finished her 30-year career in the State Patrol as District Commander in Eau Claire, Wisconsin. (Courtesy of Marsha Wiley.)

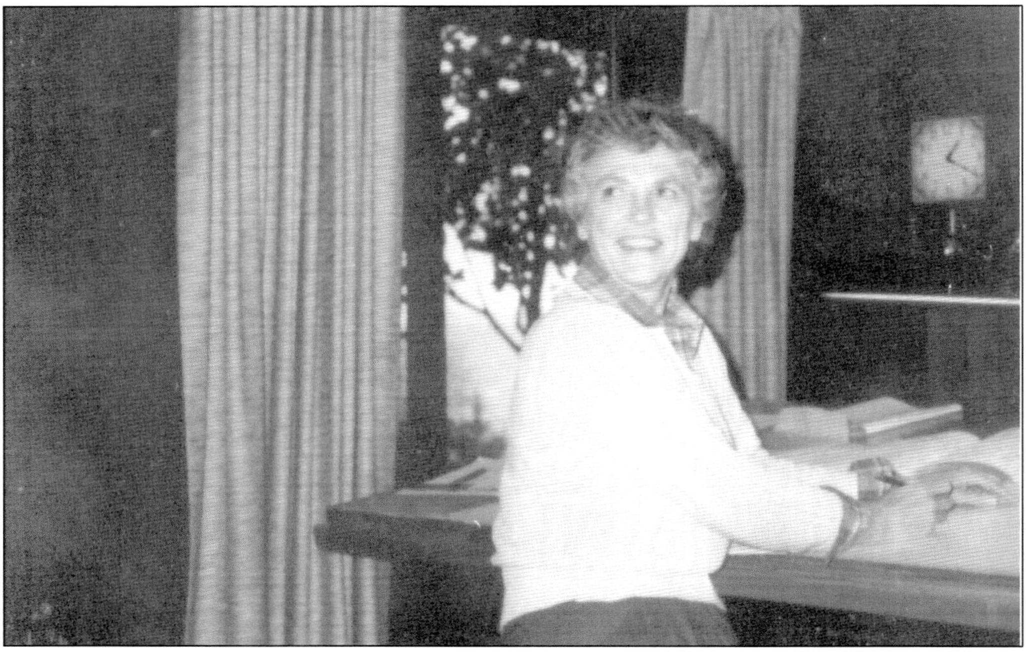

A kitchen table and a sense of adventure were key ingredients in Yvonne Brunstad's experience of working at home on the "artwork" for the Cray 2. Following original instructions, she created hand-drawn diagrams, one of the steps in designing circuit boards for the Cray 2 supercomputer. (Courtesy of CFMIT.)

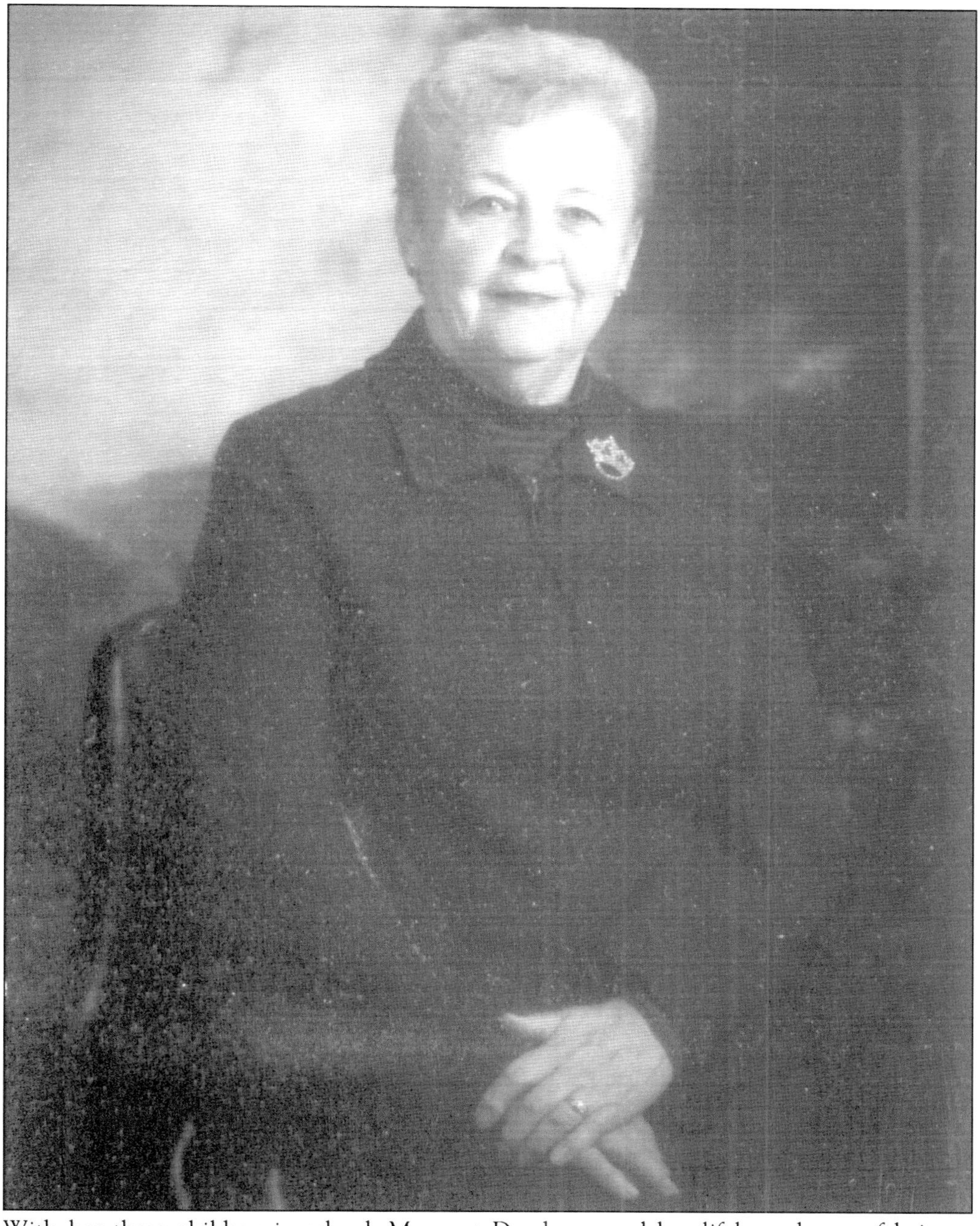

With her three children in school, Margaret Durch pursued her lifelong dream of being a teacher, earning a degree in elementary education and teaching from 1967 until 1976. During that same period of time, Margaret managed Chiptronics, a company formed in 1974 by her husband, Pat Durch. The employees, who numbered 250 at its zenith, received component parts from Control Data, assembled them in their facilities, a task called "stringing donuts," and sold them to both Cray Research and Control Data. As vice president of Tschopp Durch Camastral, Margaret Durch also managed Timber Terrace Golf Course until her retirement in 1993. (Courtesy of Margaret Durch.)

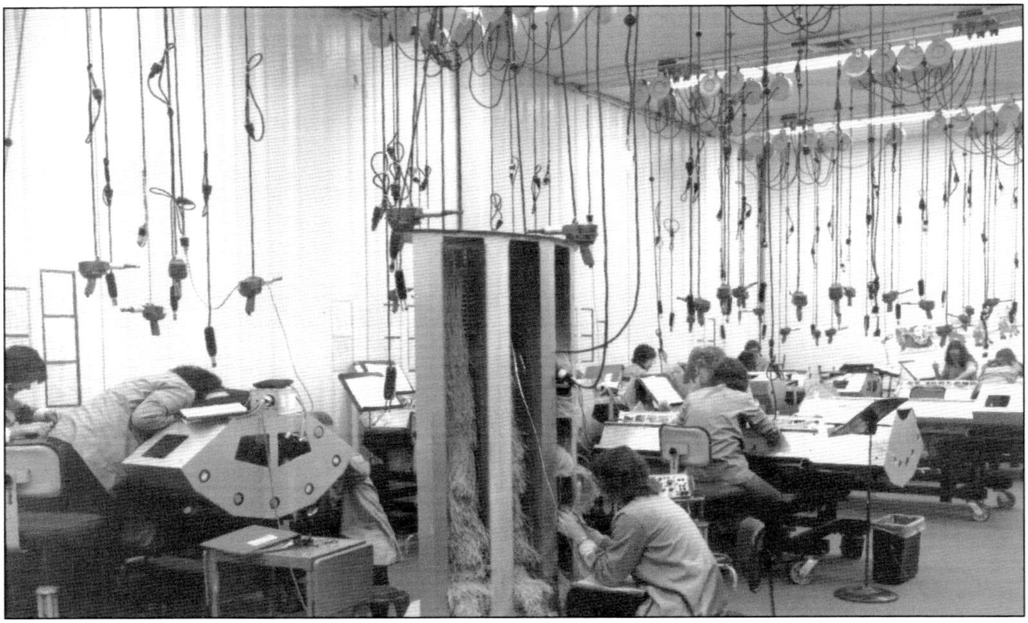

Just as women assembled piece work in their homes, sewed garments for Chippewa Woolens, and did the detail work for Mason Shoe, women became a key part of the new technology world. The Cray X-MP had 60 miles of wire and took about five months to build and another four months to test before the $11.4 million machine could be shipped to a Cray customer. (Courtesy of CFMIT.)

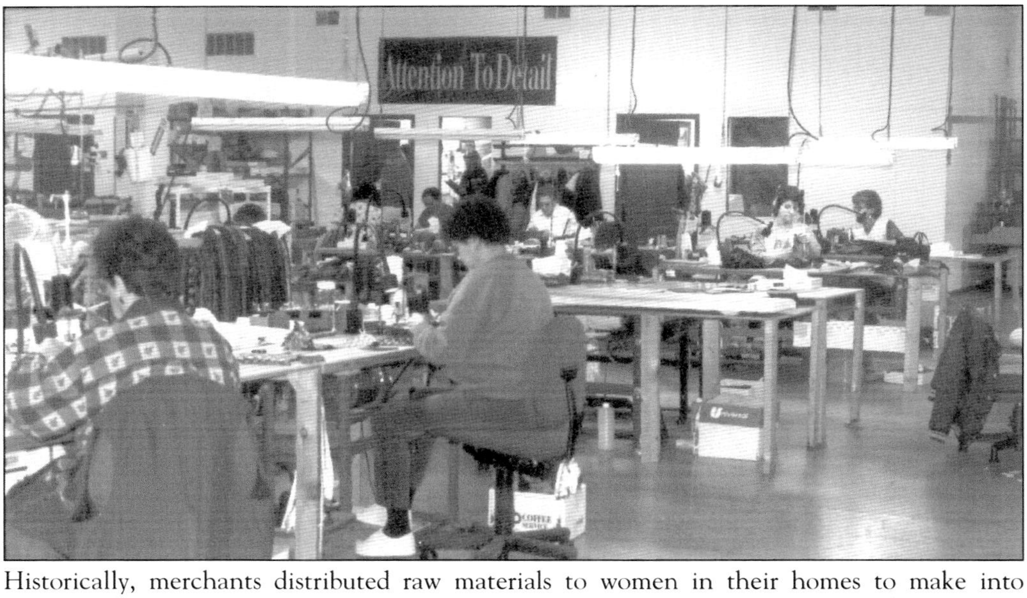

Historically, merchants distributed raw materials to women in their homes to make into ready made "put out work." When John and Alison Sazama began XMI, which stands for "extraordinary marketing idea," Alison taught the women to sew the 100% silk, handmade ties in her home. Calling the people who work at XMI their greatest asset, and stressing quality, XMI likes to think of itself as the Rolls Royce of the apparel industry. (Courtesy of CFMIT.)

Housed in the former Notre Dame Convent, which was the home of the teaching sisters of Norte Dame, the Chippewa County Historical Society and Genealogy Society work to preserve the invaluable history of Chippewa Falls. Winifred Glass Jensen, one of many volunteer directors of the Center, is pictured with an antique pump organ donated by the Kehl family. (Courtesy of the *Chippewa Herald*.)

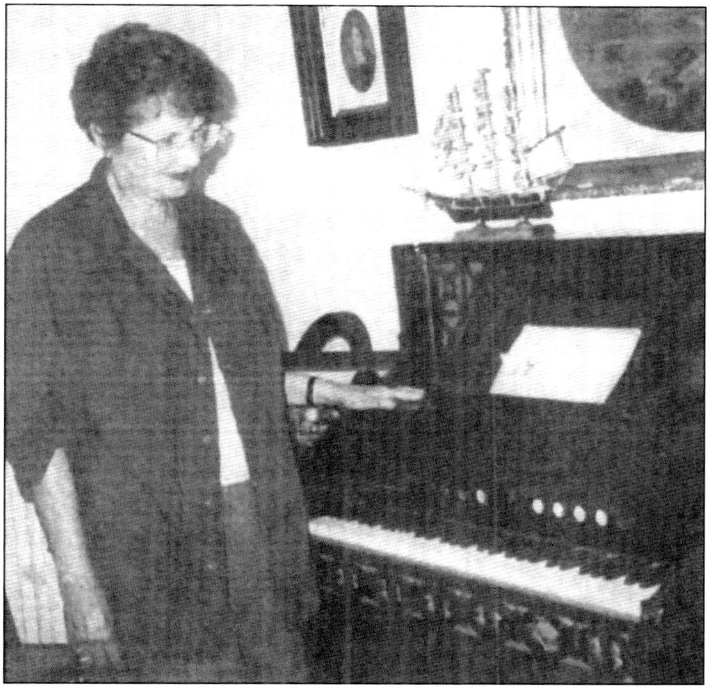

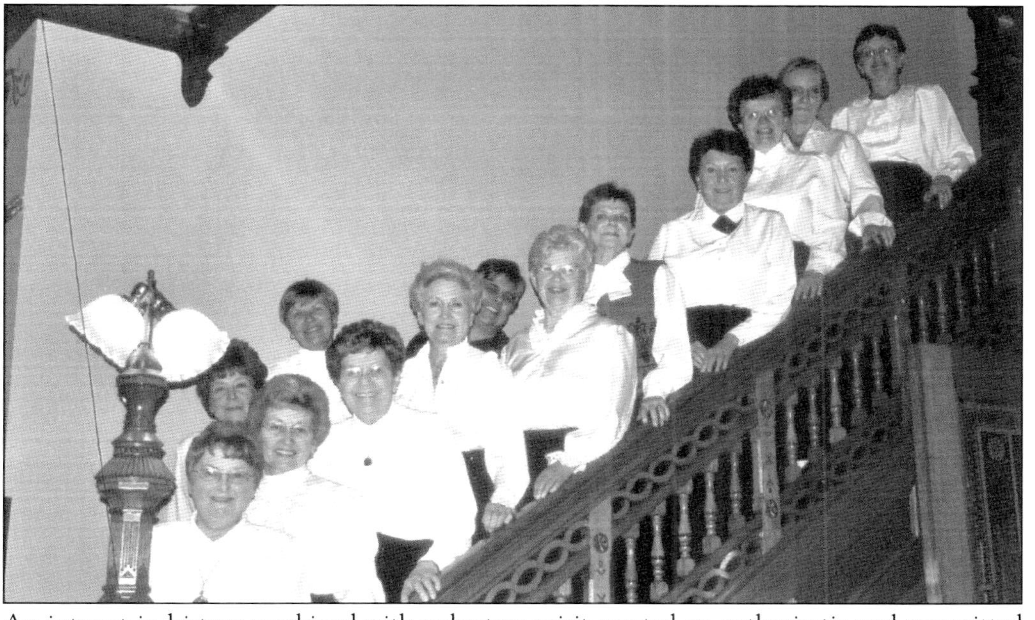

An interest in history combined with volunteer spirit created an enthusiastic and committed group of docents at the Cook Rutledge Mansion. Pictured here are, from left to right: (front row) Judy Vaudreuil, Ann Gordon, Verene Crane, Jinx Smith, Donna Kraemer, Barbara Meredith, Jean Eystad, Carol Peterson, D'Mitria Gray, and Jeanne Wright; (second row) Mona Zutter, Sara Abendroth, and Peggy Nehring. Not pictured are Melanie Berg, Edna Bunn, Lisa Farineau, Dorothy Fredrickson, Betty Girard, Ann Goodall, Joan LaRuek, Anne Sather, Calandra Szulgit, Leslie Szulgit, and Marsha Wiley. (Courtesy of the Cook Rutledge Mansion.)

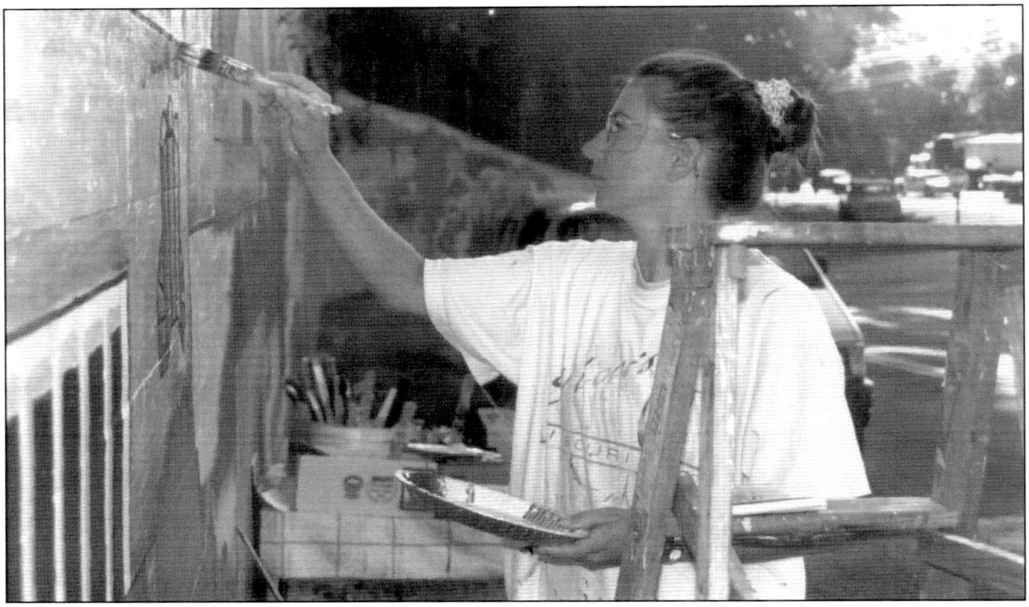

Painting the town took on a whole new meaning when the aging retaining wall along the Wagner Street Hill was redesigned by artist Jean Arneson in 1992. Jean, a self-employed freelance artist whose favorite media is oil, enjoys painting familiar scenes. On the Wagner Street wall, a collaborative effort between the schools, the public, and the Main Street organization, Jean painted her interpretation of Chippewa Falls' history. (Courtesy of the *Chippewa Herald.*)

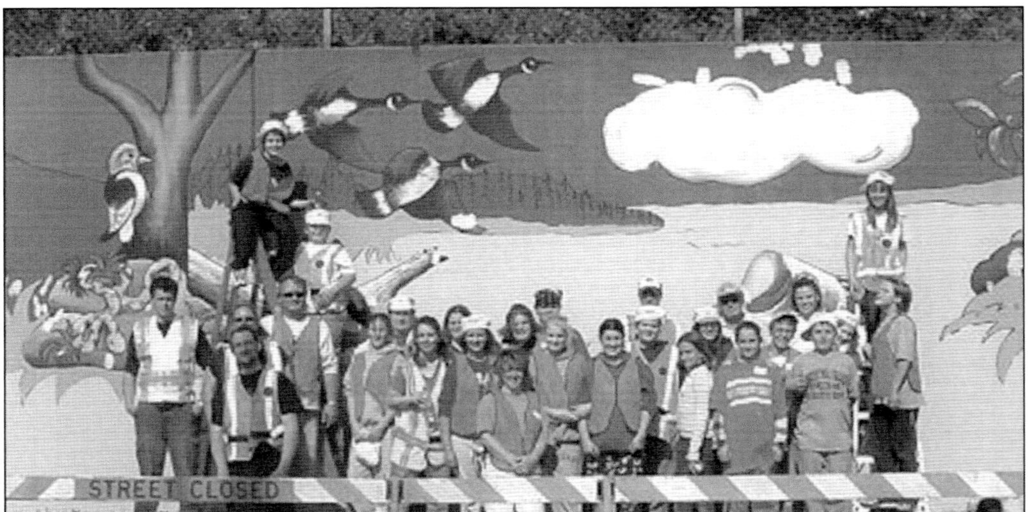

In October 2004, Main Street partnered with the Chippewa Falls Area Unified School District Voyager Community Learning Program, the Chippewa Area Mentor Program, and their Americorp members to restore the weather-damaged River Street wall mural. Sharon Cronin Fralik, the original artist on the project, returned and generously shared her talents for a second time. A grant from the American Girl Company, support from the City of Chippewa Falls, and numerous businesses contributed to this colorful and successful project. (Courtesy of CFMS.)

Seven

EVERY VOTE COUNTS

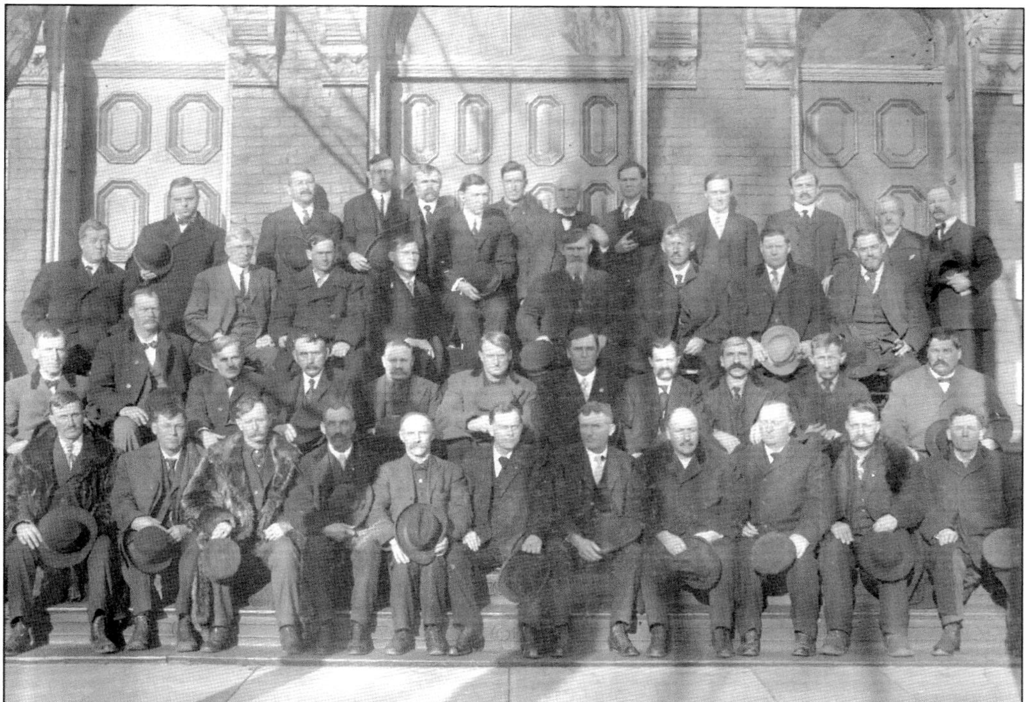

In 1900, more than twice as many newcomers settled in the United States than in all other countries combined. Rich or poor, immigrant or native born, all Americans have traditionally taken real pride in their system of government. Many of those who settled in Chippewa Falls not only created businesses, but also served their city, county, and state in the political arena. Bingham, Jenkins, Marshall, Leinenkugel, Cunningham, Raihle, Wiley, Rasmus, and Roshell all participated in political life. Politicians, from Joe McCarthy to the Kennedys and the Bushes, have visited Chippewa Falls. The active involvement of the gentlemen serving on the Chippewa County Board, pictured here in 1910, exemplified the public spirit so prevalent among those living in the Chippewa area. (Courtesy of Evalyn Wiley Frasch.)

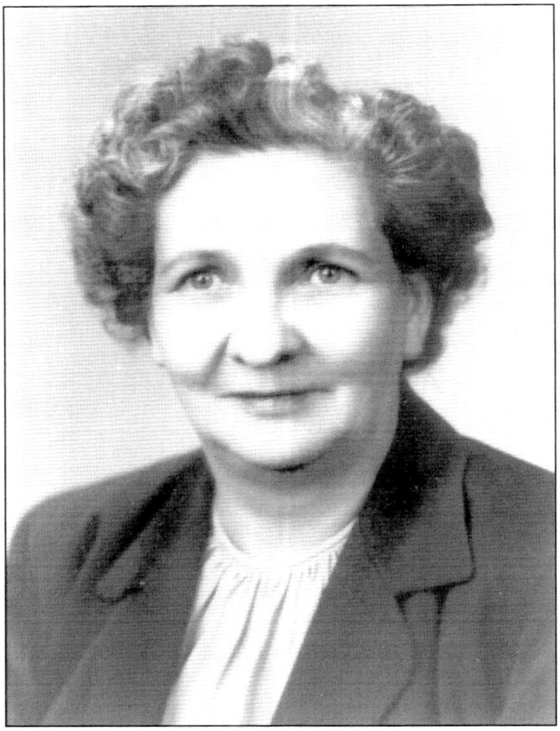

In 1869, the same year Chippewa Falls was incorporated, Susan B. Anthony started the American Woman's Suffrage Association. Sylvia Harve Raihle was born in 1892. She graduated from St. Cloud Teachers College, taught in a one-room school in northern Minnesota, built a log cabin, and then completed law school in 1927 at St. Paul College of Law. Married to Paul Raihle, they raised five children on the family farm before moving to Chippewa Falls. In 1948, Sylvia Raihle entered the political sphere when she was elected to the Wisconsin Assembly. During her three terms she was the first woman to chair a major legislative committee. (Courtesy of David and Sharon Raihle.)

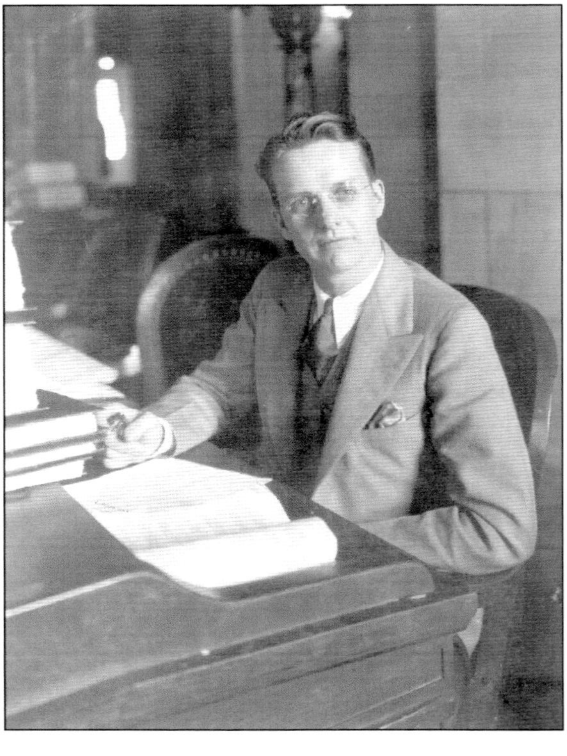

Born July 4, 1906, in the town of Eagle Point, Ingolf E. Rasmus attended the public schools in Chippewa County, Ripon College, and the University of Wisconsin Law School. He was elected to the Wisconsin Assembly in 1930 and served one term. Thereafter Ingolf Rasmus distinguished himself in the practice of law in Chippewa Falls. (Courtesy of Steve Rasmus.)

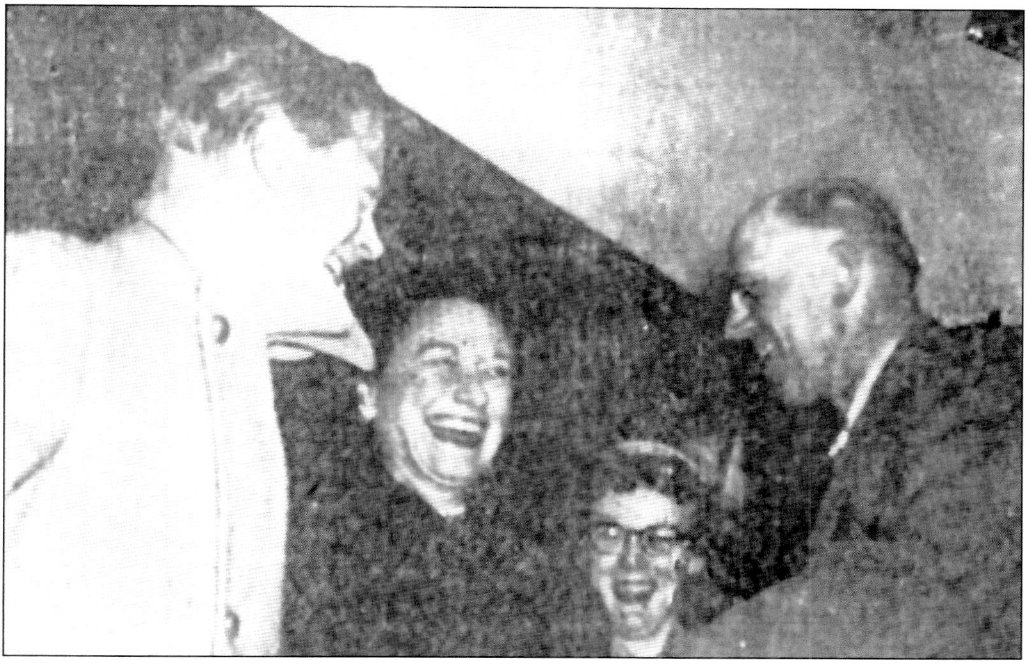

In his capacity as mayor, Harry Webb greeted the Duke and Duchess of Windsor on Easter Sunday, 1950, when their train stopped for ten minutes at the Soo Line platform. About 1,000 people watched as the Mayor and Mrs. Webb presented a bouquet of Easter lilies, a Chippewa Woolens blanket, and a case of Chippewa Springs water to the royal couple. (Courtesy of CCHS.)

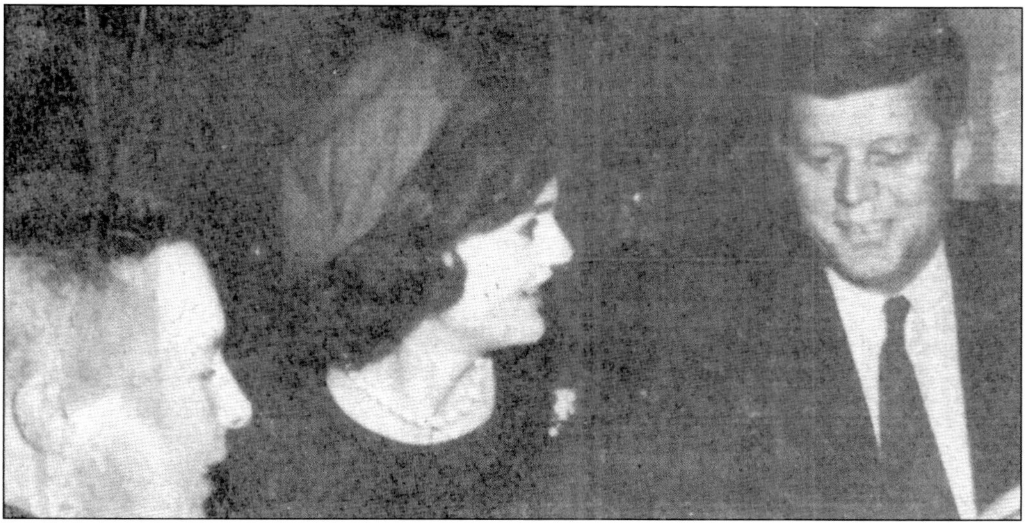

On February 26, 1960, Senator John Kennedy announced he would be a Democratic candidate for President of the United States and he and the extended Kennedy family began campaigning. On March 24, 1960, the Senator and Mrs. Kennedy greeted a large crowd at Skogmo's Café, where Kennedy outlined his five-point program to meet the needs of Wisconsin and Chippewa county farmers. The Kennedys are shown at breakfast with Peter Dugal, who was pledged as a delegate to Kennedy from the Ninth District. (Courtesy of Peter Dugal.)

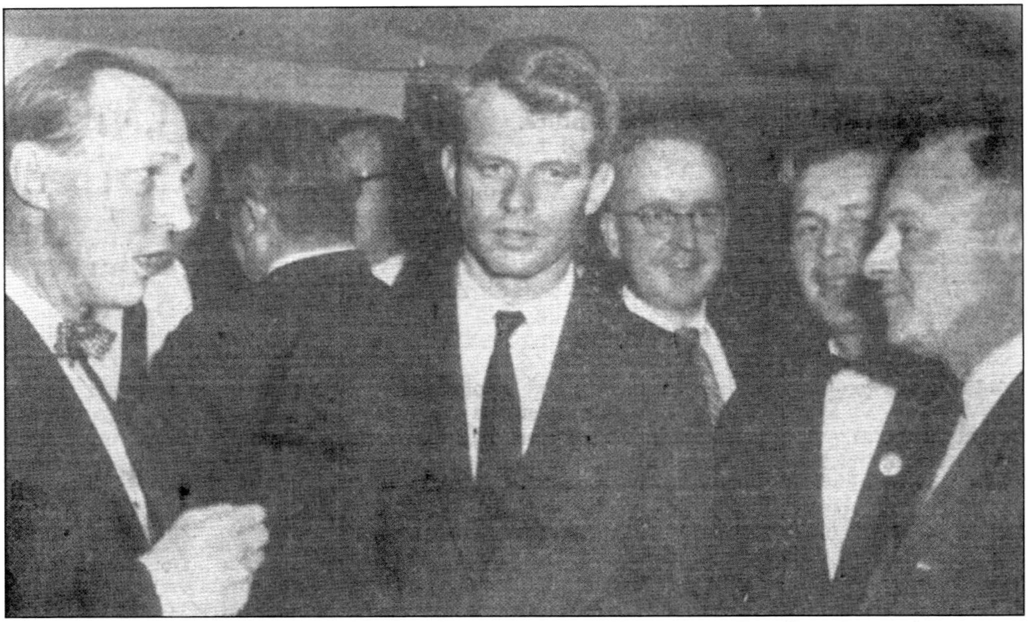

On March 17, 1960, Robert Kennedy campaigned in Chippewa Falls where he spoke to over 60 Elk members about the corruption in both unions and in certain companies. Pictured with Robert Kennedy are (from left to right) Tommy Joas, Robert Kennedy, District Attorney Eugene Jackson, Peter Dugal, and Mayor Frank Hauptmann. (Courtesy of Peter Dugal.)

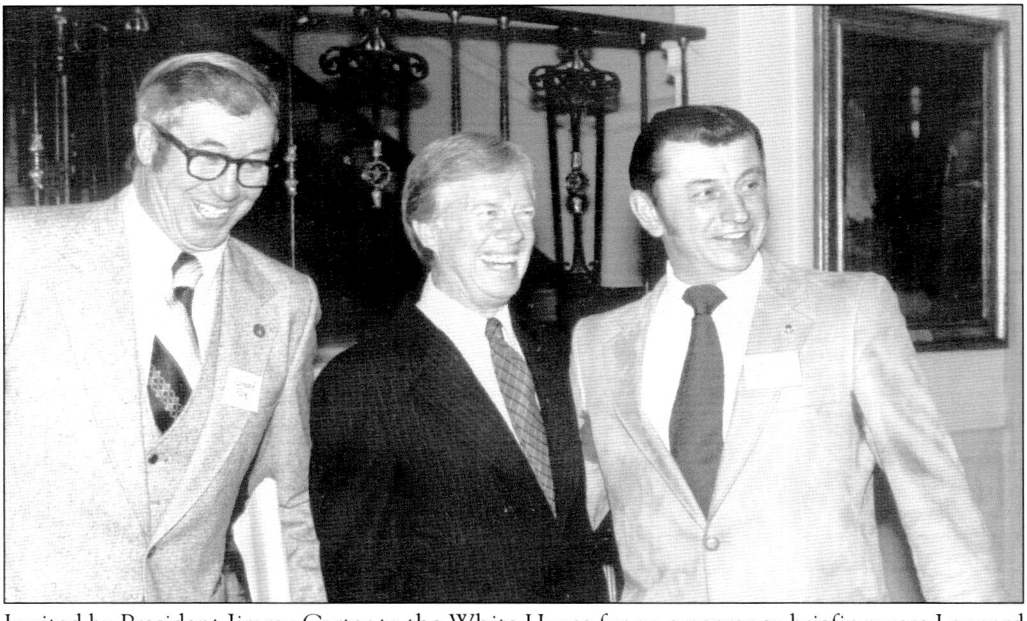

Invited by President Jimmy Carter to the White House for an emergency briefing were Leonard Peck, to the right of the President, and Marvin Roshell, former supervisor and chairman of the Lafayette town board who at the time was serving one of his four terms in the Wisconsin State Senate. (Courtesy of Marv Roshell.)

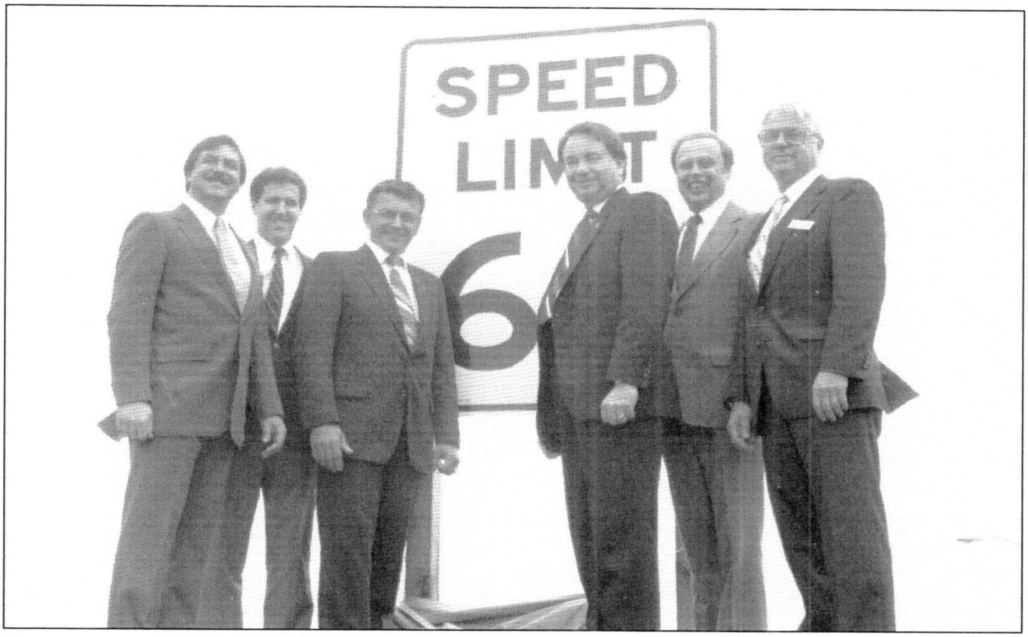

Representative Marvin Roshell introduced the bill in the Wisconsin legislature which raised the speed limit on the state's interstate highways to 65 miles per hour. Pictured celebrating that achievement are (from left to right) Assemblyman Mark Lewis, Senator Bill Berndt, Marvin Roshell, Governor Tommy Thompson, Senator Jim Harsdorf, and Secretary of Transportation Ron Feidler. (Courtesy of Marv Roshell.)

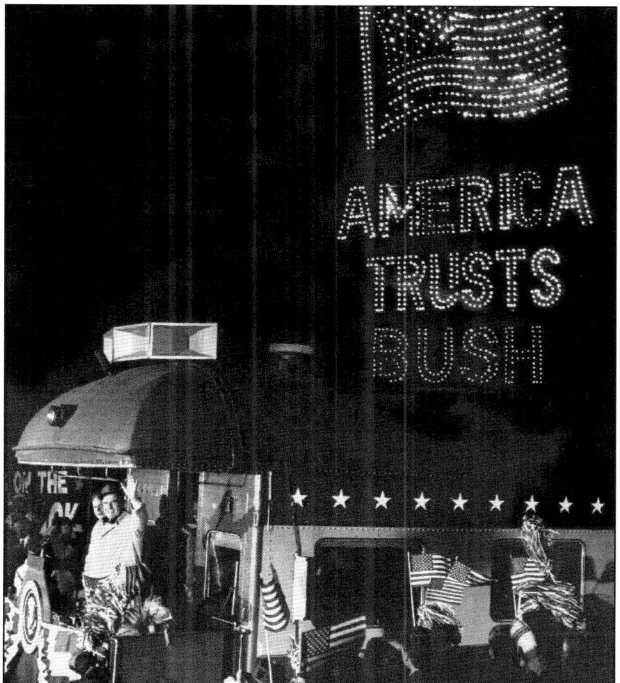

The last stop on George H.W. Bush's whistle-stop tour during his campaign for re-election was on Halloween night, 1992, in Chippewa Falls, Wisconsin. Arriving by train, the weary President spoke to enthusiastic and curious crowds who gathered along the Soo Line tracks behind the plastics plant. (Courtesy of *Eau Claire Leader Telegram.*)

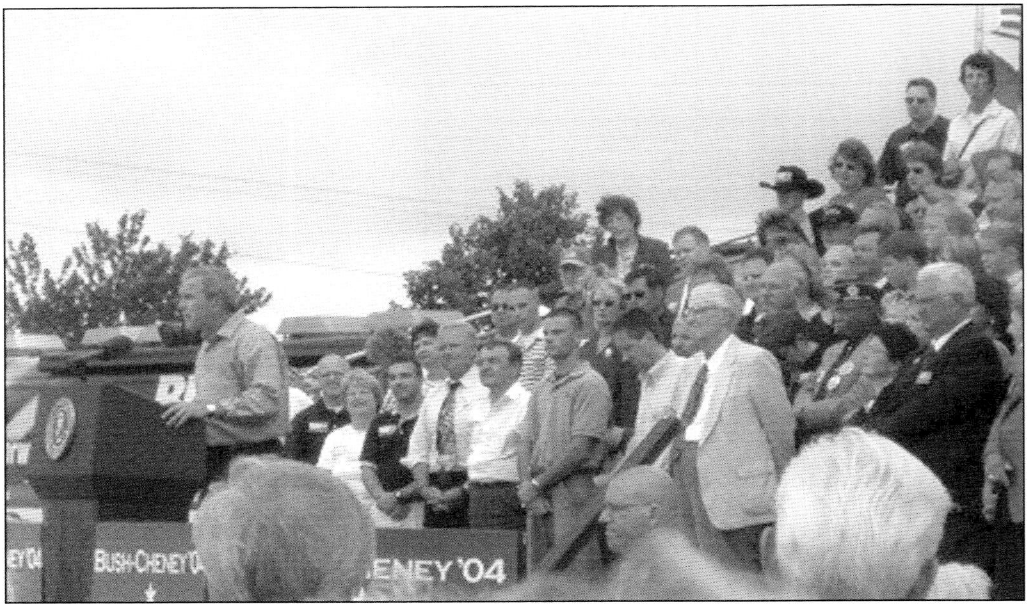

On August 18, 2004, President George W. Bush campaigned in Chippewa Falls. At Kell Container Corporation, he addressed the huge group, outlining his positions on healthcare, national security, job creation, and the war in Iraq. Earlier in the summer, Democratic candidate for President John Kerry addressed the concerns of the farming community during a campaign stop in Bloomer. (Courtesy of CFMS.)

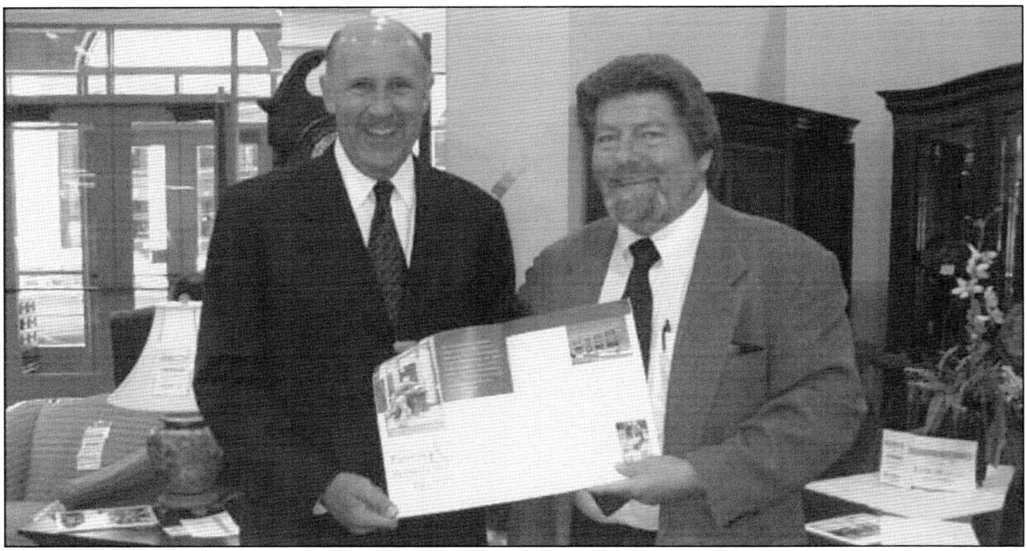

When a fire destroyed the Cobban Block in 1992, the Main Street organization and the city of Chippewa Falls worked together to find an appropriate plan for that historic block. The Korger family undertook a major business expansion and completed their award-winning building venture in 2004. Governor Jim Doyle and Chippewa Falls Main Street Executive Director Jim Schuh toured the building in the summer of 2004 and are pictured holding the National Main Street news article written about Korger's successful project. (Courtesy of CFMS.)

Eight

MADE IN CHIPPEWA

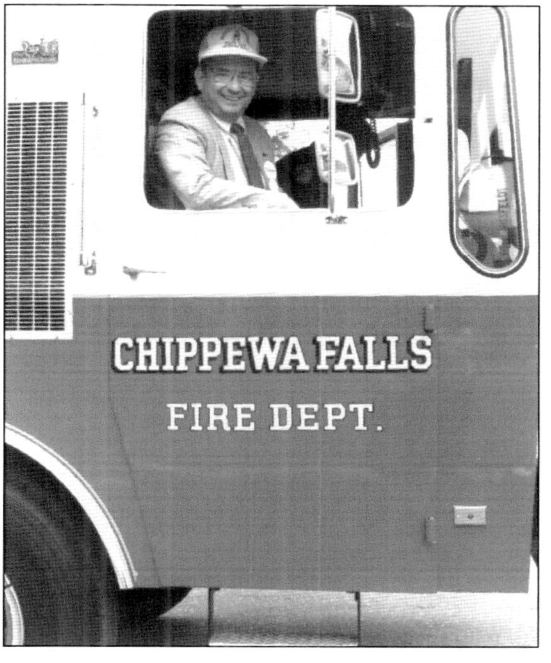

The "Made in Chippewa" label has always meant quality. Lumber planed in the Chippewa Lumber and Boom sawmill was shipped east to build houses for a rapidly-growing population. Shoes and boots from Mason Shoe and Chippewa Shoe were sent across the country. What caused the origin of a product and its eventual utility? What were the expectations and motivations of those individuals who accepted the risk of creating something revolutionary? "Made in Chippewa" is still here, although the products have changed. Governor Tommy Thompson is pictured in a Chippewa Falls Fire Department Darley fire engine equipped with a Darley pump made in Chippewa Falls. (Courtesy of the *Chippewa Herald*.)

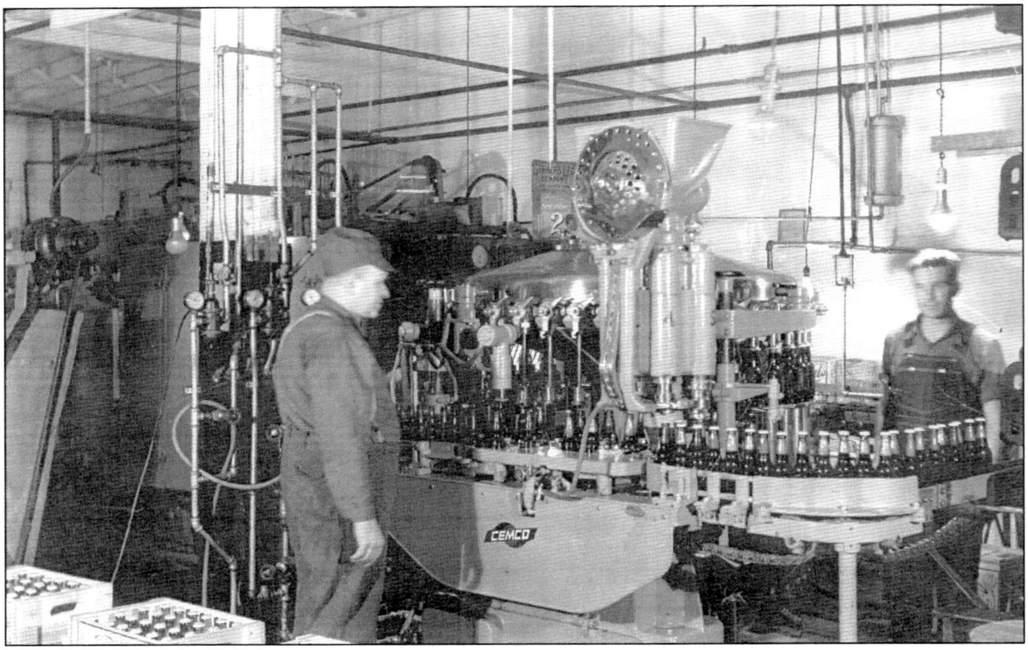

Beer containers at Leinenkugel's have undergone changes since the early brewing days. Wooden kegs gave way to steel kegs that were superseded by aluminum and finally stainless steel kegs. Bottles have gone from standard 12-ounce size to 7-ounce "shorties" to generous half-gallon bottles. Watching the operations in the bottling house is Sidney Hebert, on the right. (Courtesy of Kevin and Krista Alberts.)

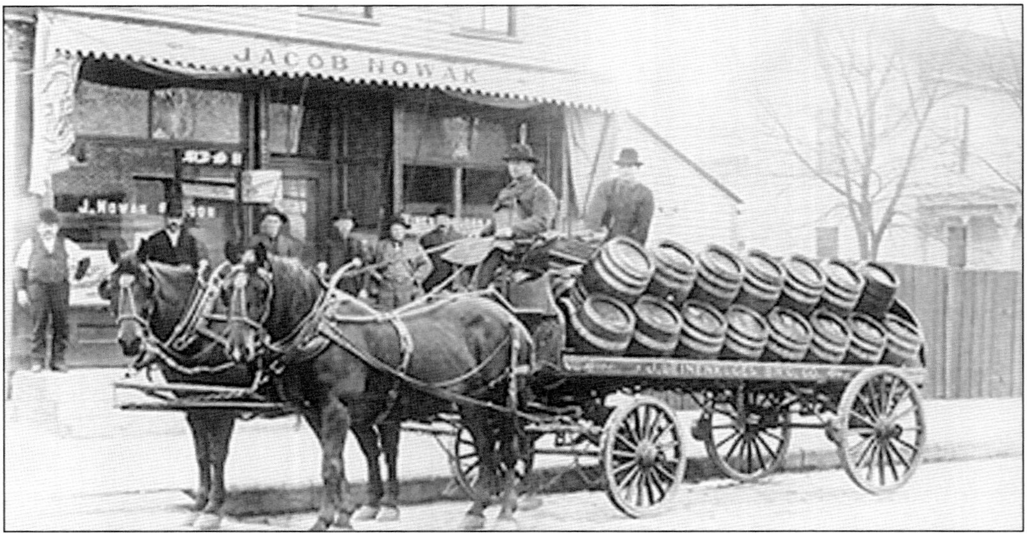

Leinenkugel's had two teams of horses which were hitched up every day to deliver kegs of beer within an eight to ten mile radius of Chippewa Falls. During the early years, Jacob Leinenkugel drove the wagon himself. In January of 1936, the delivery team ran away while the driver, Ed Price, made a delivery. Much to the disappointment of bystanders, nothing fell off the wagon. After a two-block dash, two students halted the frightened horses on High Street. (Courtesy of JLBC.)

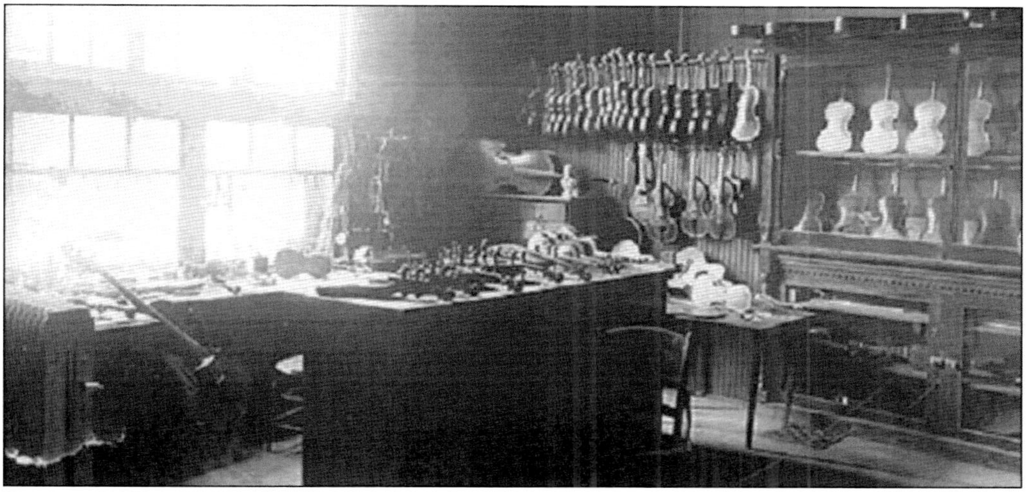

Gunnar Helland made his first violin when he was 12 years old. The workshop of Gunnar Helland, who created the beautifully-decorated and inlaid eight-stringed Hardanger violins, was the only Hardanger violin shop in the United States in 1923. Gunnar reportedly made 500 violins during his lifetime and is considered by some to be the Stradivarius of Hardanger violins. (Courtesy of CCHS.)

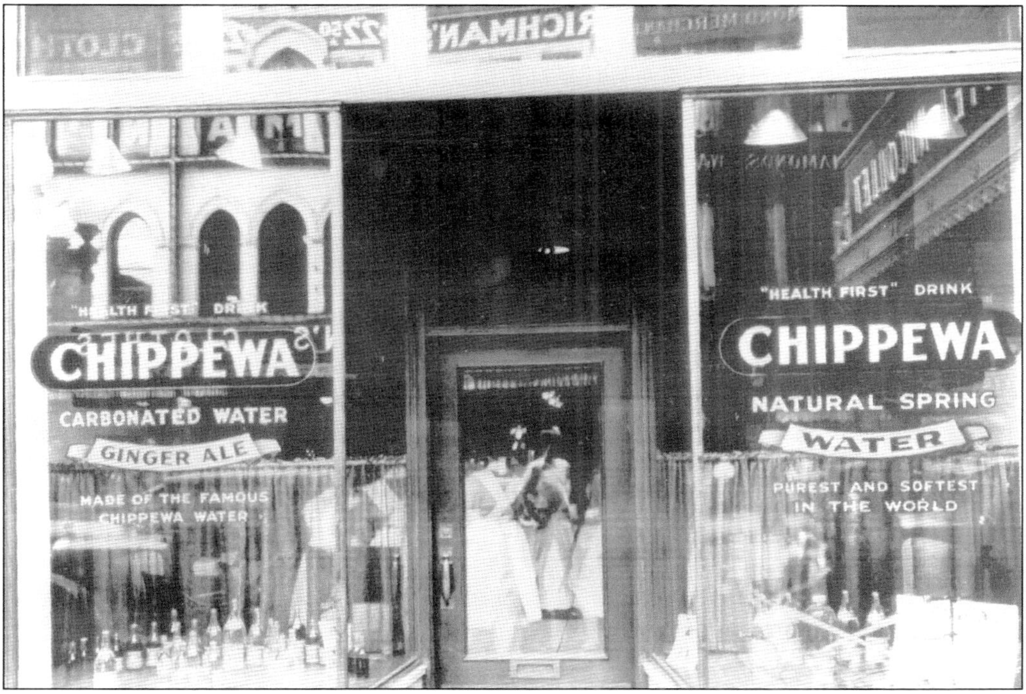

Thaddeus Pound was a true believer in the restorative qualities of the spring water on his farm. Chippewa Springs Company was incorporated in 1894 with a capital of $300,000 and, by 1889, Pound was bottling water drawn from his springs and shipping it by rail to large cities such as Minneapolis, where this storefront advertised the health benefits of Chippewa Springs water. (Courtesy of CCHS.)

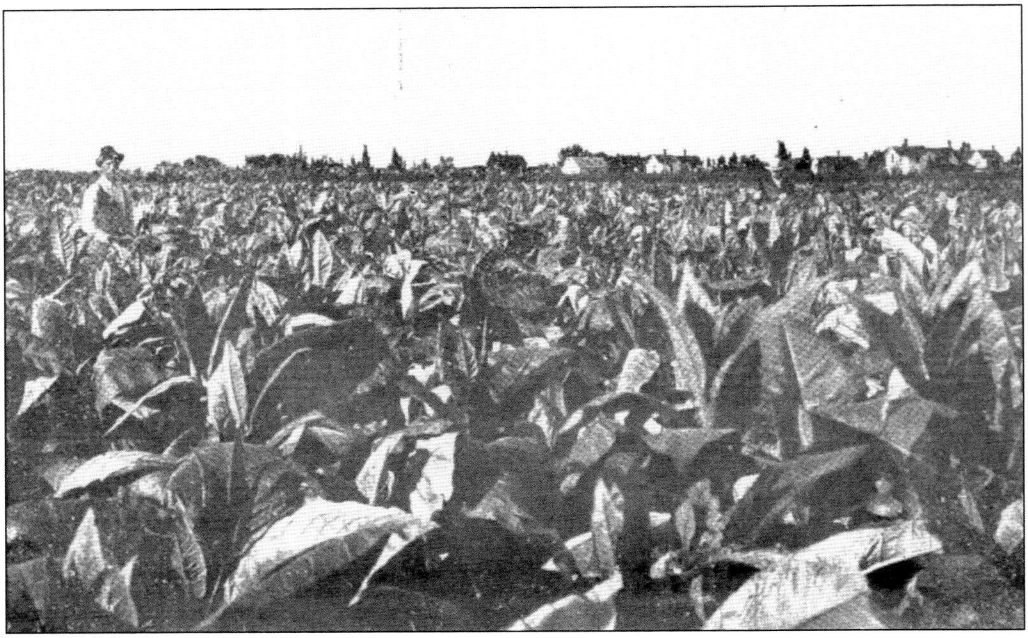

By 1906, farmers from all parts of the county adjacent to Chippewa Falls were receiving from 6¢ to 10¢ per pound for their leaf tobacco. On February 18, 1906, over 50 teams drawing loads of leaf tobacco converged on the C.M. & St. Paul freight depot where the buyer J.A. Green of Green and Sons declared Chippewa County farmers knew how to handle a tobacco crop and prepare it for market. (Courtesy of CCHS.)

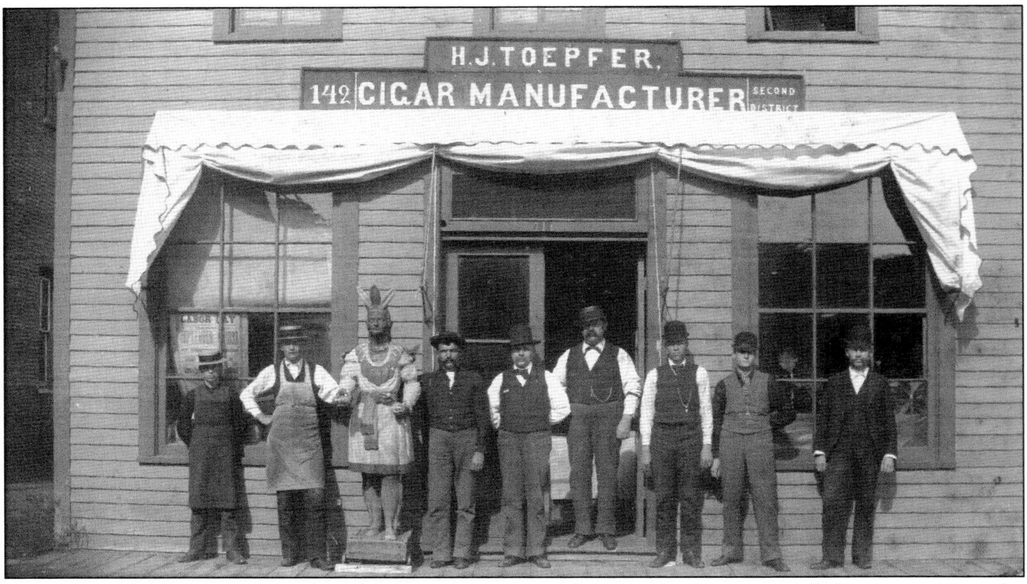

H.J. Toepfer's name appeared in the first issue of Wright's 1883 *Chippewa Falls Directory*. Toepfer was a popular cigar manufacturer who created "The Lumberman's Favorite Cigar." Employees of Toepfer's lined up in front of a window in which a poster announced events for the 1893 Labor Day Celebration. (Courtesy of Joe Joas.)

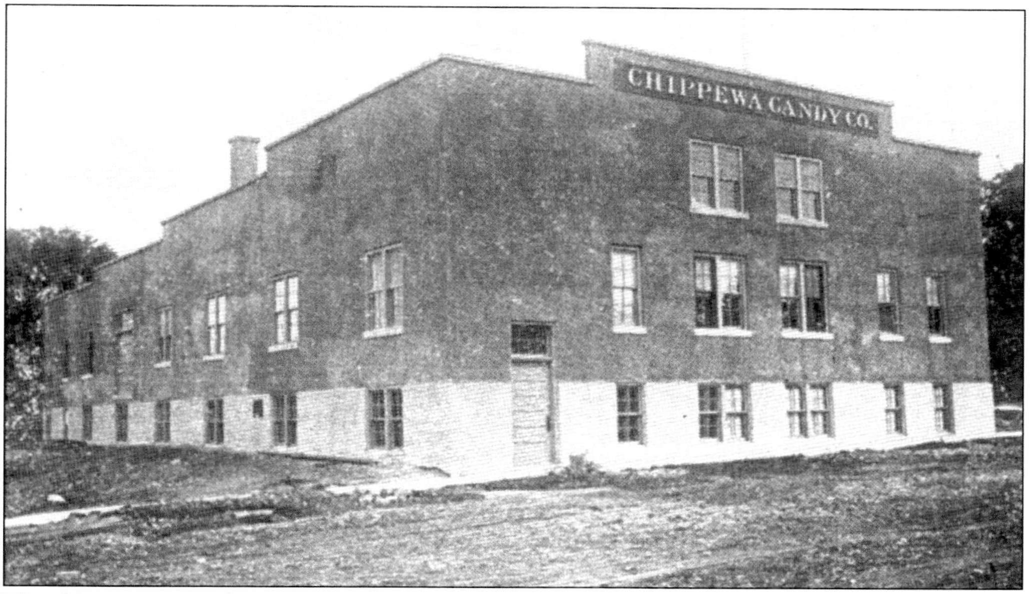

The Chippewa Candy Company, owned by John Zesiger, occupied a modern factory building designed especially "to meet every requirement of hygienic methods in the manufacture of candy." Chippewa Springs water and pure ingredients made "Chippewa Candy" known throughout Wisconsin. Located at 212 E. Columbia Street, the building now houses John's Auto Parts. (Courtesy of CCHS.)

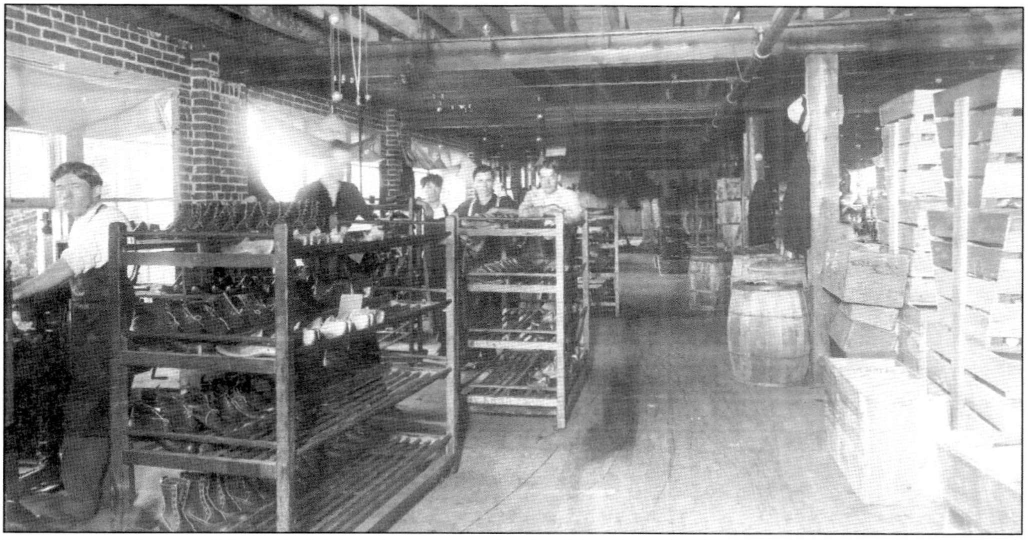

Incorporated in 1902 with $10,000 in capital, the Handmade Boot and Shoe Company was met with unprecedented success. Forty employees worked overtime to keep up with the orders. Handmade Shoe, Chippewa Shoe, Mason Shoe, and Gotzain Shoe companies made Chippewa Falls the center of shoe manufacturing. In 1903, shoemakers at the various shoe factories in Chippewa Falls were organized under the International Leatherworkers trade union. (Courtesy of Kris and David Martineau.)

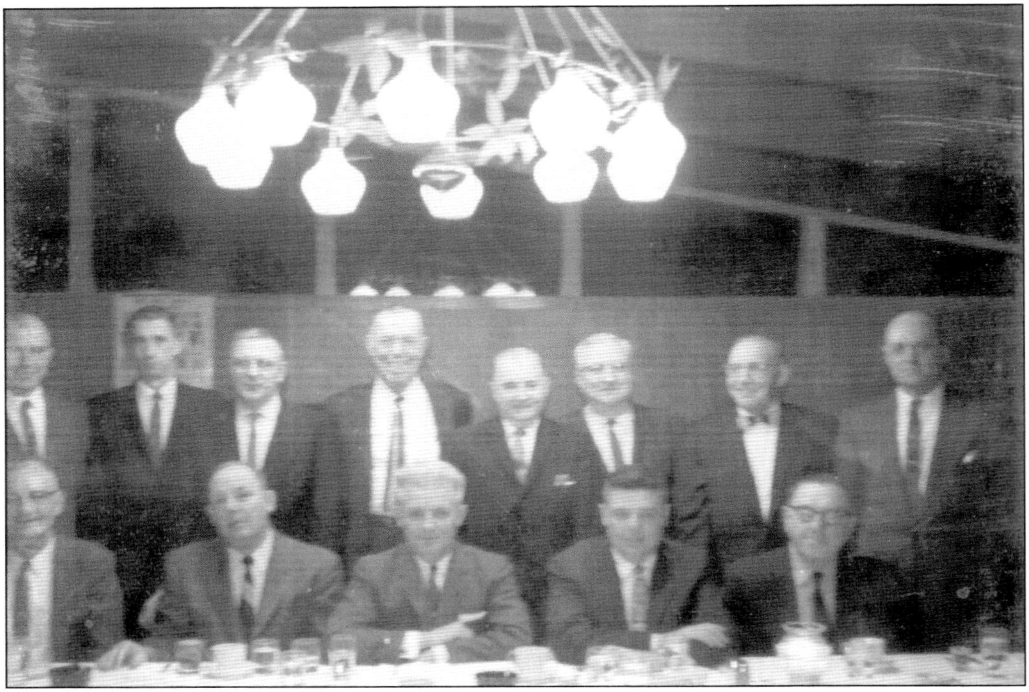

Chippewa Shoe Company officers and department heads are pictured, from left: (seated) George Dreger, Lasting Department, R.L. Jackson, Foreman: Cutting Department, Donal Keefer, Foreman: Fitting Department, Jack McDonald, Vice President of Sales, and Floyd Piotrowski, retired Secretary-Treasurer; (standing) Al Buchberger, Secretary-Treasurer, Lloyd Eckes, Superintendent, Vince Cinquegrana, Sales Manager, T.A. McDonald, President and CEO, Ed Jasper, Shipping Foreman, Joe Fliehr, Sales Department, Peter Stenseth, retired Superintendent, and Rudy Ruples, Goodyear Department Foreman. (Courtesy of Lloyd Eckes.)

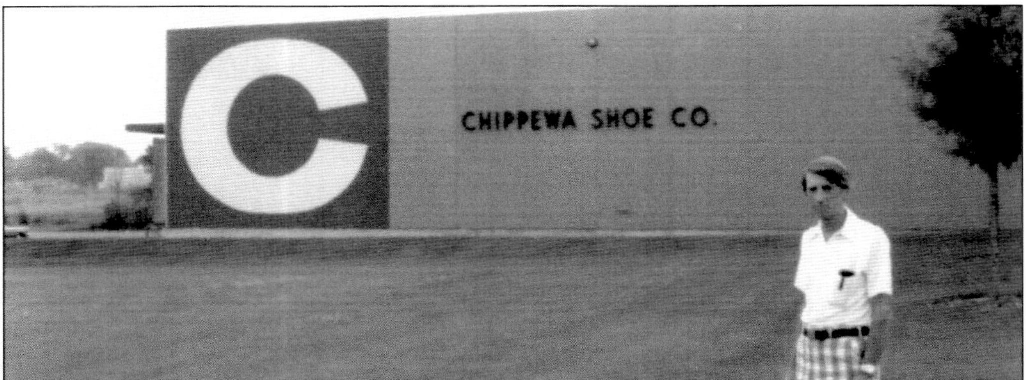

The Chippewa Shoe Company pioneered in introducing Chippewa shoes to the world. From its modest beginning in 1901, it became the backbone of the shoe industry. Lumbermen, miners, sportsmen, ranchers, and farmers appreciated the "splendid wearing qualities" of the original Chippewa work shoes. Lloyd Eckes is pictured in front of the Chippewa Shoe Company building on First Avenue, complete with its distinctive "C" logo. The building later housed Cray Research and Celestica. (Courtesy of Lloyd Eckes.)

In 1948, while visiting relatives in Eau Claire, Don Williams, an employee of Dow Chemical's plastics technical service department, realized that no plastic extruder existed west of Chicago. He formed Chippewa Plastics with his friend, Ken Fleming. With a couple of hand-operated molding machines, the company at first made poker chip molds, molds for key chain fobs, and small "glow in the dark" stars. (Courtesy of CFMIT.)

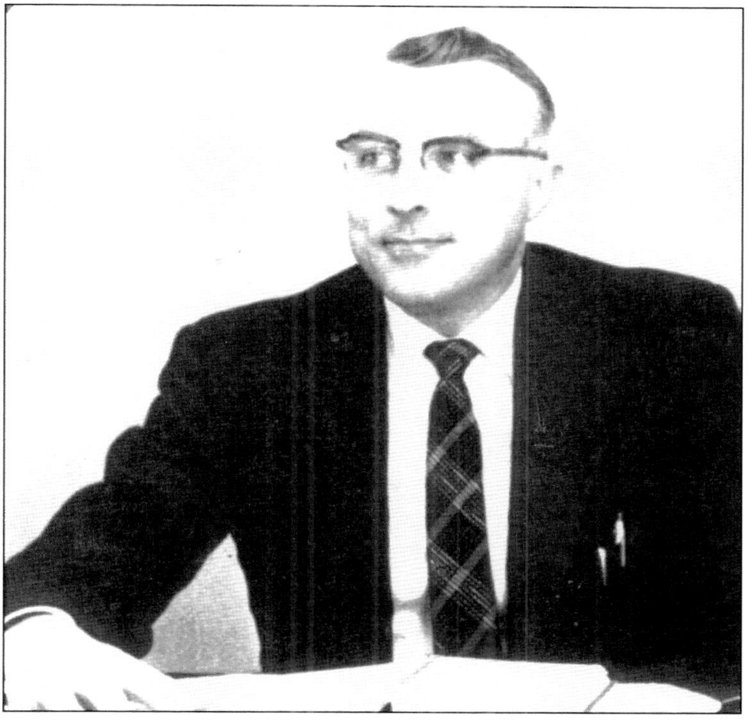

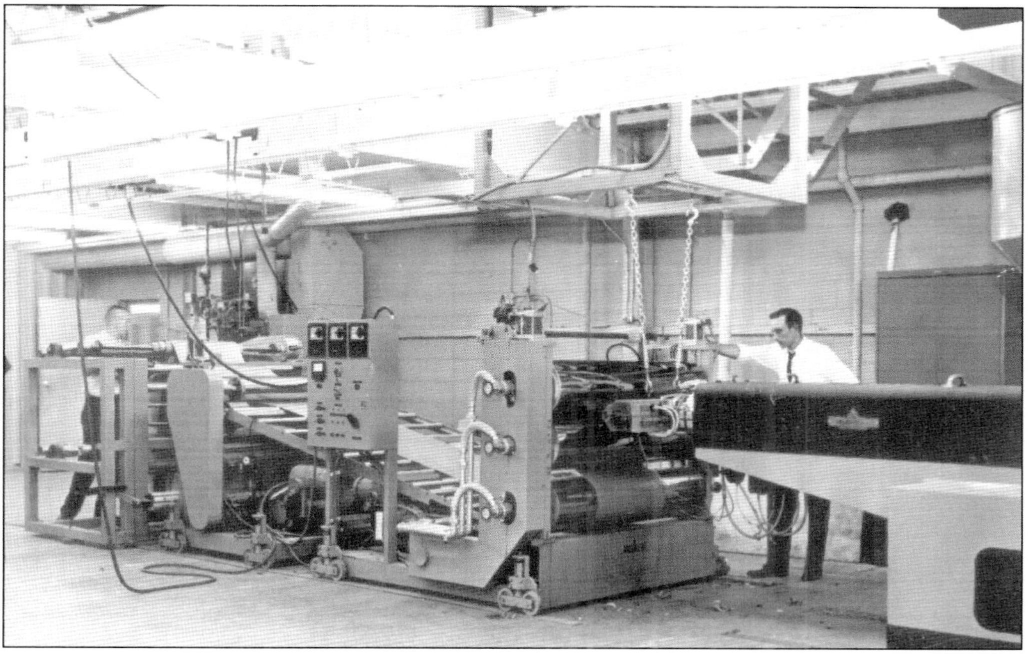

The plastic technology that started with Chippewa Plastics evolved into the technology of polystyrene foam extrusion and spawned many plastics-related businesses, such as Johnson Plastics, which in turn spawned Extrusion Dies. Pictured in the 1960s is the Johnson Manufacturing sheet line for producing plastic film. (Courtesy of Extrusion Dies.)

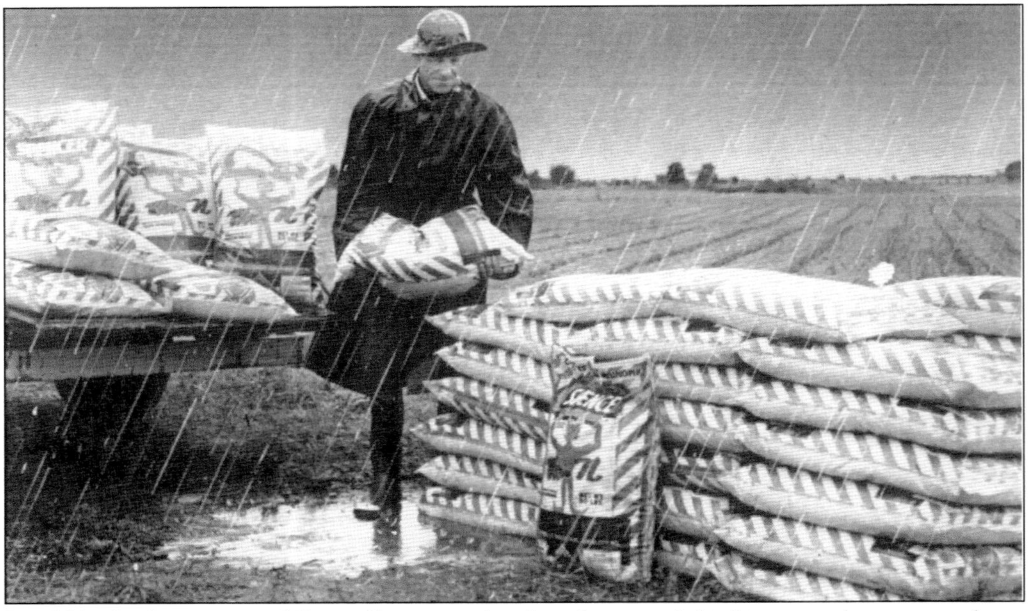

In 1908, the International Paper Company developed a waxed drinking cup that was so cheap it could be thrown away after use. By the 1950s, Chippewa Plastics was making plastic products that were less expensive, more durable, easier to manufacture in large quantities, and were disposable. The advertisement above extolled the strong and protective qualities of their plastic bags. (Courtesy of CFMIT.)

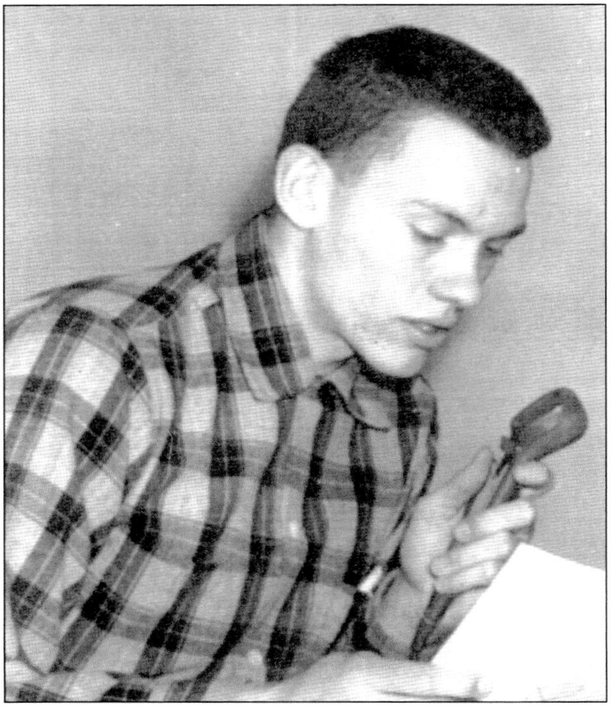

As product research director at Chippewa Plastics in 1958, Dave Hancock and co-workers pioneered the extrusion of polystyrene foam. As a founder of Applied Research and Development Corporation that manufactured food containers, plastic food trays, and interior packaging for fragile items, he helped spawn other plastics related companies. He acquired Hubbard Scientific in 1976 and started Spectrum Industries, which manufactures office furniture for today's needs. (Courtesy of CFMIT.)

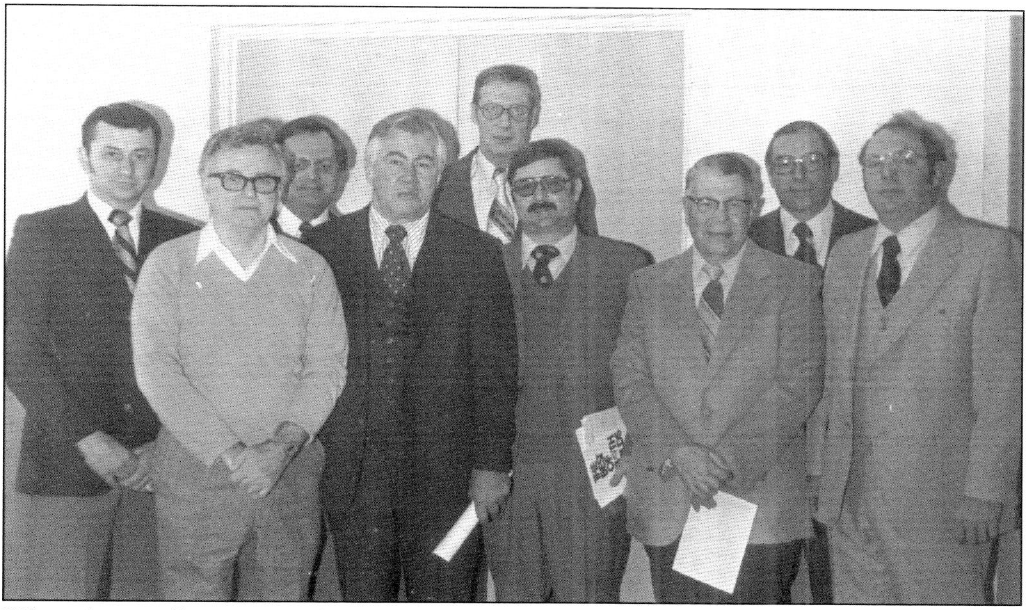

When the rapidly-growing Chippewa Plastics company needed a larger facility and help with financing, it became a catalyst for the formation of the Industrial Development Corporation in 1953. The IDC developed "industrial parks" and by 1957, it was marketing the land. Pictured at a 1979 IDC Annual Meeting are (from left to right) Marvin Roshell, Victor Mason, Don Whiting, John Willut, Franklin Kurth, Jim Colbert, Francis Seyforth, Gene Mower, and Don Stumpf. (Courtesy of CFACC.)

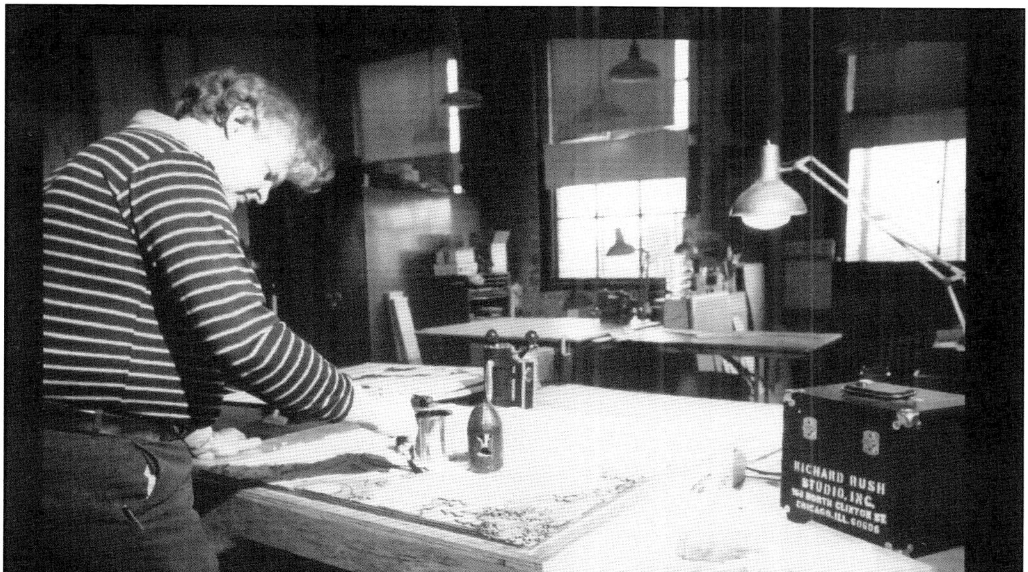

When Hubbard Scientific was purchased in 1976 by Dave Hancock, he moved the manufacturing facility from Chicago to Chippewa Falls, where he knew the strong work ethic would benefit the company. Today, Hubbard Scientific, which creates educational products for teachers, is the largest manufacturer of raised relief maps in the world. (Courtesy of CCHS.)

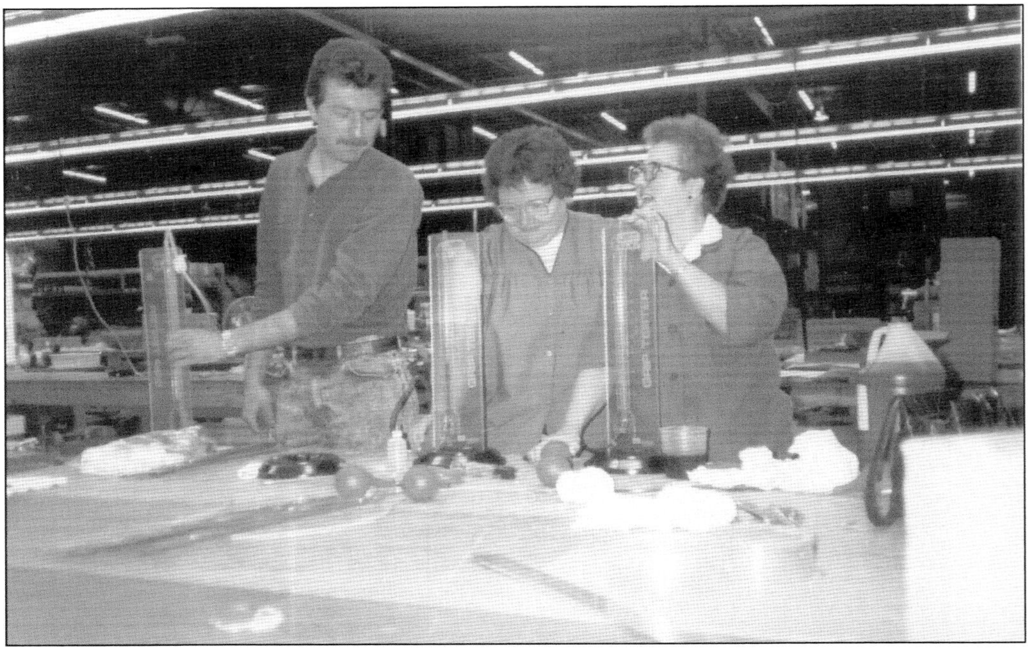

A safe environment is stressed at Hubbard Scientific. Along the production lines, employees assembled anatomy models, terrariums, orbiters, and other educational products. Employees (from left to right) Paul Taylor, Jean Parkhurst, and Lorraine Horel say "coming to work at Hubbard Scientific is like coming to play every day." (Courtesy of Tom Halblieb.)

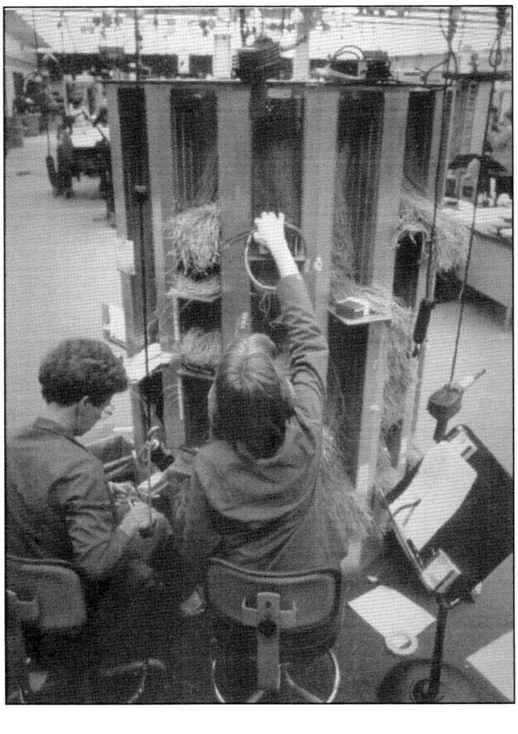

In 1985, Cray Research announced the Cray-2, a 12-foot-square machine weighing 5,500 pounds, with fluorocarbon cooling technology. Over half the Chippewa Falls employees worked in the manufacturing department where the computers were physically put together. (Courtesy of CFMIT.)

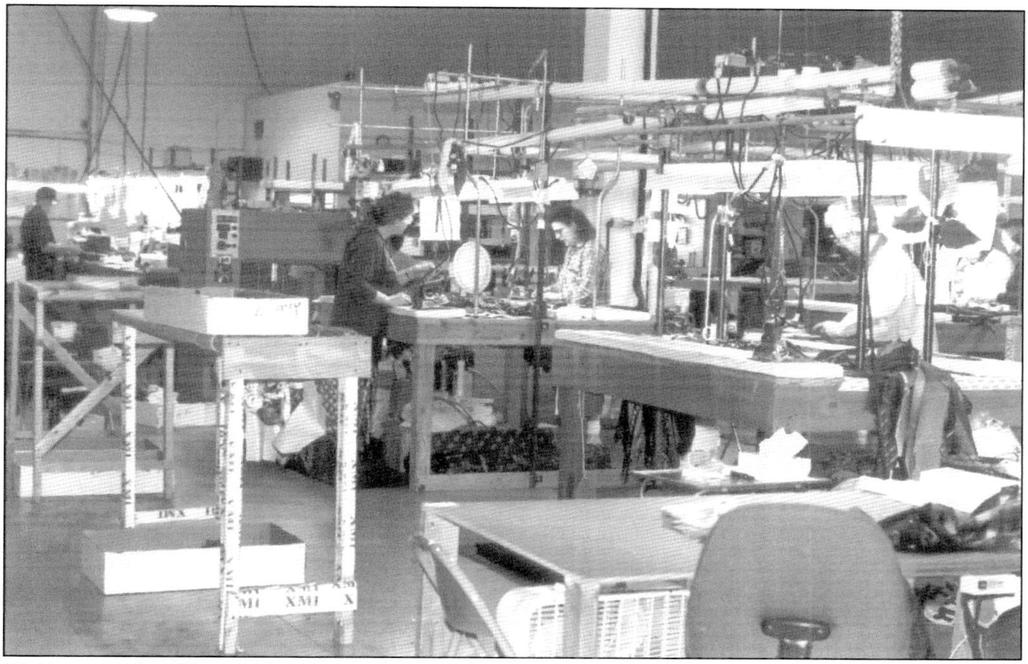

XMI stands for "Extraordinary Marketing Idea." Fabrics for the ties are imported from Italy and England, the designing is done in New York, and the ties are manufactured in Chippewa Falls. Within the factory, men cut the fabric with round knives and women sew at their own tables, creating handmade ties worn by television personalities such as *The West Wing*'s Martin Sheen and ESPN sportscasters. (Courtesy of CFMIT.)

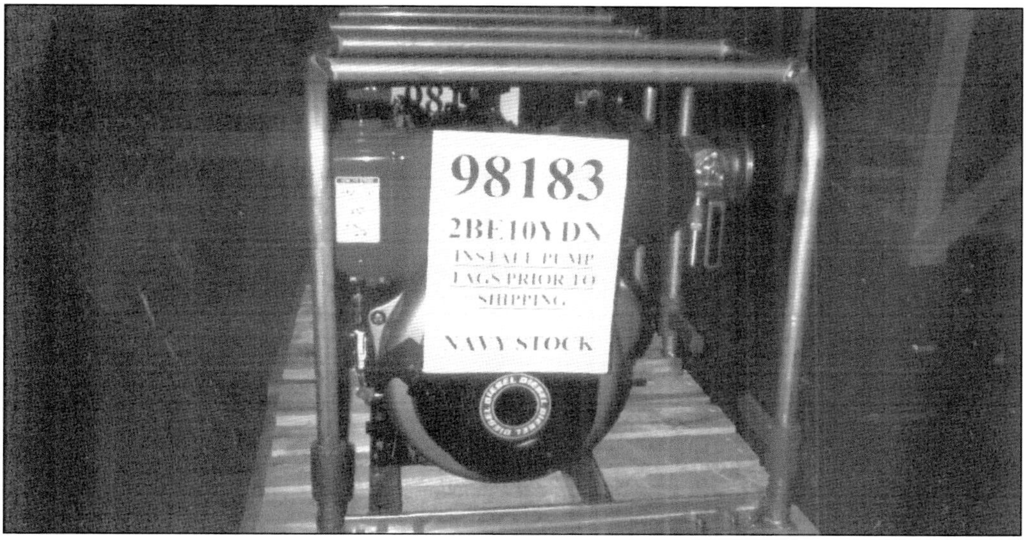

On January 20, 1944, W.S. Darley & Company and its employees received the Army-Navy "E" award in recognition of Darley's production record on military contracts. For two years during World War II, Darley operated around the clock, with 90 employees producing 40 pumps a day, thus earning the company the gratitude of the military that relied on the pumps in battleships and on military bases. (Courtesy of CFMIT.)

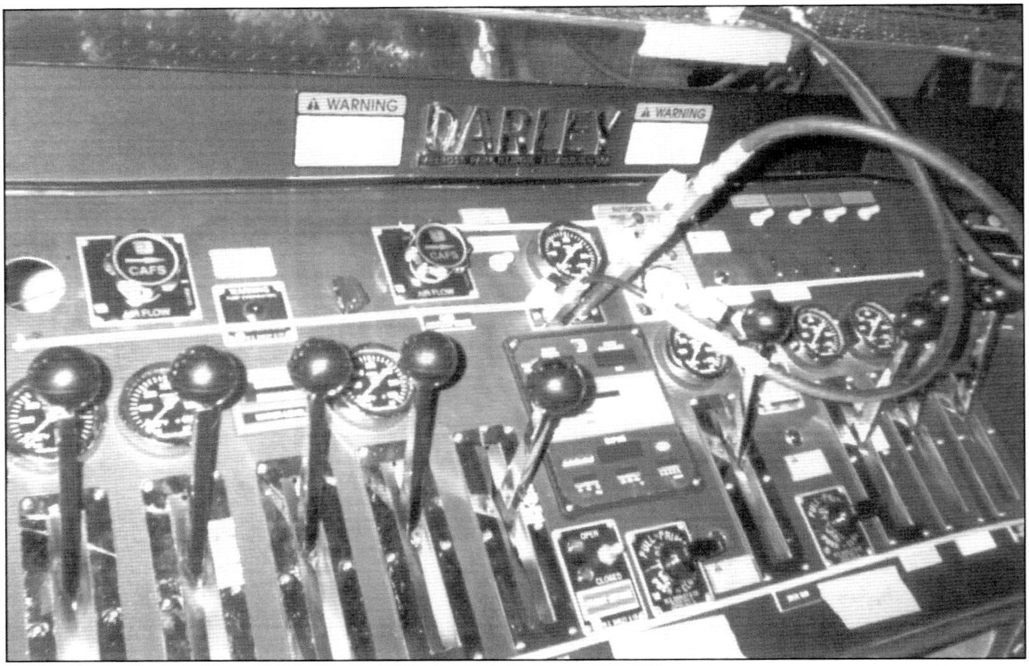

The "one of a kind" specialty fire trucks are manufactured by a Darley company in Augusta, Wisconsin. When Darley expanded its sales to New Zealand, Taiwan, South Africa, the Philippines, and Australia, the company created what it called "the best exporting system in the world." It is not unusual to see a fire truck destined for the Ghana Fire Department taking a test drive through Chippewa Falls. (Courtesy of CFMIT.)

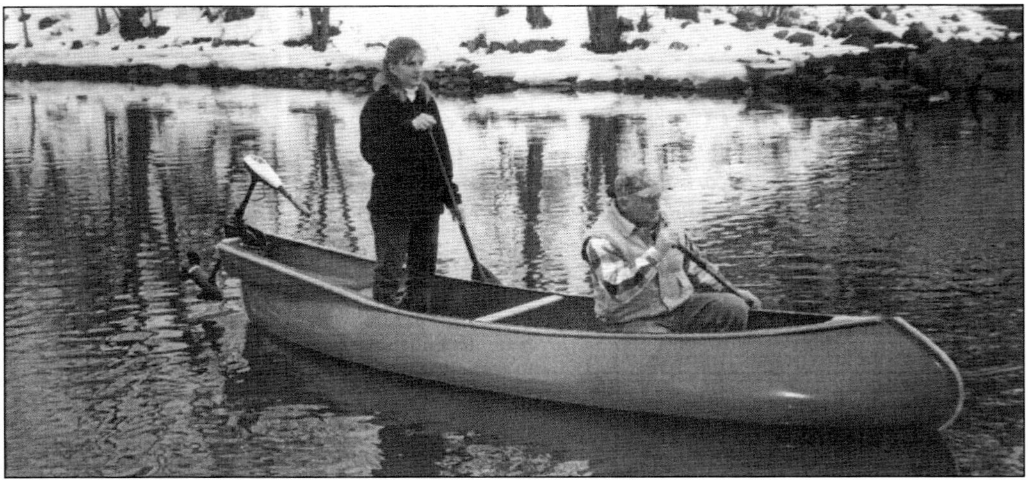

Marvin Belknap, following instructions in *Boy's Life* magazine, made his first canoe out of orange crates and his father's best canvas when he was 10 years old. After a career in the plastics business, he built a stable canoe, using Frank Lloyd Wright's theory of designing around function. His Golden Hawk canoes became popular with fishermen, duck hunters, trappers, and participants in the April Fool's Day canoe race he started in 1970. Marvin Belknap is pictured with his daughter, Susan, testing the waters. (Courtesy of CFMIT.)

Nine

Main Street Revisited

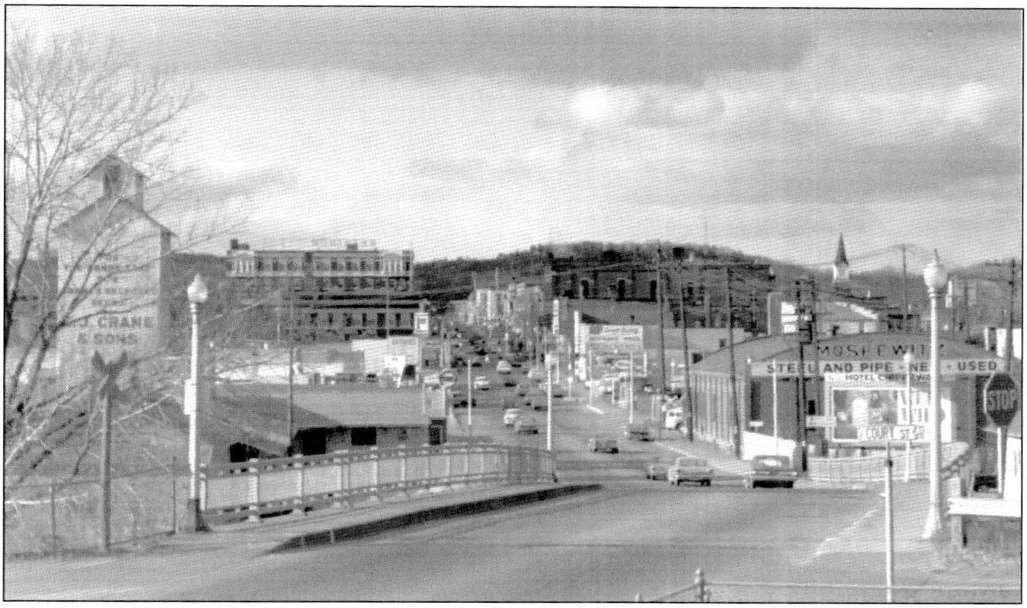

When the Village of Chippewa Falls was incorporated as a city in 1869, there was only a ferry boat connecting Frenchtown, on the south side of the Chippewa River, with the growing City of Chippewa Falls on the north side of the river. The first bridge over the Chippewa River was completed in 1870, creating the first of many "bridges of Chippewa Falls." Each bridge had a name and a purpose, each carried cars, trains, and people to and from the downtown area, and each offered a unique view of Chippewa Falls. The "Blue Bridge" provided the first glimpse of downtown Chippewa Falls and its main thoroughfare, Bridge Street. Lined with many diverse businesses, Bridge Street reflected the ebbs and flows of an industrial city, from the lumbering era to the present. Buildings constructed for one specific business housed quite a few different ones over the years. Buildings and character were lost to fires, neglect, and modernization efforts, but with education and encouragement from the Main Street Program since 1989, Chippewa Falls has renewed its commitment to preserving and restoring what remains. (Courtesy of CFACC.)

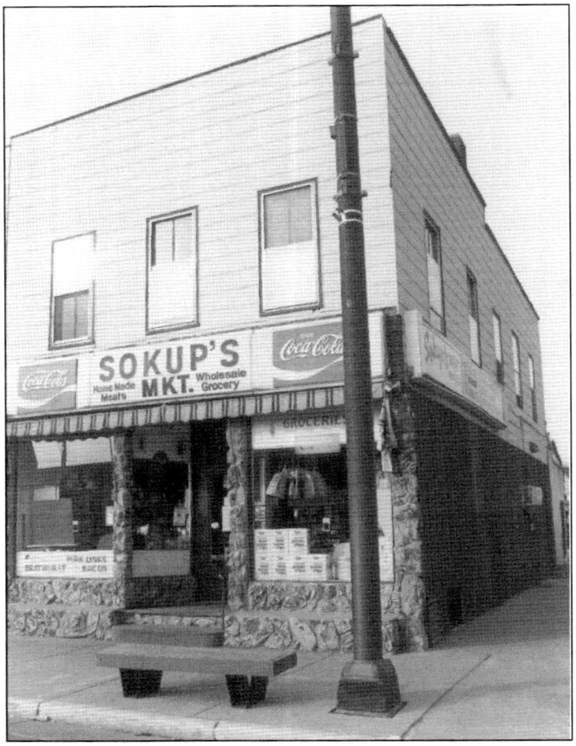

The corner of North Bridge and Spruce Streets may well be called Sokup's Corner for there has been a Sokup's Market there since 1894. Founder Joseph Sokup turned the business over to his son, Peter, who retired in 1963 and turned the grocery store over to his son, John, who, along with his hard-working wife, Angie, remains active in the business today even after turning the business over to their own son, Peter. (Courtesy of CCHS.)

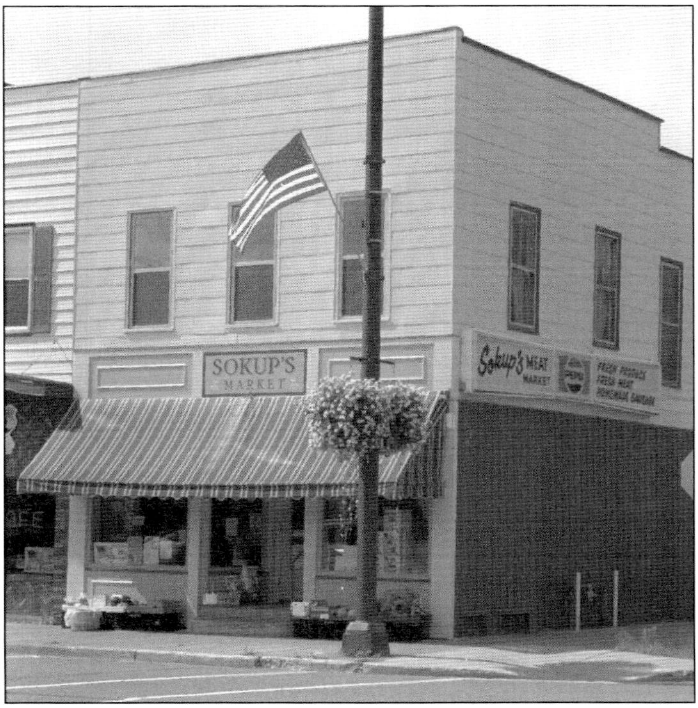

Peter Sokup, the fourth generation operator of Sokup's Market, had the opportunity in 2003 to restore the storefront after the driver of a car lost control and struck the building, causing major damage. The "new" exterior was designed to more closely resemble the original façade, complete with baskets of fruits, vegetables, and nuts placed just outside the front door. (Courtesy of Dave Gordon.)

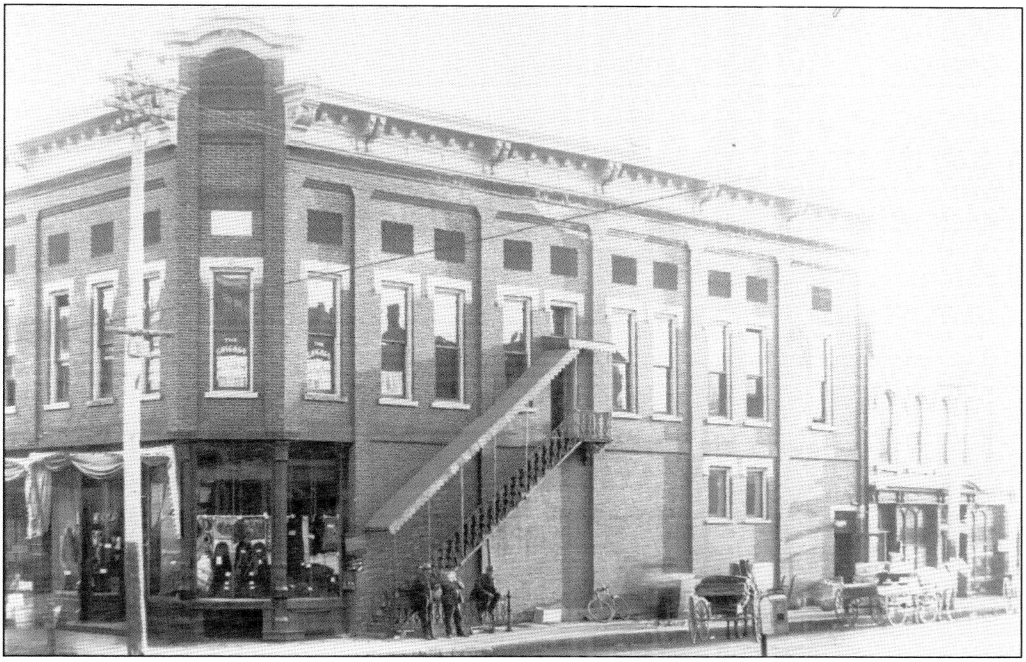

In 1873, the French Lumber Company was incorporated. In 1885, the French Mercantile was housed in the massive brick building at 124 N. Bridge Street, a site considered one of the best business locations in the city. It provided groceries, shoes, clothing, and lumber to the growing Chippewa Falls community. The building has since been in continuous use by a variety of businesses, including McNulty's, Waterman's, Schultz Brothers, and PB Office Supply. (Courtesy of CCHS.)

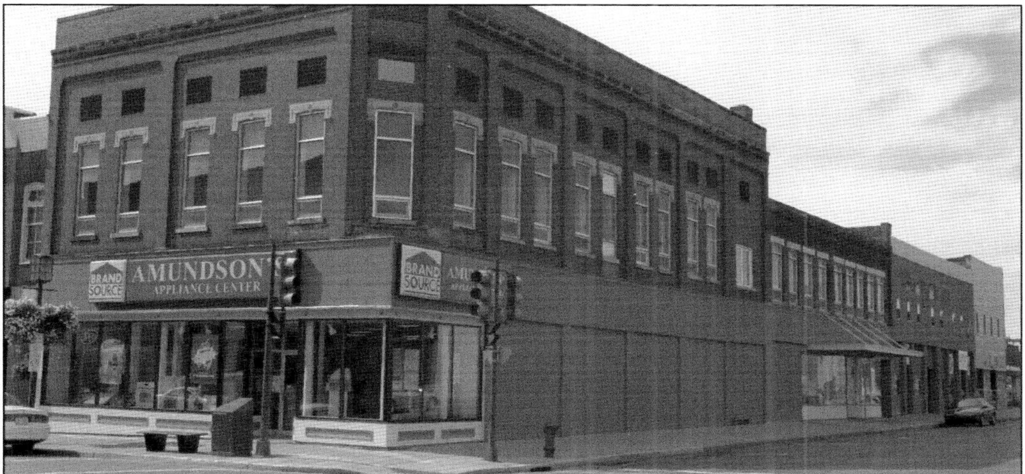

PB Office Supply, which opened in November 1954 in the former Krause's Café at 214 N. Bridge Street, later relocated to the former French Lumber Company building. After PB Office Supply closed, investor Steve Harmon renovated the original building and leased it to Amundson's Appliance from Rice Lake, continuing the productive history of the French Lumber Company building. (Courtesy of Dave Gordon.)

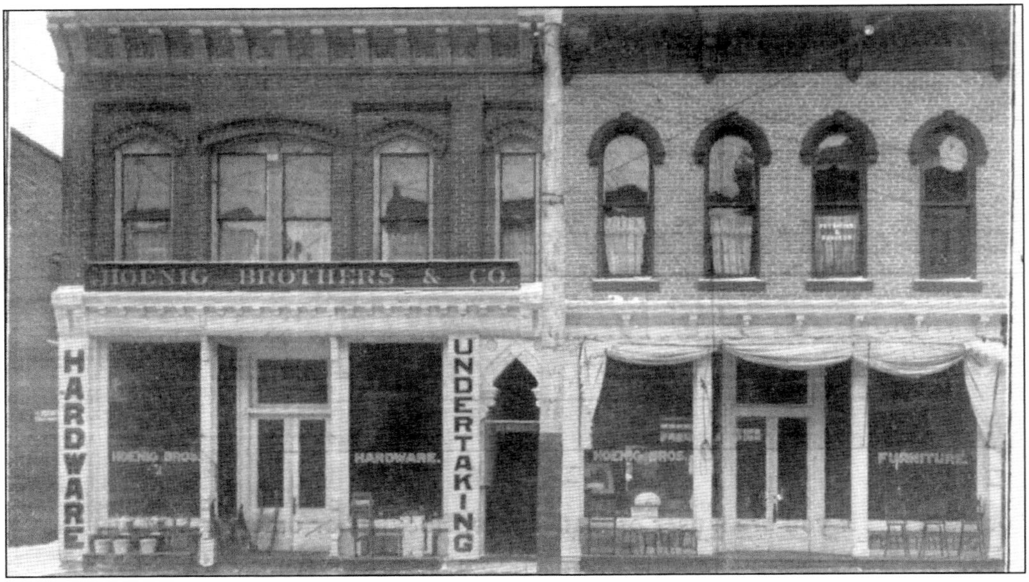

Early stores and businesses were found along Spring and River Streets. As the city flourished, so did its downtown and buildings were soon erected along both sides of Bridge Street. The 1903 buildings pictured at 114, 116, and 120 N. Bridge Street were home to Hoenig Brothers Hardware, a furniture store and undertaking parlor, and to Riester and Dettloff's Drug Store. Second floors were used as offices by real estate agents, dentists, doctors, and lawyers. At 114 1/2 N. Bridge Street, piano lessons were taught in the studios of Robert Fowler and Eleanor Jacobson. (Courtesy of CCHS.)

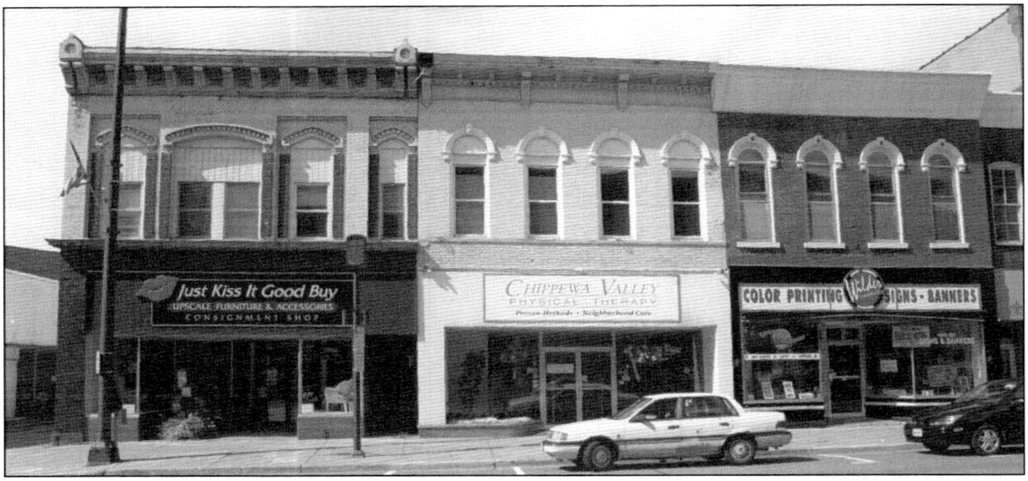

The businesses presently located at 114, 116, and 120 N. Bridge Street are: Just Kiss It Good Buy, Chippewa Valley Physical Therapy, and Wilder Graphics. At 114 N. Bridge Street, the corbelled brick over the windows and the ornamental brackets on the upper windows contributed to the beauty of the former Hoenig Brothers store. Architect Steve Playter—an innovative and energetic individual who appreciates the historical nature of downtown buildings—and his partner Roger Rudy are the owners of the former Hoenig Brothers store, which is now occupied by Just Kiss It Good Buy. Storefront improvements include an eye-catching sign and a chrome sculpture. (Courtesy of Dave Gordon.)

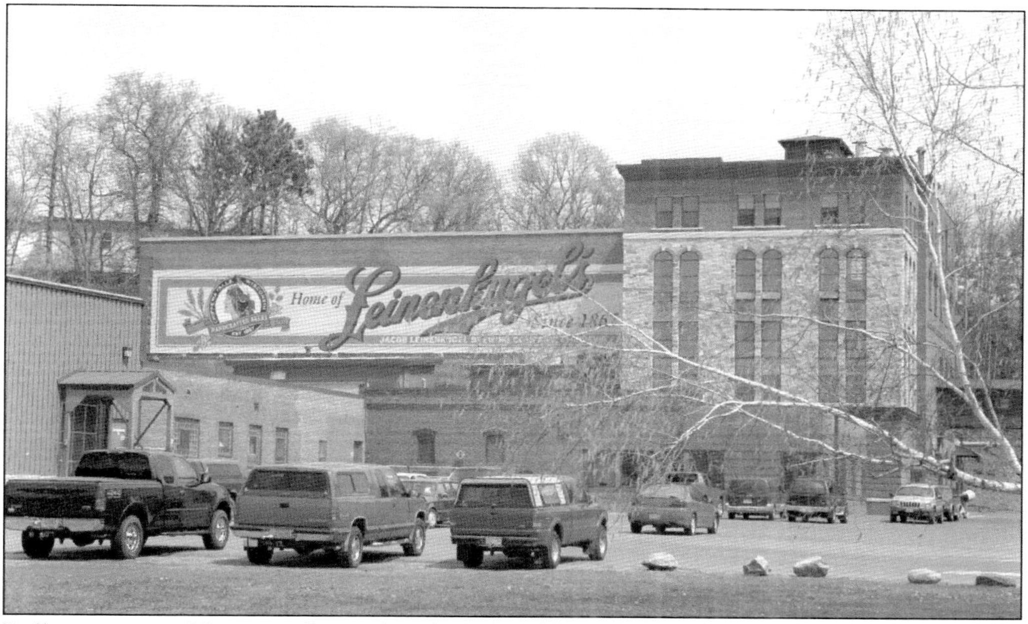

Still in its original location, Leinenkugel's is the oldest industry in existence in Chippewa Falls. The original brewery was housed in a 24-by-50-foot building and the lumbermen were the first customers. Through astute management, it survived Prohibition, tended to its customers, and expanded its operations to include a four-story brew house, storage facilities, and a bottling plant. Leinenkugel's is a multi-generational industry with the fifth generation still involved in the brewery today. (Courtesy of Dave Gordon.)

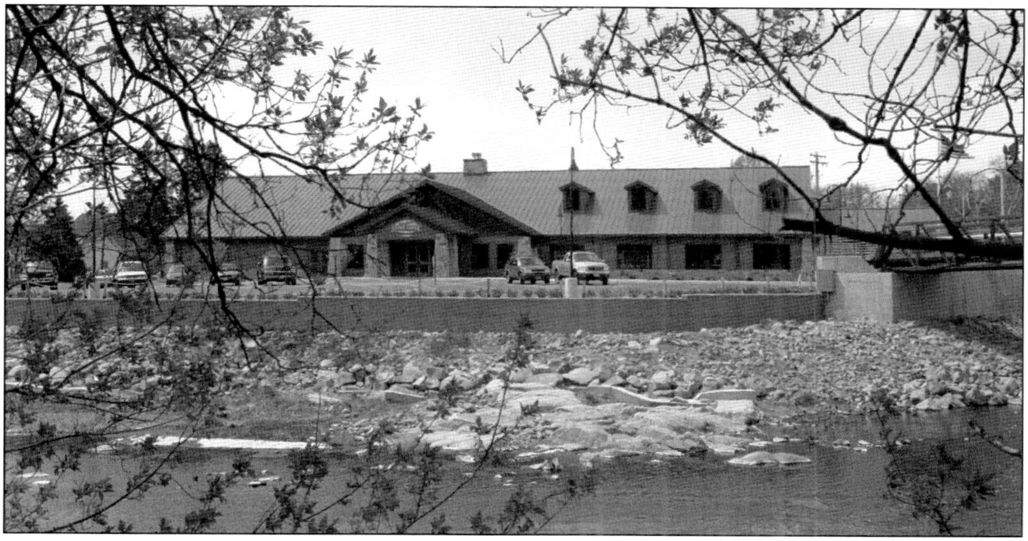

Within the walls of the Leinenkugel Brewery, there used to be a tasting room where tourists, thirsty after a brewery tour, could sample Leinenkugel's beer at its freshest. In 2003, in keeping with their desire to provide the best hospitality to visitors and the community, Leinenkugel's built a new Leinenkugel Hospitality Center, known as the Leinie Lodge, on the site of the Chippewa Woolen Mill across Duncan Creek from the brewery. (Courtesy of Dave Gordon.)

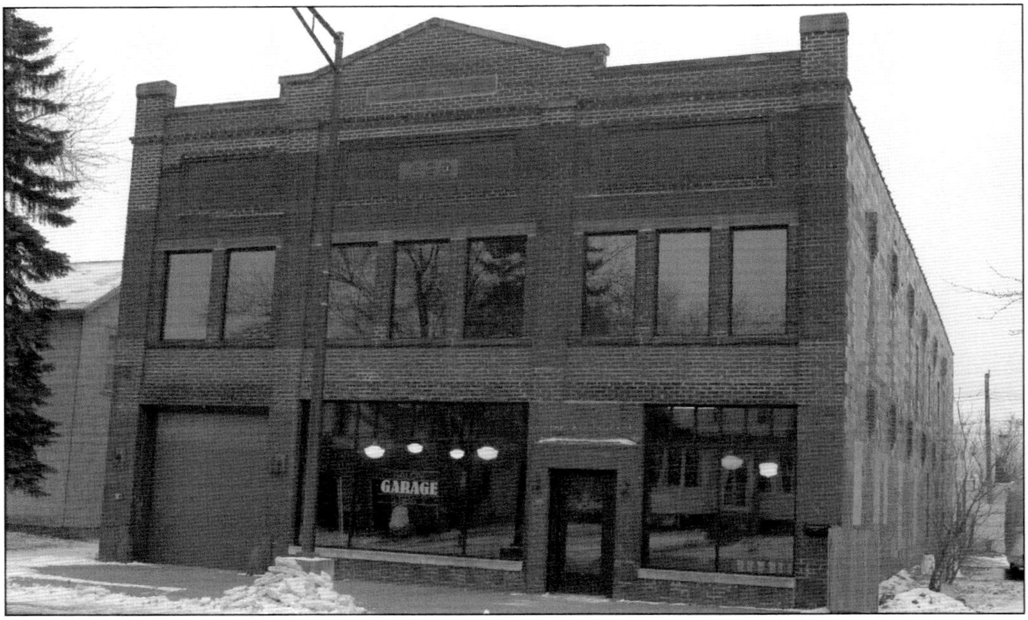

In the past, stagecoaches, horse-drawn wagons, and buggies rumbled along the streets of Chippewa Falls. On July 23, 1903, Henry Ford sold his first Model A, called a "family horse," for $850. Chippewa Falls soon embraced the automobile and dealerships proliferated in the city. In 1920 the Saitta-Lunde Motor Company became the sixth dealership in Chippewa Falls when it opened in this building at 45 E. Elm Street. Since then, the building—whose architectural style was representative of early automobile dealerships—has served as the National Guard Armory and a school system warehouse. Cheryl and Troy Story purchased and, with sensitivity to its historic character, renovated the structure and opened the Garage Salon & Spa in July of 2004. (Courtesy of Dave Gordon.)

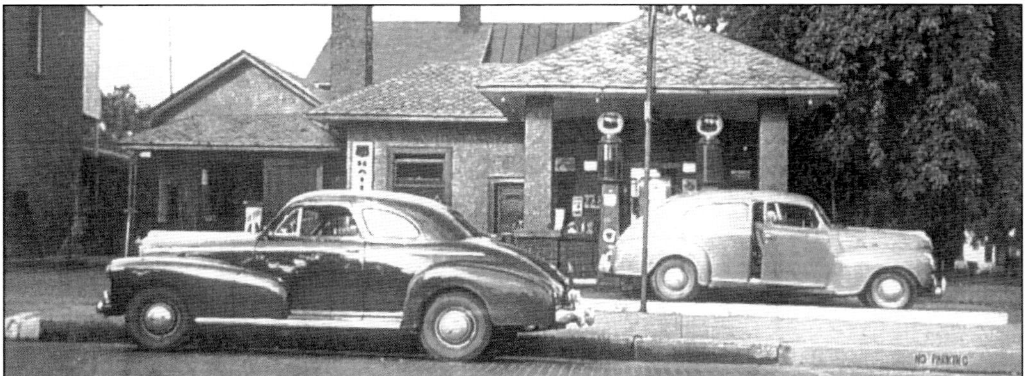

As automobiles became more popular, car dealerships proliferated in Downtown Chippewa Falls. Service stations necessarily followed. On North Bridge Street, Northside Shell, Grammont's Cities Service, and Thomson Oil Station were joined by Eystad's Phillips 66 Station, which is pictured here at 603 N. Bridge Street. Eystad's promoted itself with the slogan, "We Have Kept Chippewa County Rolling for 26 Years." This location is now home to the Medicine Shoppe. (Courtesy of Tom and Karen Olson.)

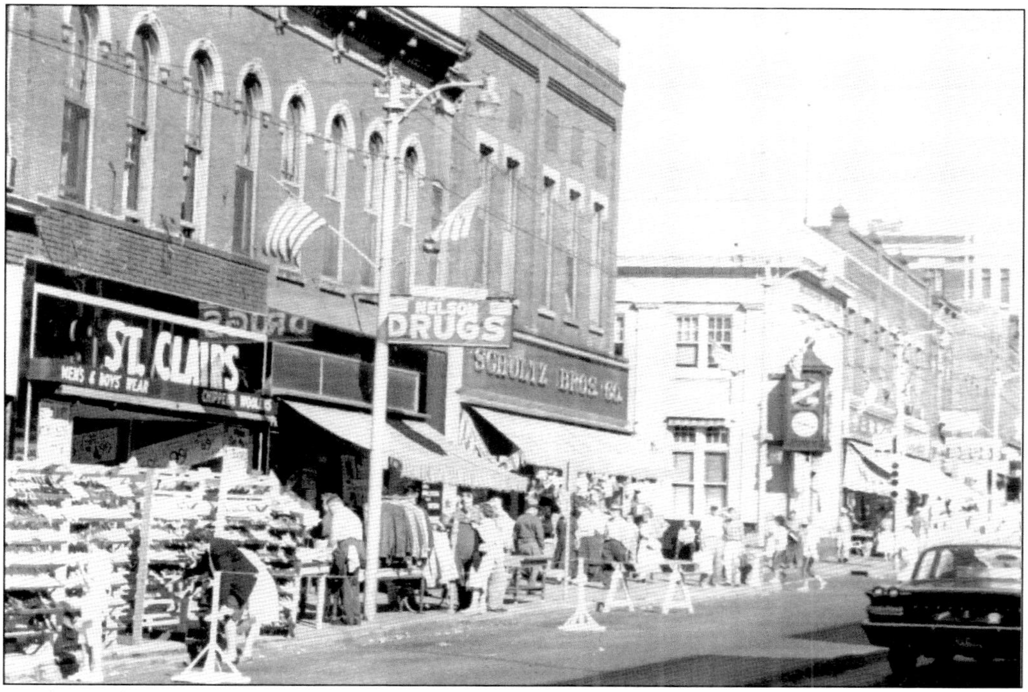

Traditionally held during Fair Week, Crazy Days, named for the "crazy" priced merchandise piled on tables in front of downtown stores, became a much anticipated summer event. St. Clair's store, which carried nationally-known men's and boys' apparel, displayed racks of footwear on its sidewalks, while Schultz Brothers Dime Store actually had items for sale for 10¢. Main Street continues the tradition of assisting downtown merchants with "Krazy Daze" and other year-round retail promotions (Courtesy of CFACC.)

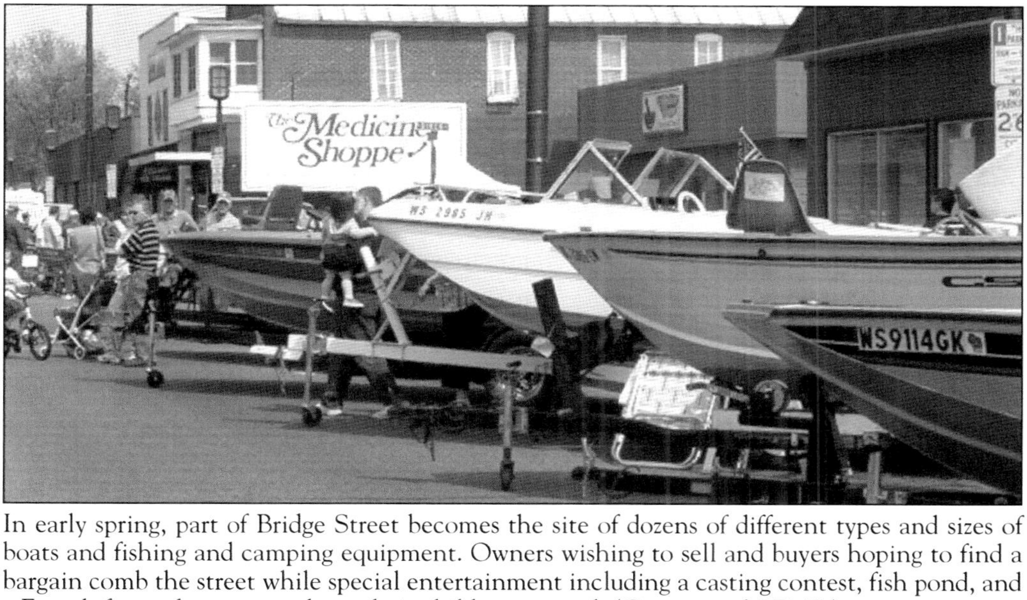

In early spring, part of Bridge Street becomes the site of dozens of different types and sizes of boats and fishing and camping equipment. Owners wishing to sell and buyers hoping to find a bargain comb the street while special entertainment including a casting contest, fish pond, and a French fur trade-era camp keep their children amused. (Courtesy of CFMS.)

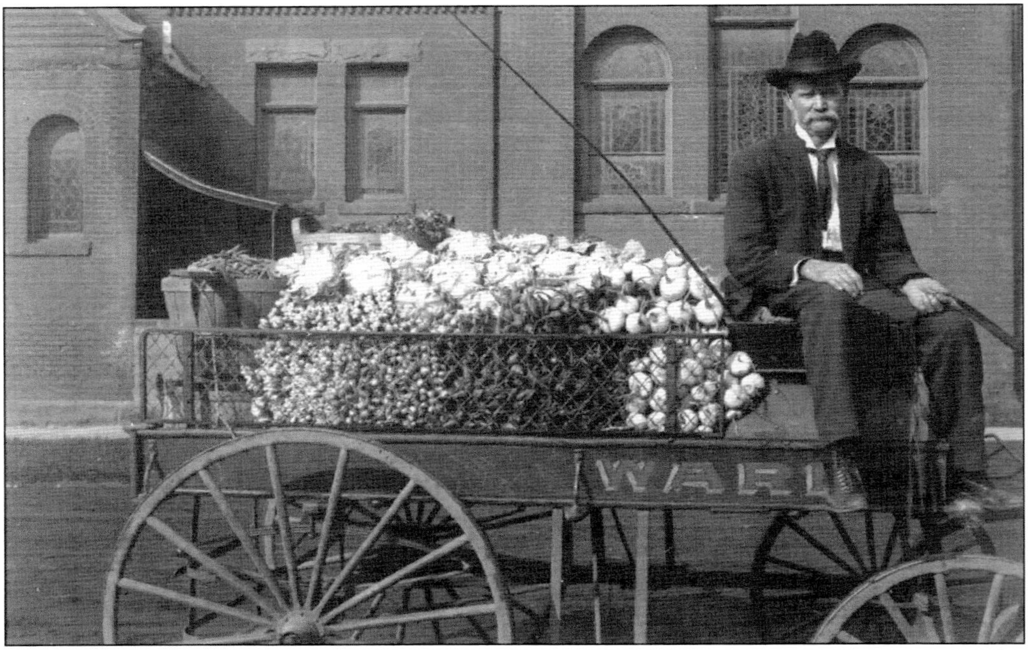

The Chippewa Falls Commercial League, an outgrowth of the Progressive League, erected a public market with rest rooms, horse sheds, and other accommodations for farmers and their horses. The market day programs included music, prizes, and special inducements. The first Wednesday of the month was set aside for city market day and the last Wednesday was for the farmer's market. (Courtesy of CCHS.)

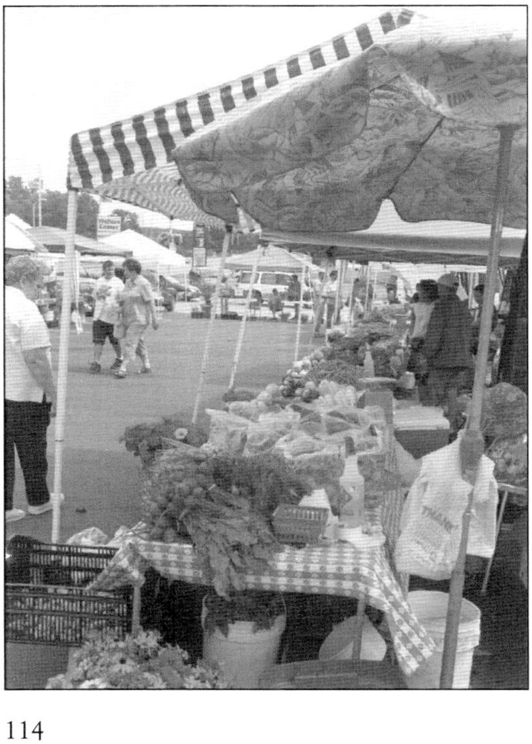

Chippewa Falls Main Street has brought back the tradition of a "Farmer's Market." Every Thursday throughout the summer and fall, beautiful flowers, fruits, vegetables, baked goods, and other items attract appreciative buyers to the Farmer's Market in Downtown Chippewa Falls. (Courtesy of Dave Gordon.)

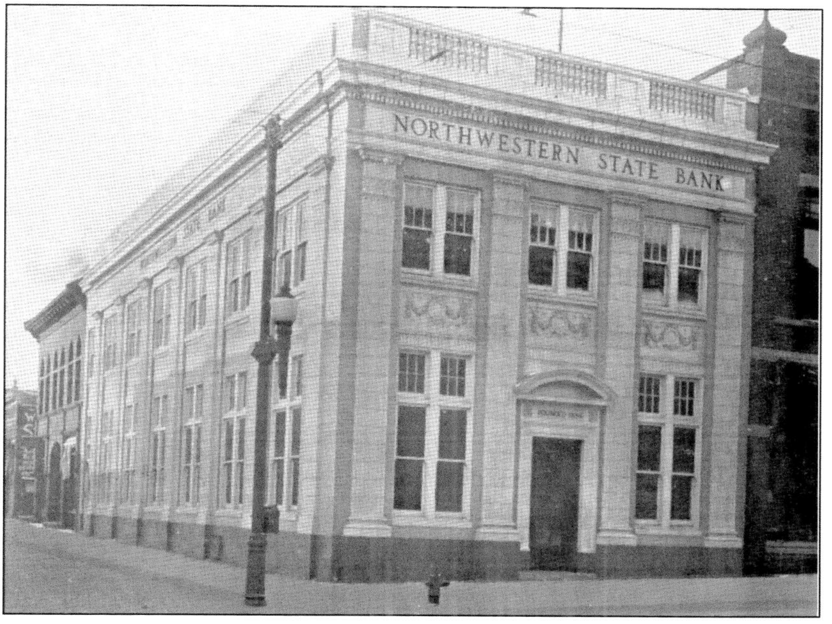

Northwestern State Bank was organized in 1904 with a capital of $80,000. S.C.F. Cobban was president and Thomas Kelly was vice-president. It first opened at 202 N. Bridge Street in the old Seymour Bank building that had been erected in 1883. The Seymour Bank closed in 1893. In 1925, a neo-classical cream-colored brick building was constructed on this site. The new building, reflecting progress, stability, and perfection, was designed and constructed by A. Moorman and Company of St. Paul, Minnesota. (Courtesy of the Northwestern Bank.)

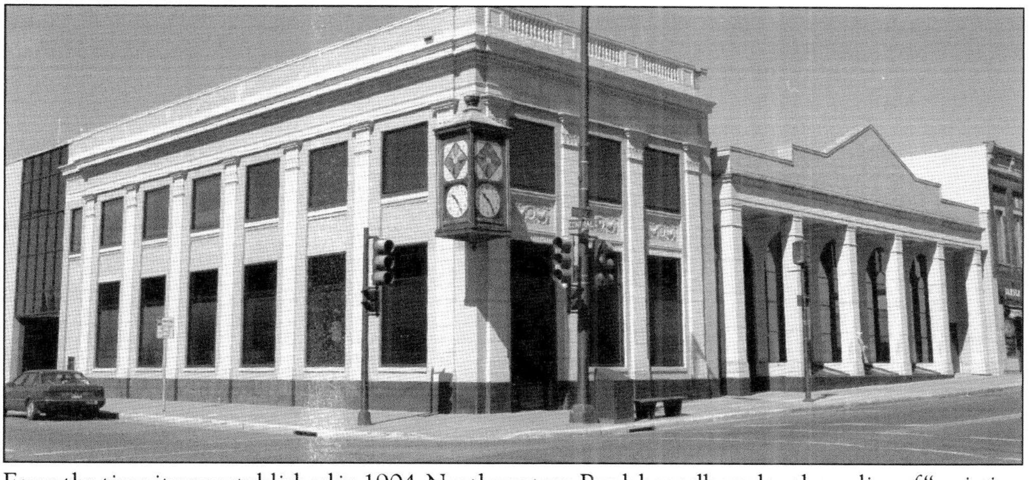

From the time it was established in 1904, Northwestern Bank has adhered to the policy of "assisting in the growth and development of Chippewa County through the constant improvement of our banking facilities." Those facilities were indeed improved in 1991 when the bank expanded its building onto the site of the F.W. Woolworth store. By incorporating architectural components found in the original building, the cream-colored brick, large windows, and stately columns enhanced the locally-owned and independent bank that remains an "anchor of strength" in downtown Chippewa Falls. (Courtesy of Dave Gordon.)

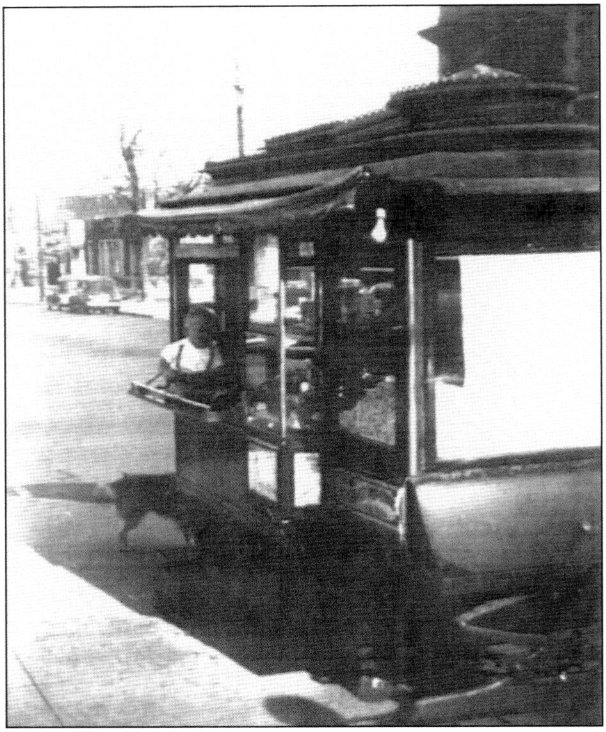

Reverend Roger Patrow, in a letter to the *Chippewa Herald Telegram* in December of 2001, fondly recalled that after seeing a Saturday night movie he would buy popcorn from Paddy Jenkins who operated his popcorn wagon on the corner of Bridge and Columbia Streets at the Edward Rutledge Charity Building. He and his friends then sat on the Rutledge wall, watching the cars "cruise" Bridge Street. (Courtesy of Don Frenette.)

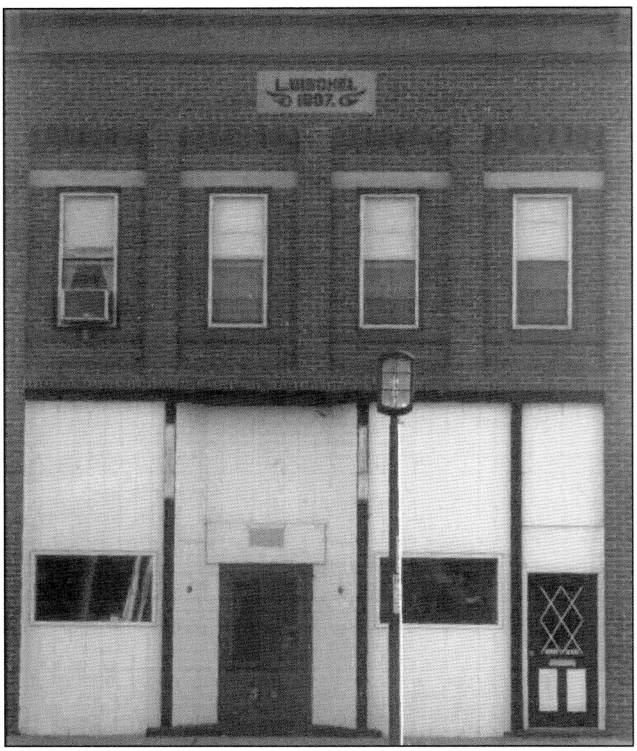

Lorenz Bischel was born in Germany and moved to Chippewa Falls in 1863. After farming for two decades, he started his meat market in 1883 at 522 N. Bridge Street. In 1907, Lorenz built and moved into a new building at 514 N. Bridge Street. Members of his family continued to live upstairs until the early 1950s when the property was bought by Ken Grothe and it became the location of Grothe's Electric. (Courtesy of CFMS.)

Ken Grothe, an active member of the Main Street program from its inception, attended the National Main Street Education conferences for several years, and became a strong and vocal advocate of downtown revitalization efforts. In early 1990, he restored the historic character of the building at 514 North Bridge Street. Brent Talledge became the next owner of the historic property when he opened his business, Chippewa Frame and Art Gallery, thus ensuring the future of a building that has housed 98 years of service to Chippewa Falls. (Courtesy of CFMS.)

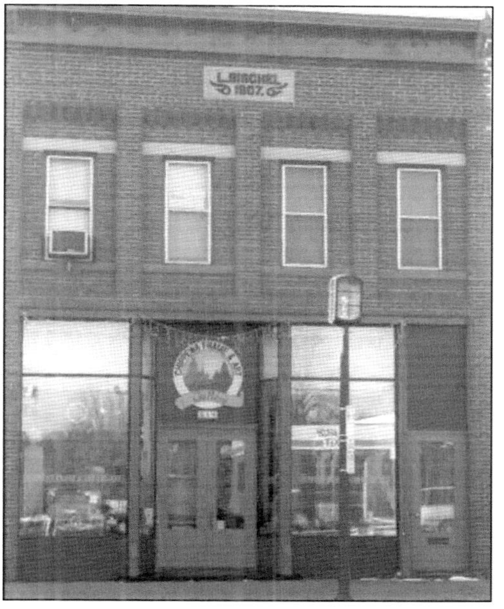

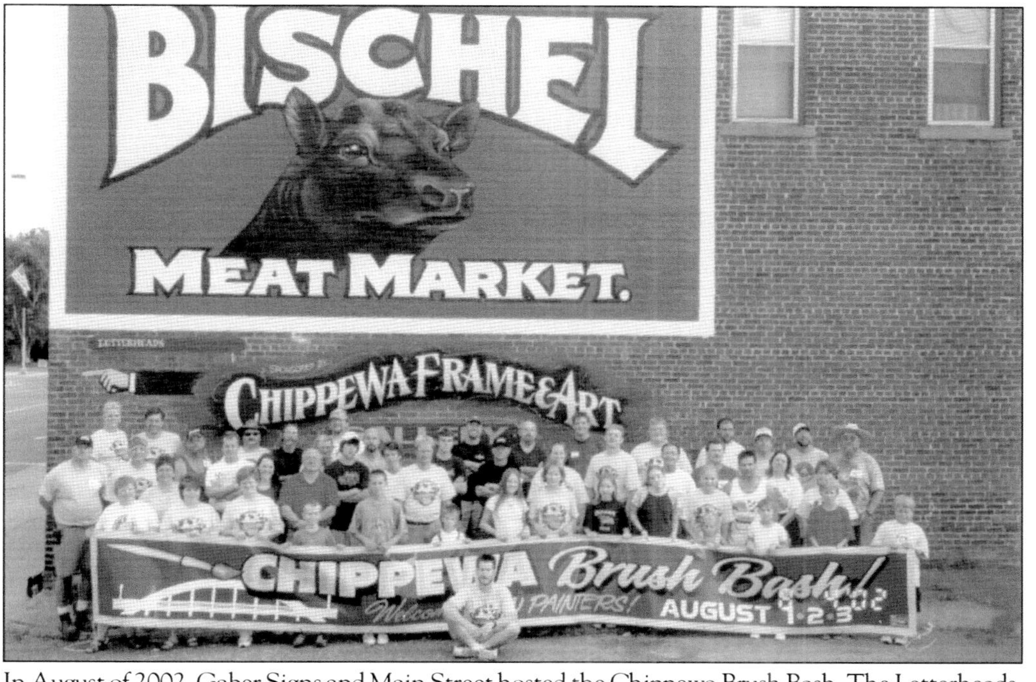

In August of 2002, Gaber Signs and Main Street hosted the Chippewa Brush Bash. The Letterheads, an international organization of sign painters, recreated the Bischel Meat Market sign which had been covered with white paint after the meat market closed. An original meat market "ghost sign" is still visible on the south side of the building. Several other public art projects benefiting downtown were also completed by the Letterheads volunteers. A second Chippewa Brush Bash is scheduled for 2006. Kurt Gaber is seated in front of the sign. (Courtesy of CFMS.)

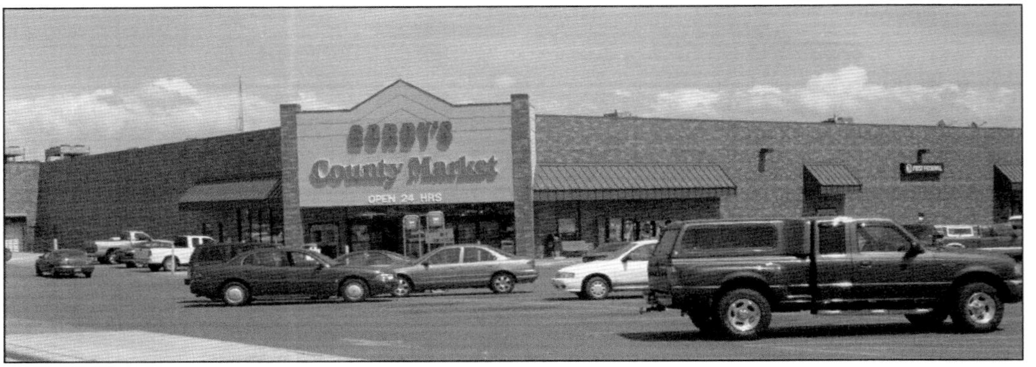

Gordy Schafer has always understood the importance of community and the need to support its efforts for growth and change. From modest beginnings in his grocery store at 419 South Main Street, Gordy expanded into the Lake Wissota area and Downtown Chippewa Falls where he and members of the Schafer family have operated two major downtown stores for decades. In 1998, he doubled the size of his downtown supermarket, renewing the commitment of the Schafer family to supporting a strong and vital downtown. (Courtesy of Dave Gordon.)

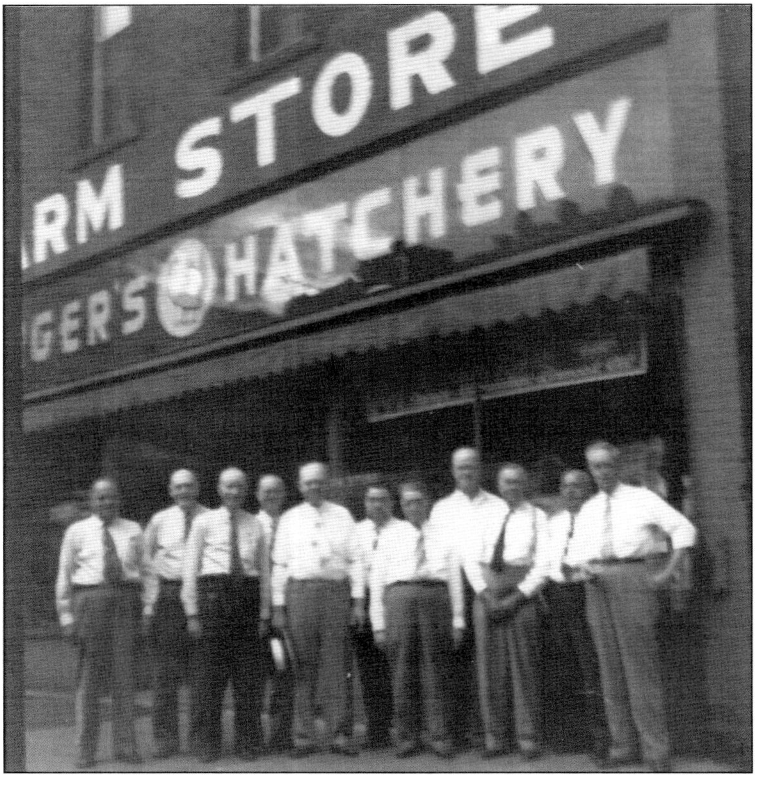

Henry and Agatha Korger began business as a chick hatchery and farm implement dealer in the early 1930s and the hard-working Korger family never looked back. Joe and Lucille Korger expanded into paints and home decorating, training the next generation for even greater challenges. (Courtesy of CCHS.)

The first library to serve the needs of a growing community was located in the former McBean building at 19 E. Central Street. In 1903, the new Carnegie Library, a stone structure of Romanesque architecture with two pillars flanking the front doors, was opened. When the library, described in 1933 as "a building to be proud of" was demolished in 1978, the two distinctive pillars were saved, only to be incorporated into the National Supermarket built on the site of the junior high school. Finally, the still-beautiful pillars were installed beside the front doors of the store the Korger family, themselves pillars of the community, built on the Cobban block in 2004. (Courtesy of CFMS.)

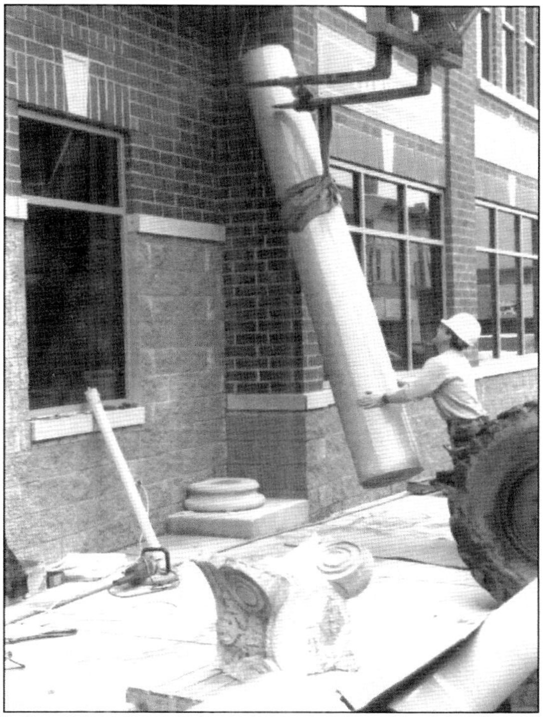

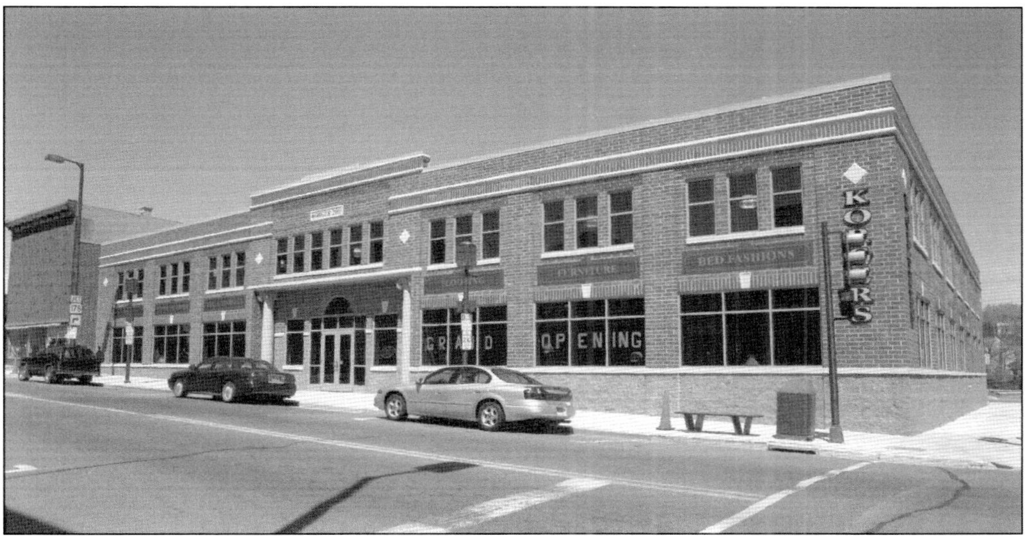

In 2004, siblings Carol Korger Christenson and Bill, Tom, and Gary Korger created a beautiful 17,000-square-foot, two-story building in which to carry on the family tradition. The Korger Block building won the Phoenix Award at the 2004 Wisconsin Commercial Real Estate Women's Showcase Awards in Milwaukee. Architecturally, the new building fits the style of the 48 neighboring properties located in the Bridge Street Commercial Historic District which Chippewa Falls Main Street had listed on the National Register of Historic Places in 1994. The Wisconsin Main Street Small Business Development Specialist assisted the Korger family with their business expansion plan and the building project financing proposal. (Courtesy of Dave Gordon.)

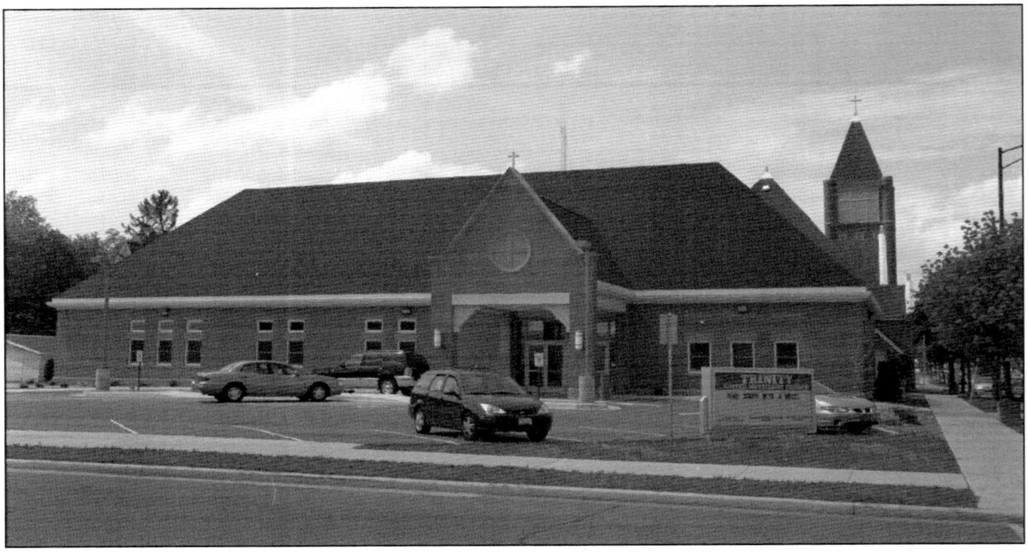

On May 18, 2003, a ribbon-tying ceremony was held to symbolize the relationship of two historical Chippewa Falls churches—Trinity United Methodist (shown above) and First Presbyterian (shown below). The churches confirmed their commitment to the vitality of Downtown when they each completed $1.6 million renovation and expansion projects that were compatible with their historic architecture. The Methodist Church's 9,000 square foot addition includes a drive-through canopy (porte-cochere), handicap access to all floors, dining hall, kitchen, office complex, restrooms, library, music room, and youth room. Architecturally, the new building blends perfectly with the 1892 church. The Presbyterian Church successfully incorporated a new architecturally-compatible design for the previously mismatched 1950s education building. The flat roof was removed and wooden roof trusses created a pitched roof to blend with the original church building's Gothic style roof. The entire 1883 building's exterior was restored and functional advantages were created with a new floor plan. (Courtesy of Dave Gordon.)

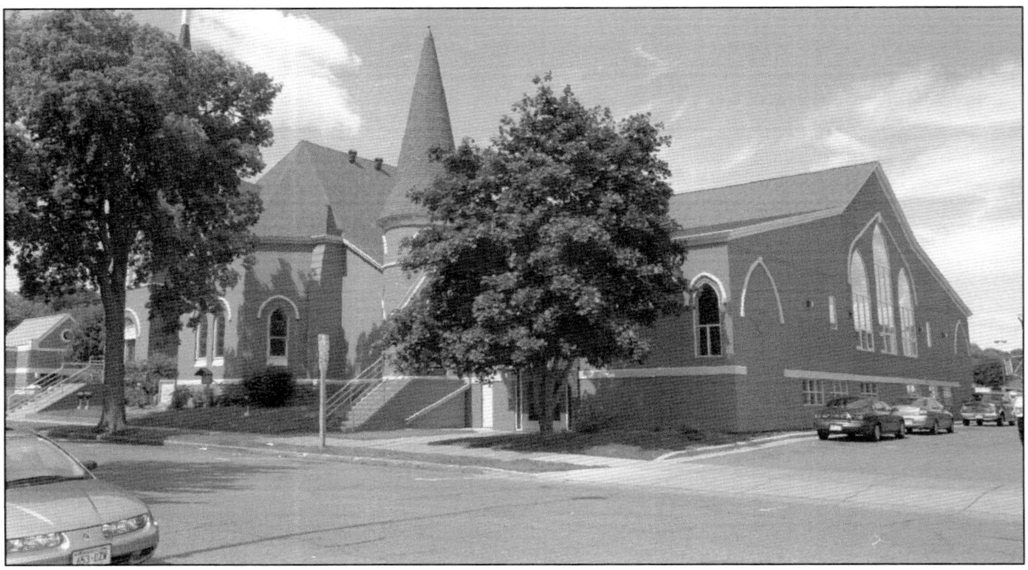

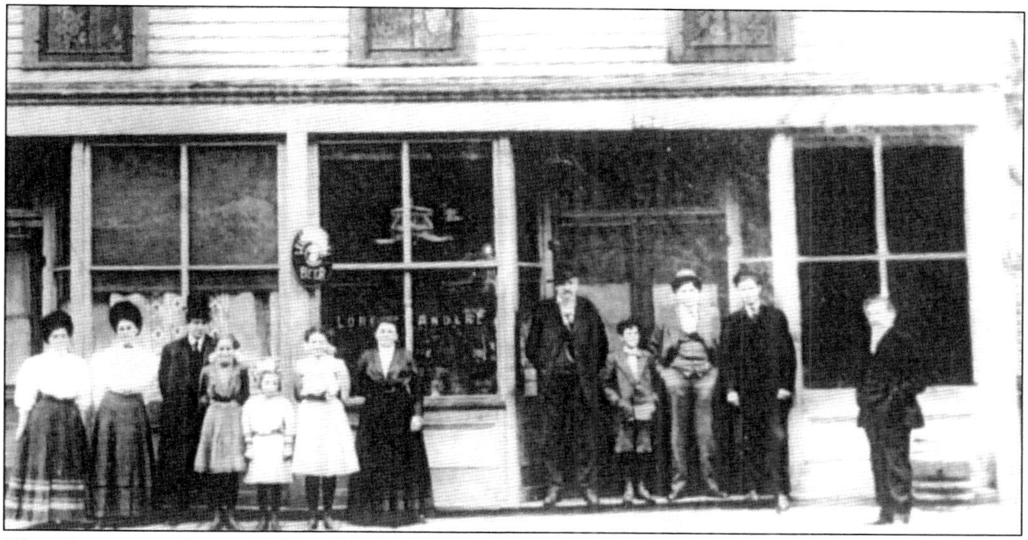

This photo was taken c. 1909 in front of the original Metropolitan Anderl Hotel. The hotel catered to the needs of the "transient public." Steam heat, running water in every room, and the very best of furnishings were advertised. Daily meals were served and bedding and quilts were handmade on site. A saloon occupied the south side of the first floor and a Western Union office was on the north. Pictured (from left to right) are Wilhelmina Anderl, Katherine Anderl, Henry Anderl, Florence Anderl, Florence Rieman, Emily Anderl, Lorenz Anderl (owner), Hugo Albert Anderl, William Anderl, and handyman Peter Morgan. (Courtesy of Jan Zutter.)

Through extensive restoration by owner Brian Johnson, of Ritter Companies, the former Anderl Hotel was transformed with architecturally-appropriate construction components in late 2004. Main Street Design Committee members volunteered their assistance to the owner. An early 1900s advertisement showing the original brick building façade was provided, with an elevation sketch of how the building should be restored and a pallet of primary and accent colors. On the interior, the suspended ceilings have been removed, revealing the original ornate embossed metal ceiling. (Courtesy of CFMS.)

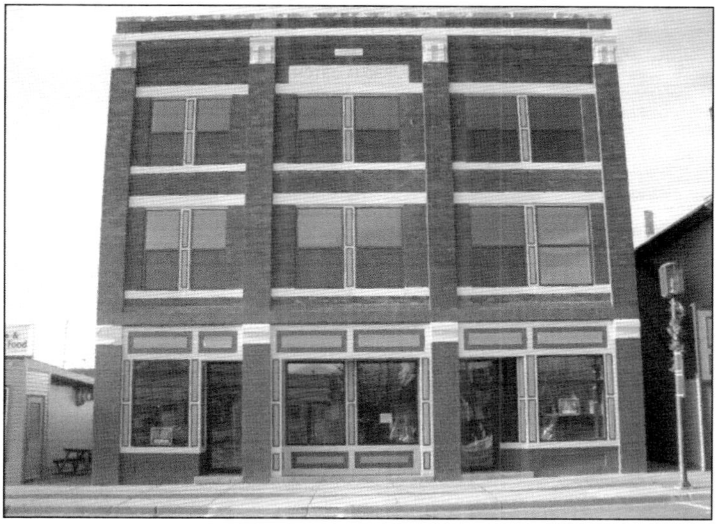

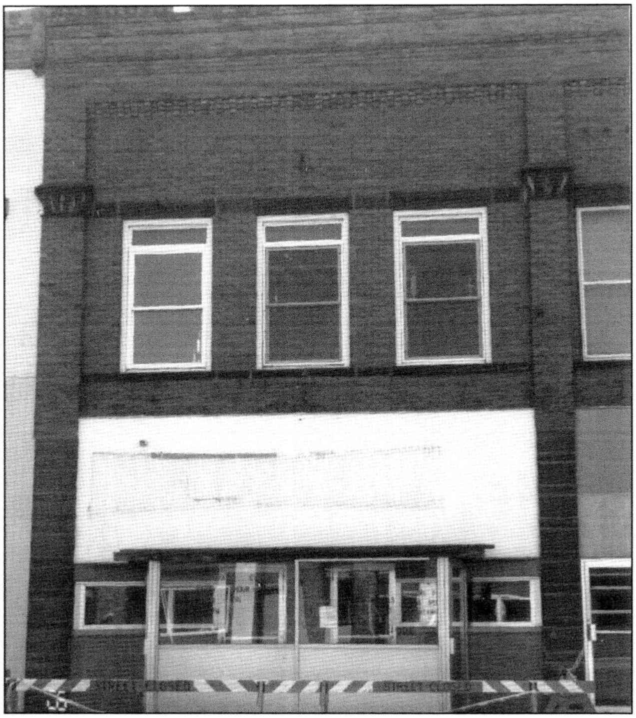

Many individuals have contributed to the growth of the Chippewa Falls community, by investing in land, in buildings, and in businesses, many located first along River Street, then Spring Street and Bridge Street. Buildings on Spring Street reflected the diverse need of a growing community and, over the years, changed hands and served different purposes. Some were neglected while others were remodeled and "modernized," an example of which is the building at 17 W. Spring Street. (Courtesy of CFMS.)

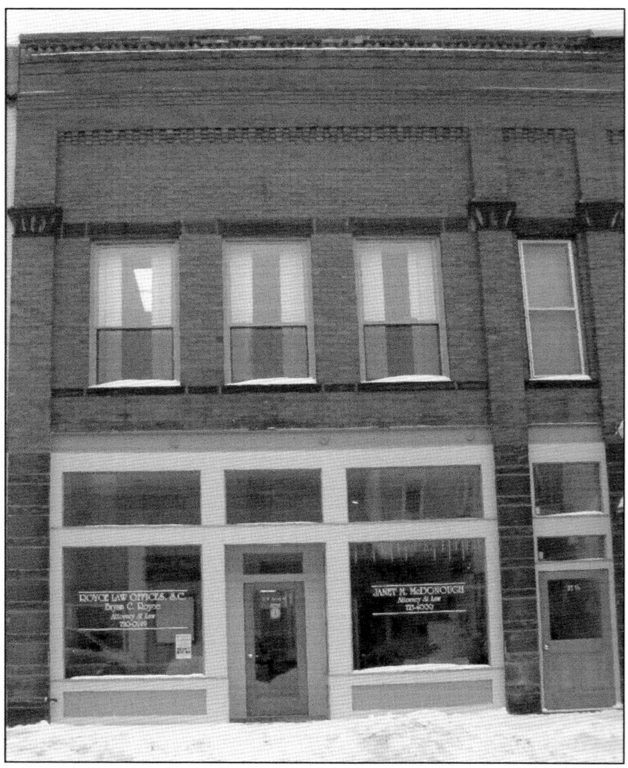

David Raihle Jr. understood the importance of keeping historic areas of Chippewa Falls intact when he accepted the challenge of renovating the entire building at 17 W. Spring Street. The substantial project included the removal of concrete block, the installation of both a new wooden storefront entrance and the original size display windows. The completed project provided for two upstairs apartments with high ceilings and skylights and office space on the first floor. Nominated for the Best Façade Rehabilitation in 2003, the restored building reflected David Raihle Jr.'s commitment to preserving all aspects of his hometown. (Courtesy of CFMS.)

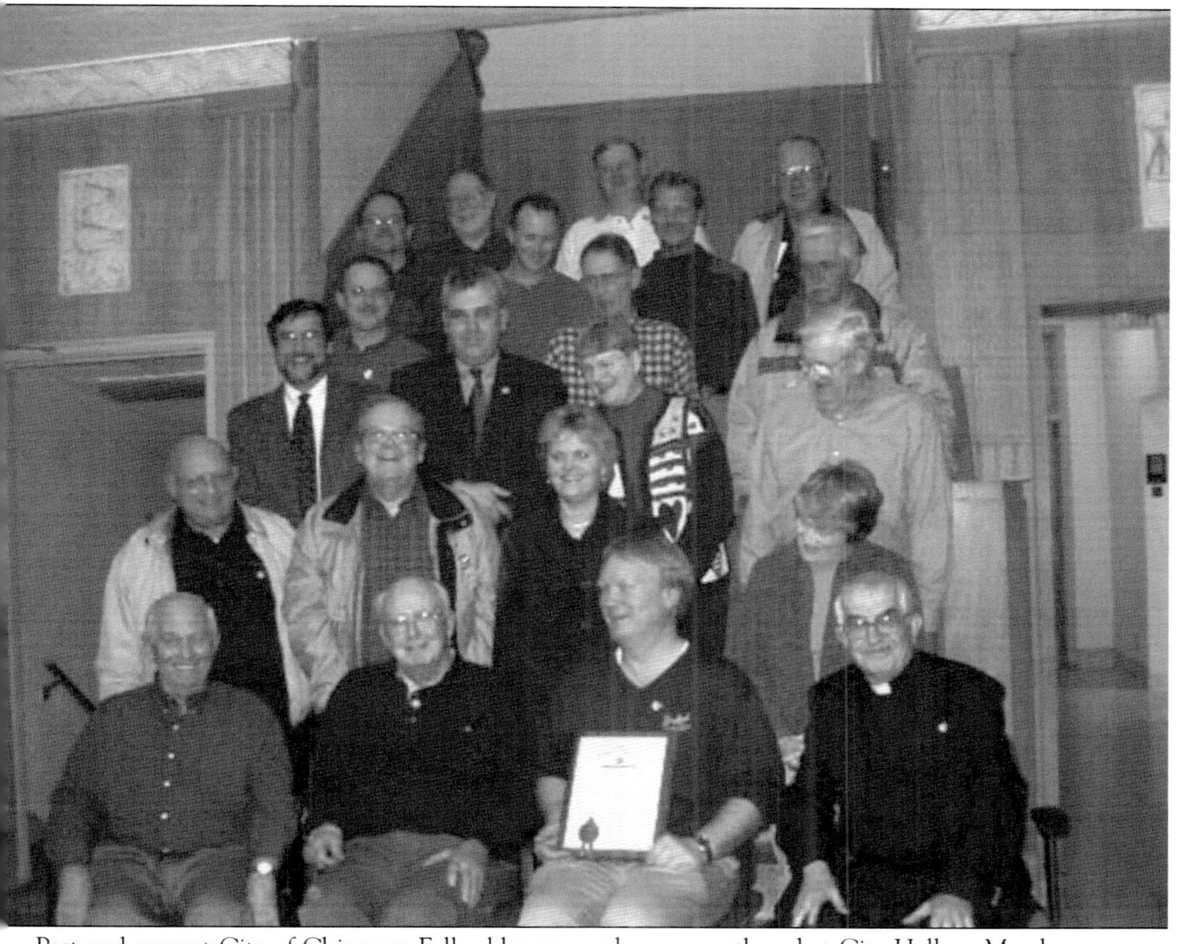

Past and present City of Chippewa Falls aldermen and mayors gathered at City Hall on March 25, 2004, to celebrate the city's 135th anniversary. Pictured are, from left to right: (front row) Howard Olson, Leo Hamilton, Doug Sandvick, and Father Jeremiah Cashman; (second row) Leo Eichinger, Tom Armstrong, Debra Waldusky, and Evelyn Maloney; (third row) Tim Normand, Bob Hoekstra, Donna Meier, and Bob Sommerfeld; (fourth row) Steve Hamilton, Paul Peters, and Scott Trippler; (back row) Steve Dean, Terry Giordano, David Grinnell, Dennis Roshell, Troy Thomas, and Cal Myrman. (Courtesy of CFMS.)

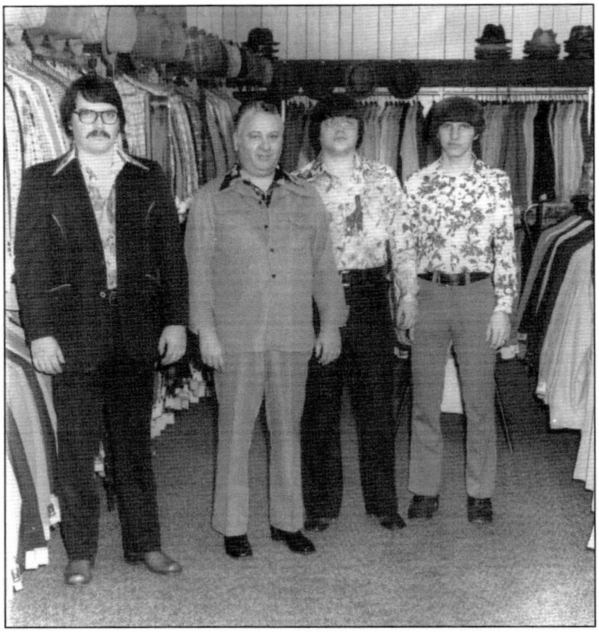

When Robert Rada purchased Stum's Men's Wear in 1967, Rada's soon became a fixture in downtown Chippewa Falls. Offering quality menswear, Bob, Rick, and John Rada were "proud to be part of the fabric that makes Chippewa Falls . . . home." Rick and John took over the family business when their father retired in 1981. Rick Rada became owner in 1997 and continued the tradition of providing regular, big, and tall sizes to area men. Pictured wearing men's styles popular in the 1970s are, from left, Rick Rada, Bob Rada, John Rada, and employee Steve Hofkes. (Courtesy of Rick Rada.)

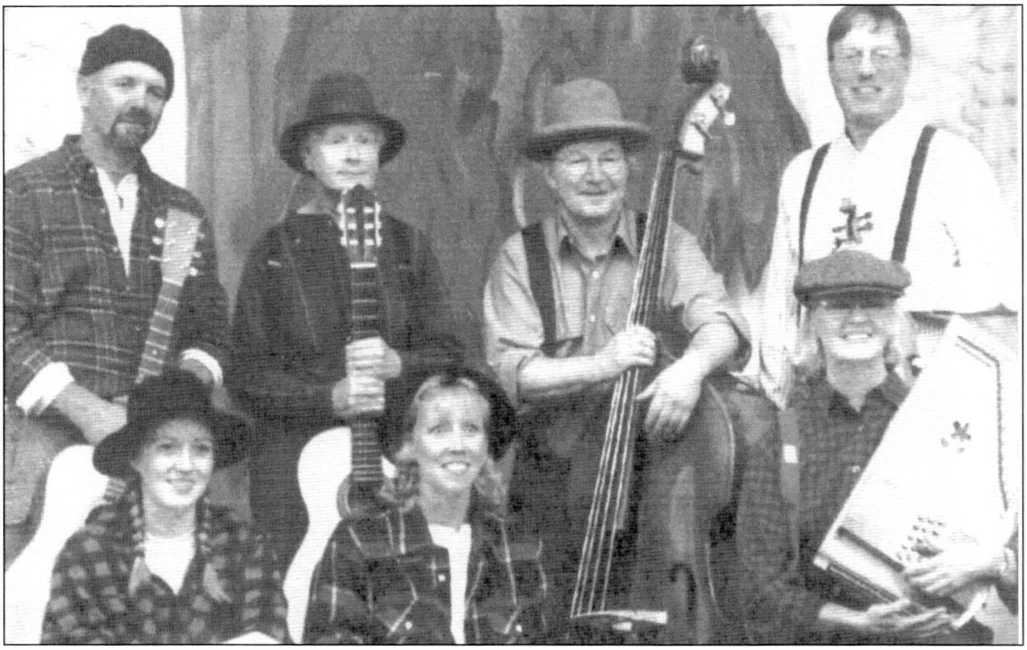

Gerald Way created the play, *Pioneers at the Falls*, performed at the Heyde Center to sold-out crowds. The play brought to life the ethnically diverse individuals who populated Chippewa Falls from its inception until the turn of the century. Eleven original songs composed by Gerald Way were sung by "The Swampers," pictured here in period costumes. They are, from left to right: (first row) Casey Danielson, Kathy Danielson, and Judy Ganser; (second row) Tim Danielson, Judy Brist, Jerry Way, and Rob Kuchta. Jerry Way won the Wisconsin Main Street 2002 Best Cultural Preservation Project Award for *Pioneers at the Falls* (Courtesy of The Swampers.)

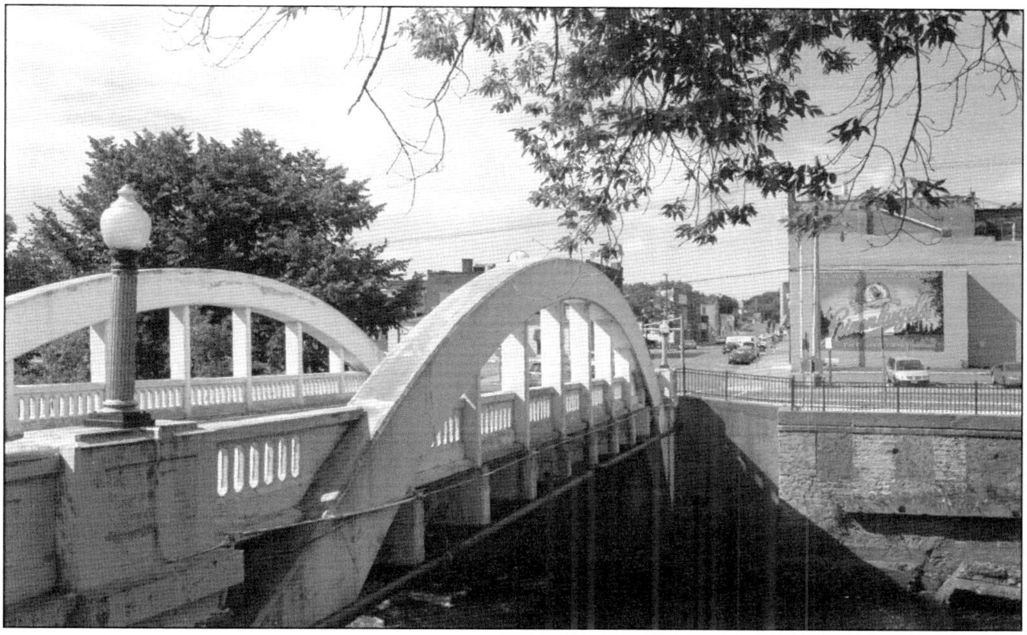

The Marsh Rainbow Arch Bridge built in 1916 at a cost of $13,950 is the only bridge of this style still remaining in Wisconsin. It was the only Downtown bridge to withstand the devastating 1934 flood. It was placed on the National Register of Historic Places in 1982. Looking west where the bridge crosses over Duncan Creek, a wall sign is visible on the side of the American Legion Post 77. The sign was sponsored by the Jacob Leinenkugel Brewing Company "as a salute to the military veterans of the Chippewa Valley." (Courtesy of Dave Gordon.)

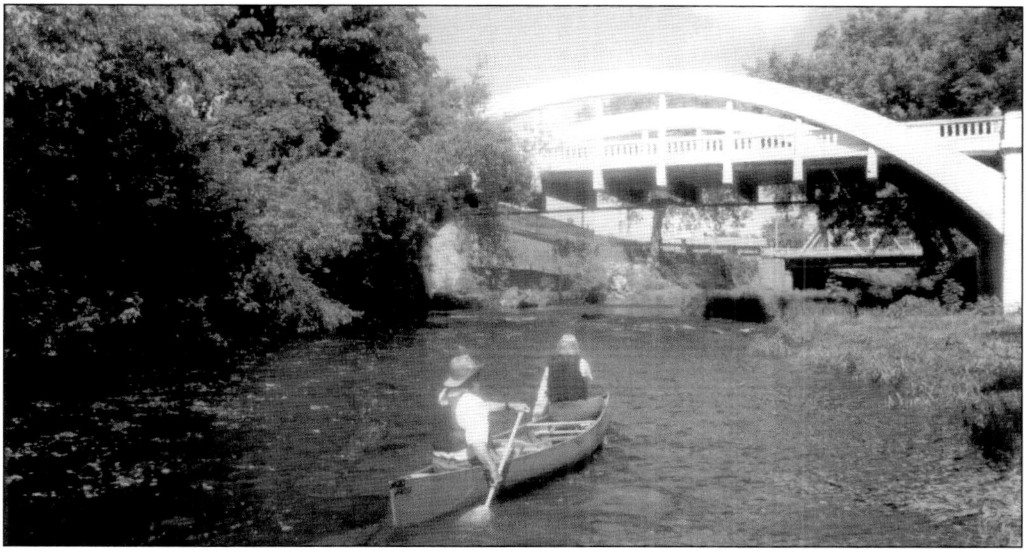

One of the founding fathers of Chippewa Falls Main Street, Chuck Card and downtown business owner and resident Judy Ganser paddle upstream in Duncan Creek after portaging from the Chippewa River above the hydro-electric dam. They are heading toward the Marsh Rainbow Arch Bridge in historic Downtown Chippewa Falls. (Courtesy of CFMS.)

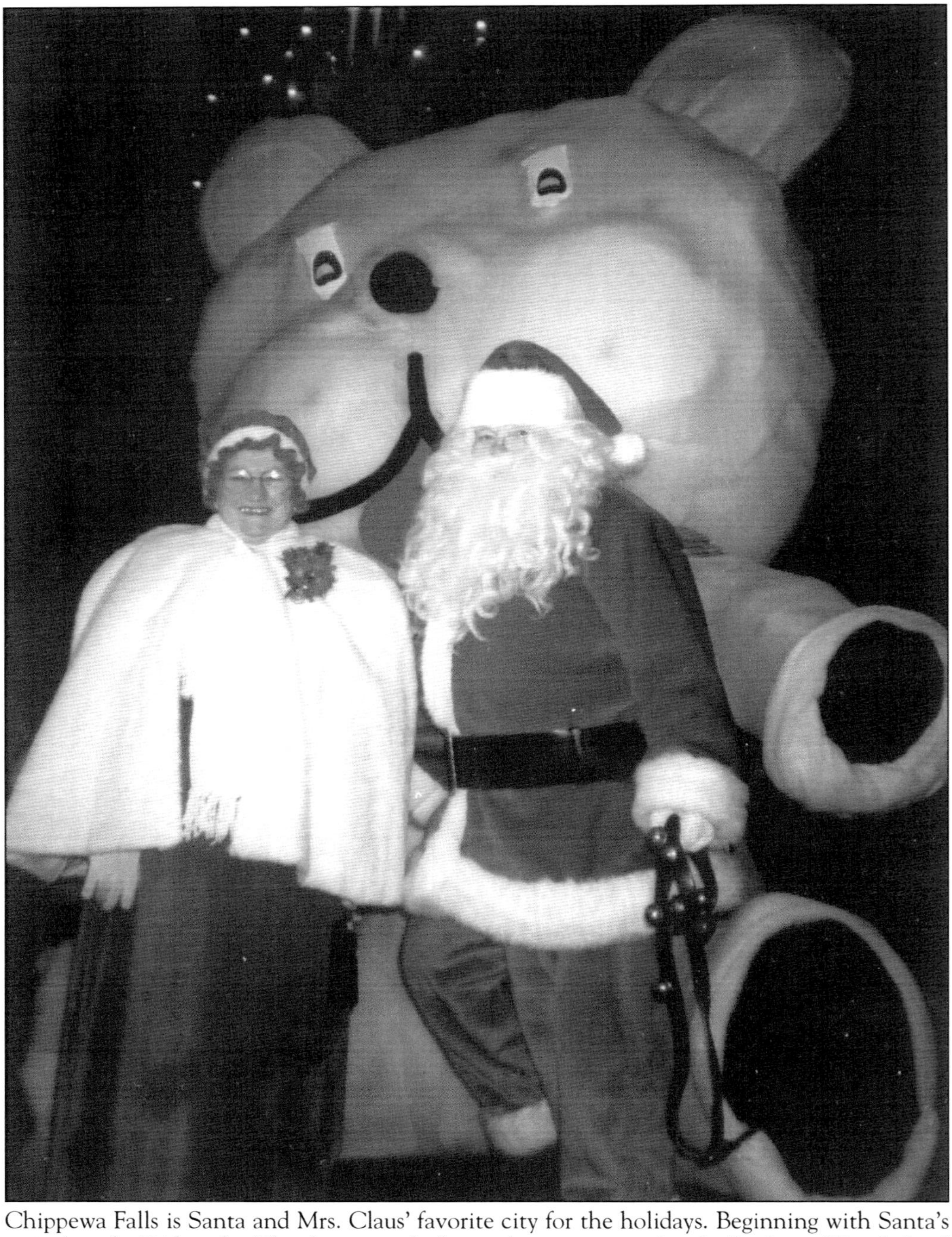

Chippewa Falls is Santa and Mrs. Claus' favorite city for the holidays. Beginning with Santa's arrival on the Friday after Thanksgiving, the horse-drawn wagon rides, the Bridge to Wonderland Parade, and visits with children at their headquarters at the Rutledge Charities building, events keep Santa and Mrs. Claus very busy. After 13 years as Santa's spouse, Marie Meinen, shown above, retired in 2002. Main Street is grateful to Marie Meinen and Chuck Card (Santa) for the many years they have brought joy and excitement to the children of Chippewa Falls. (Courtesy of CFMS.)

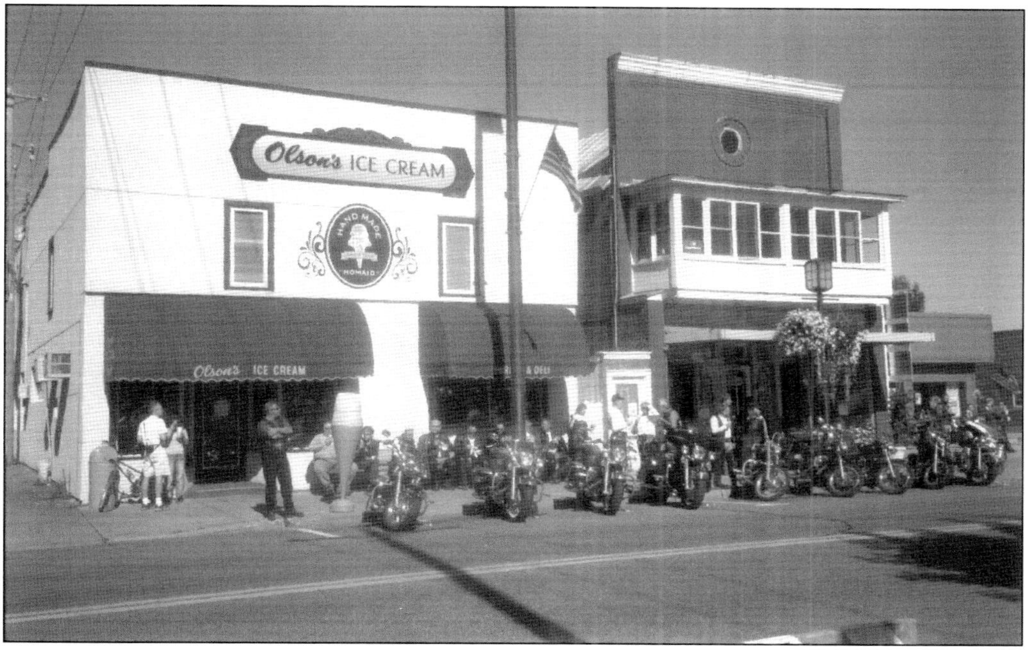

Downtown rumbled with excitement during the Wisconsin Hog Rally held in August of 2004. As part of the rally, Main Street held a pancake breakfast, coordinated a downtown poker walk and took souvenir photos in front of the Leinenkugel mural on the side of the Town Pump. Shown here are Hog Rally participants taking a break for refreshments at Olson's Ice Cream and Deli. Rally coordinator Nelson Schaller said, "They loved the grounds and the friendly people in the stores and restaurants. This is one of the best rallies we have had." (Courtesy of CFMS.)

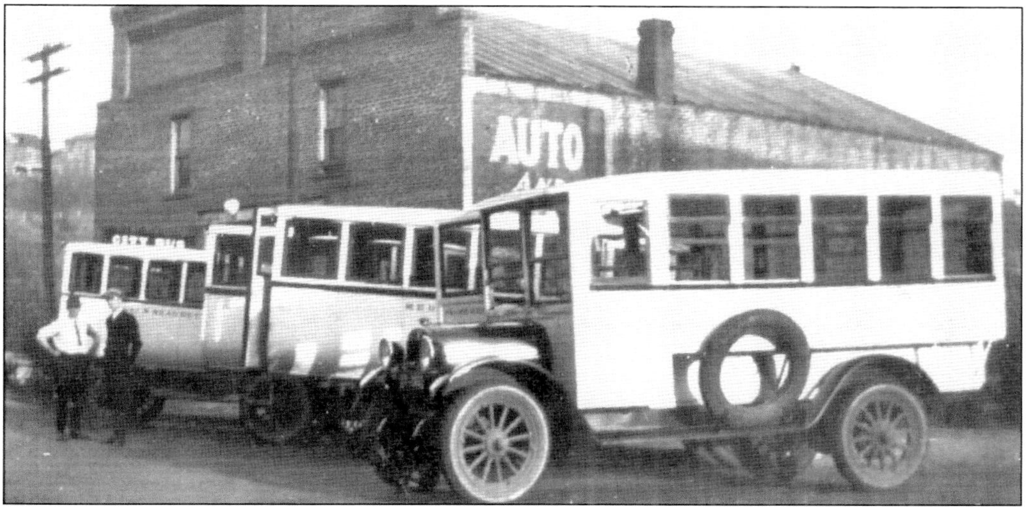

Chippewa Trails has been providing motor coach service to the Chippewa Valley since 1920. This c. 1920 photo showed their well-maintained fleet of buses in front of their company on East Spring Street in downtown Chippewa Falls. Their reputation for service has been built over five generations and the full-service bus company continues to offer charter service, customized tours, and school transportation. (Courtesy of Chippewa Trails.)

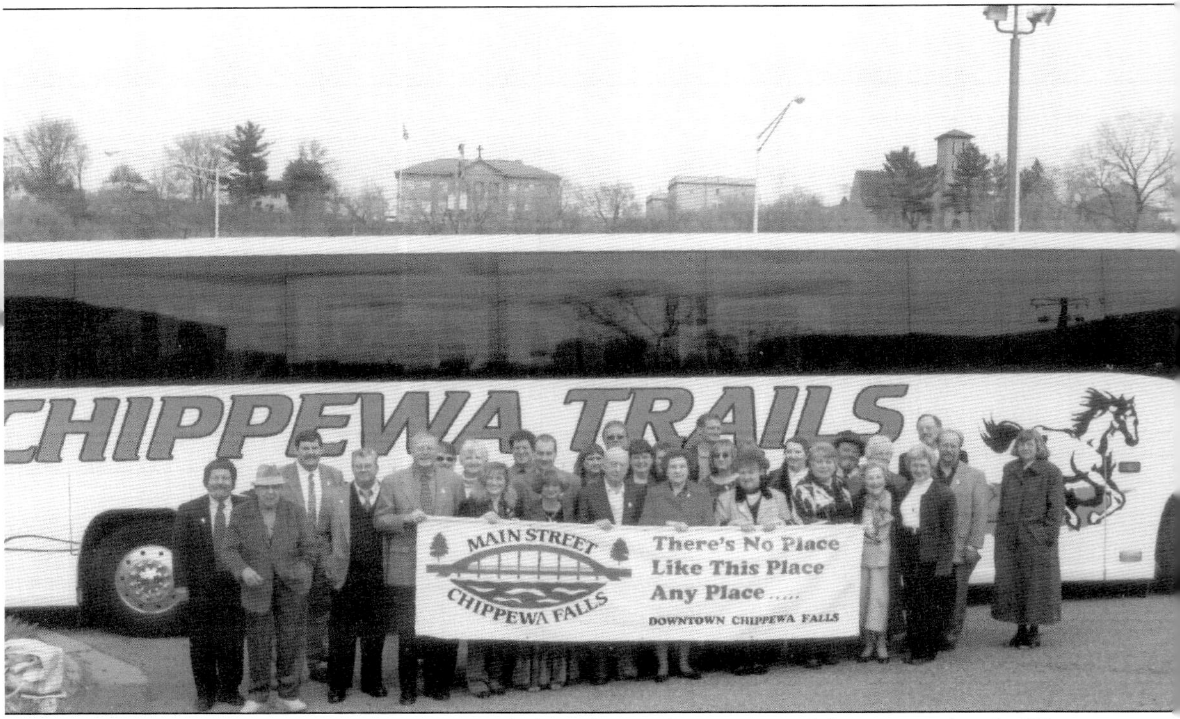

Chippewa Falls Main Street chartered a brand new Chippewa Trails bus to travel to the Wisconsin Main Street 14th Annual Awards Banquet in Waupaca on April 30, 2004. Spirits were high and smiles were big. The group of volunteers and staff accepted the Wisconsin Main Street Spirit Award which is given to the community that has demonstrated the commitment and enthusiasm to make the Main Street program a top local priority, to be a positive downtown revitalization model, and display leadership in state-wide advocacy. Education, volunteer involvement, and support of downtown improvement activities are all considered when choosing the winner of this award. The Best Public Private Partnership Award in Downtown Revitalization was also received by Chippewa Falls. Pictured are (from left to right) Jim Schuh, Steve Playter, Dave Kuhn, Dennis Brown, Fred Kuss, Teri Opsahl, Joyce Pugh, Kelly Roshell, Steve Pigeon, Jayson Smith, Barb Smith, Nancy Schuh, Joe Joas, Doug Sandvick, Louise Bentley, Sandy Furst, Lucy LeCleir, Dave Cihasky, Kelly Zimmerman, Carolyn Williamson, Lavon Thompson, Laura Franta, Mary Brown, Chuck Card, Char Card, Willi Holm, Ann Gordon, Dave Gordon, Brent Talledge, and Virginia Smith. For more information visit our website at www.ChippewaFallsMainSt.org. (Courtesy of CFMS.)